Neurodiversity in the Workplace

Maximizing Success through Inclusive Dynamic Workplace Design™

Susan Fitzell

Praise for *Neurodiversity in the Workplace: Maximizing Success through Inclusive Dynamic Workplace Design™*

Perspective matters and this book changed mine. Too many leaders and organizations approach talent from a deficit perspective. They evaluate talent based on how people are different and why an individual doesn't fit into a familiar box. Here's the thing—neurodiverse individuals (up to one-third of your team according to Susan Fitzell—don't fit into our familiar boxes. In other words, organizations miss the unique talents and capabilities of a significant portion of their team because of their perspective.

This book can be "traditionally labeled" in the category of diversity and inclusion. But, that is missing the bigger perspective. This book challenges us to unlock the power of a significant percentage of our workforce to help us achieve more. In the process, we can create a culture where everyone grows, develops, and flourishes. I loved how this book challenged my thinking and opened the door to new ideas about building a culture that can flourish in the face of today's complexity, uncertainty, and change. You will enjoy it, too.

– Randy Pennington, Pennington Performance Group

This book is an important read! From the first chapter, I was struck by Susan's insight: 'Adding divergent thinkers to the workplace may be a company's best investment to increase its competitive advantage.' This book is a roadmap to creating workplaces that are both inclusive and high-performing. Susan breaks down complex concepts into actionable steps, showing leaders how to harness neurodiversity to foster innovation and adaptability. I'd recommend this book to any leader committed to building a truly inclusive, forward-thinking organization.

– John A. DeMato, Visual Storytelling Expert

By championing neurodiversity, you will enhance the well-being of your workforce and position your company as a leader in innovation and inclusivity. By combining heartfelt storytelling with actionable strategies, Susan Fitzell reframes neurodiversity as a strength to celebrate rather than a challenge to overcome. Fitzell, draws from her personal experience as a neurodivergent individual, and emphasizes shifting from a deficit mindset to a GIFTS-mindset.

Her concept of Inclusive Dynamic Workplace Design (IDWD) offers practical solutions like quiet spaces, hybrid work options, and sensory-friendly areas to meet diverse employee needs. Embracing neurodiversity is not only ethically important but also a strategic advantage. This book is an inspiring and practical resource for HR professionals, managers, and leaders seeking meaningful change.

– Sabrina Sterling, Ed.D., Instructional Technology Specialist

As a neurodiversity advocate, I was delighted to see this book. It's got simple tips and tricks for everyone in the workplace. Fitzell, being neurodivergent herself, brings authentic insights that bridge the gap between neurodivergent employees and traditional workplace expectations. The strategies for self-advocacy and workplace navigation are invaluable.

– Monica Harding, Assistant Project Executive Content Consumer and Business Services Division at IDA Ireland

A MUST READ for HR Professionals looking for a clear roadmap on designing a physical workspace and culture that unlocks the potential of neurodivergent employees in a way that is uniquely tailored to their needs yet provides benefits for all employees. Susan Fitzell's deep and personal knowledge and experience of charting the waters of neuro-inclusive initiatives in workplaces and academia is apparent, as she provides impactful insights to back up her Inclusive Dynamic Workplace Design system. She reminds us that, despite our best efforts, initiatives can fall devastatingly flat absent training and preparation. This book seeks to provide input into both the "Why" and the "How" of implementing a neuroinclusive workplace and does so in clear terms that are easily understood.

– Julie Laum, PHR, SHRM-CP, ACE-CHC

Finally: A Book That Spotlights Those Beautiful Divergent Minds In The Workplace.

Susan Fitzell's *Neurodiversity in the Workplace: Maximizing Success through Inclusive Dynamic Workplace Design* is a game-changer for organizational inclusivity. As a humanistic psychiatrist working in behavioral neuroscience, I'm impressed by her practical strategies for harnessing the unique strengths and untapped potential of neurodivergent individuals. Fitzell's Inclusive Dynamic Workplace Design™ offers a comprehensive, actionable framework that can transform how businesses approach diversity and innovation. This book is essential reading for any leader committed to building a genuinely inclusive and high-performing workplace. The ability to think-out-of-the-box and not adhere to conformity thinking should be nurtured and applauded and it's time to spotlight those beautiful divergent minds in our respected industries.

– Dr. Reef Karim, Human Performance Expert, Humanistic Psychiatrist

Great advice for inclusion of neurodivergent people with on-point real-world anecdotes. As the father of neurodivergent children, I hoped Susan Gingras Fitzell's book would deliver ideas on how to help them and others like them in the working world. What I found was that she did that...and so much more!

Her ability to illustrate through examples really helped reveal pitfalls we should all avoid. A great example was when she was called out by a trainer for being distracted when, in reality, she was accommodating her auditory processing disorder by connecting the lecture's discussion points to key information on her iPad. I am so glad to have this book in hand as I work to build positive work culture and strategize how to assist my children as they navigate early adulthood. Wonderful book! Highly recommend!

– Michael G. Neece

A Must-Read for Understanding and Supporting Neurodiversity at Work. As a neurodivergent novice, I found this book incredibly enlightening and valuable. The author's personal stories and clear explanations made complex concepts easily digestible. The Dynamic Workplace Design™ concept is outstanding and addresses issues like open office layouts that don't suit everyone's needs. The section on neurodivergent women was particularly insightful and well-researched.

What really impressed me was the discussion on accommodations versus favoritism—it was handled with great clarity and wisdom. If I were a CEO, I would be taking extensive notes on implementing these workplace design concepts. The author's ability to weave real-life stories with practical workplace solutions makes this an invaluable resource for understanding and supporting neurodiversity in the workplace.

– Katharine Giovanni, Partner, The Giowell Group

Neurodiversity in the Workplace

Maximizing Success through Inclusive Dynamic Workplace Design™

Susan Fitzell

Neurodiversity in the Workplace: Maximizing Success Through
Inclusive Dynamic Workplace Design

ISBN: 978-1-932995-42-8 (softcover)
Library of Congress Cataloging-in-Publication Data

Published by

Cogent Catalyst Publications
PO Box 6182
Manchester, NH 03108
www.SusanFitzell.com
sfitzell@susanfitzell.com
603-325-6087

Book design by: Nick Zelinger
eBook Interior design by: Rebecca Finkel
Editing by: Laura Jorstad

First Edition

Printed in the United States of America

Dedication

To Jeffery Sullivan

My steadfast friend, guide, and champion for the past quarter-century. Your unwavering belief gave me the courage to bridge worlds and share this message. Through every high and low, your wisdom and encouragement have been my north star. This book exists because you helped me believe it could—and should. For always putting my best interests first and being the wind beneath my wings, I dedicate this work to you, with deep gratitude and admiration.

Contents

Compelling Points for Decision-Makers

Who Should Buy This Book

Are you facing any of these situations?

- Have you interviewed a talented candidate whose interview didn't go as well as expected?
- Do you have a team member who hyperfocuses on specific tasks or interests?
- Is your company starting a program to hire individuals on the autism spectrum?

ROI of Neurodiversity: What This Book Offers Your Organization

This book is for you if:

- You're an employer looking to fill a skills gap.
- You're a manager of neurodivergent employees.
- You're a human resources (HR) professional aiming to hire, train, and support neurodivergent workers.
- You're an employee wanting to understand neurodiversity and its workplace benefits and challenges.
- You're a neurodivergent employee who wants strategies to advocate for yourself and be successful no matter your challenges.

This book addresses all these needs. It's written by a neurodivergent adult with experience in both education and business, navigating—and helping others navigate—neurodivergence in both settings.. This book isn't pie-in-the-sky. It's reality-based, practical, and founded on current research.

Strategic Takeaways for Organizational Success

- How companies support and mentor neurodivergent employees.
- Strategies to adjust recruitment and selection policies to identify and hire neurodivergent talent.
- Why neurodivergent employees often hide their diagnosis and how it affects their career.
- How to lay the groundwork for a supportive neurodiversity program in your company.
- How managers can support all their employees, manage them effectively, and be mentors to neurodivergent team members.

Why You Should Buy This Book

This book will help you accelerate employee support programs, build strong neurodiversity at work initiatives, and support employees from historically marginalized backgrounds in their career growth and success.

Table of Abbreviations

ADA	Americans with Disabilities Act
ADHD	Attention deficit hyperactivity disorder
AI	Artificial intelligence
APD	Auditory processing disorder
ASD	Autism spectrum disorder
CIO	Chief information officer
DEIA	Diversity, equity, inclusion and accessibility
DSM	Diagnostic and Statistical Manual of Mental Disorders
HBR	Harvard Business Review
HI	Human intelligence
HR	Human resources
ID	Intellectual disability
IP	Intellectual property
IT	Information technology
JAN	Job Accommodation Network
LMS	Learning management system
ND	Neurodivergent
NT	Neurotypical
OCD	Obsessive-compulsive disorder
ROI	Return on investment
STT	Speech-to-text
TACT	Teaching the Autism Community Trades
TTS	Text-to-speech
UDL	Universal Design for Learning
UK	United Kingdom
VP	Vice president

Book Icons

Icon	Description
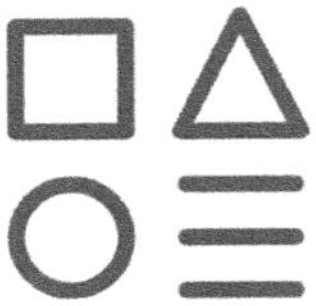	**How To –** Practical instructions and actionable guidance
	**Story –** Lived experiences from the author and employee interviews from around the world.
	**Assets –** Free downloadable content to support your journey
	**Reflection –** Questions to deepen your understanding and insight.

Foreword

When I first studied Susan Fitzell's work, I was struck by her deep understanding of how people learn and, more importantly, how they think.

With over three decades of experience in education, Susan is someone who has dedicated her life to unlocking potential, particularly in neurodivergent individuals. While many would see her extensive background in education as a hurdle when stepping into the corporate arena, I saw it for what it truly is: a tremendous advantage.

Susan's expertise in neurodiversity offers an invaluable perspective that organizations desperately need today. She understands not only the unique strengths that neurodivergent individuals bring to the table but also the challenges they face in traditional workplace environments.

As someone who identifies as neurodivergent herself, Susan brings firsthand knowledge to her work, which gives her an extraordinary ability to connect with both individuals and organizations looking to foster more inclusive workplaces.

What makes Susan's approach so powerful is that she never saw neurodivergence as something to be "accommodated" in a token way. Instead, she recognizes that by authentically welcoming varied ways of processing and learning, organizations can unlock a wealth of creativity and innovation that typically goes untapped.

Her insights aren't just theoretical. They're grounded in years of practical experience helping people thrive in environments that weren't originally designed for them.

In *Neurodiversity in the Workplace: Maximizing Success Through Inclusive Dynamic Workplace Design*, Susan distills her vast knowledge into clear, actionable strategies that leaders at all levels can apply immediately.

This isn't just a book for HR professionals or C-suite executives—it's for anyone who cares about building a workplace where every person's strengths are recognized and harnessed.

Susan's work has already sparked change in organizations across industries, and this book will take her message even further. I'm excited to see the impact it will have on the future of workplace design and leadership. The strategies and insights she shares will be a gamechanger for companies looking to create environments where everyone, no matter how their brain works, can contribute at their highest level.

—Mark Levy
Differentiation Expert, Levy Innovation LLC
LevyInnovation.com

About the Author

Susan Fitzell, M.Ed., CSP, is an internationally recognized speaker, author, and consultant specializing in neurodiversity and workplace inclusion. With over four decades of experience in education and business, she helps organizations harness the strengths of neurodivergent talent, driving innovation and productivity.

As a neurodivergent individual and parent of a neurodivergent child, Susan brings lived experience to her work. Her expertise bridges the gap between education and the workplace, equipping leaders with practical strategies to foster inclusive, high-performing environments.

Susan has authored more than a dozen books, including *Neurodiversity in the Workplace: Maximizing Success Through Inclusive Dynamic Workplace Design.* She holds a master's degree in education with a focus on conflict resolution and the prestigious Certified Speaking Professional (CSP) designation. Her consulting and speaking provide actionable solutions for companies seeking to reduce turnover, enhance team collaboration, and fully leverage diverse cognitive strengths.

Beyond her work in neurodiversity, Susan applies discipline and adaptability in all areas of life, drawing from her background as a martial artist and competitive ballroom dancer. She and her family proudly embrace their 'geek' status, with a household of engineers, including her husband, who is a software engineer, and her two children, who are both mechanical engineers and have benefited from the strategies she shares.

Susan's mission is simple: to help leaders implement inclusive practices that unlock human potential, ensuring workplaces where all employees, especially those who think differently, can thrive.

Contact the author:

For more information, visit *www.SusanFitzell.com* or call 603-625-6087.

Assets:

Free downloadable content to support your journey are available at *https://www.neurodiversityatwork.biz*

Preface

My Origin Story and the Business Case for Neurodiversity

Introduction: Who I Am Now

I'm an international speaker and author. I aim to help people reach their full potential in schools and businesses. I work with organizations to create inclusive cultures that boost innovation and bring out the best in employees.

I've lived with neurodivergence my whole life. This gives me a unique view of the world. I've been diagnosed with dyslexia, ADHD, and central auditory processing disorder. I'm also late-diagnosis autism. My journey has been one of both challenges and insights, positioning me as a neurodiversity expert who recognizes the inherent value of neurodivergent individuals within professional settings. I've seen firsthand the value differently wired brains bring to the table.

My Origin Story and the Business Case for Neurodiversity

From the time I was a child, I saw things differently from those around me. Although I lacked the words to describe it, I knew I was different. These differences became apparent early on.

I first wondered what was wrong with me when I was five or six. My father was building something in the basement, and I would startle every time he'd hit the nail with a hammer. I remember noticing that there was a rhythm as he hammered, and I knew when the next nail would be hit. Yet I still startled. What was wrong with me? Why would I still startle even when I knew what was coming?

I couldn't handle jack-in-the-boxes, either. My friends loved them, and I hated them. Every time a jack-in-the-box came out, I would startle—and not a little one but a huge startle with sound effects! Even then, I realized it was an overreaction and was embarrassed.

I remember being in third grade, and the class was out of control. I became so overwhelmed that I put my hands over my ears and screamed, "Would everybody please shut up!" I'll never forget the look on my teacher's face. To this day, I wonder why I didn't get in trouble. Instead, she quieted the class.

I have always been sensitive to sound and noise. This sensitivity has been a lifelong companion, intensifying at family gatherings where the noise would overwhelm my senses despite my own tendency to be loud. It didn't make sense to me then, and it took years to understand that I was on sensory overload.

As I've gotten older, my noise sensitivity has not improved. It's gotten worse. Lots of noises bother me. I try to ignore the agitation I'm feeling and get through it. And my startle reflex? It is still over the top. Years later, a diagnosis of central auditory processing disorder and the suggestion of misophonia began to explain these lifelong experiences.

Alongside these auditory challenges, I faced attention deficit hyperactivity disorder (ADHD). I often got in trouble as a kid when I was sent on errands to pick up a few things at the corner store. By the time I got there, I'd forgotten what I was supposed to buy! I was labeled flaky by teachers and peers because I masked my inner turmoil with a bubbly exterior. My struggles with focus and memory were compounded by depression, a hollow feeling that a compassionate guidance counselor helped me navigate.

Dyslexia was another piece of my puzzle, explaining my slow reading and difficulty keeping up with academic demands. Despite loving to read, I could only manage a few pages before fatigue set in. I was different, and I didn't fit in. I just wanted to fast-forward through my life and reach adulthood, where I believed my life would be better.

My Point of View

Until recently, I didn't understand that my differences were an advantage. It was hard for me to watch people around me suffer. I know that I am different. I grew up challenging the status quo, defending the underdogs, and trying to protect the people that I loved. All these traits backfired on me at different points in my life. I've always seen the world differently from most people around me.

Maybe that's why I've always felt the need to fight for the underdog. Maybe that's why I became a teacher. I've always taught students who struggled in school. Even though they could not write well, pass a test, or read fast enough to keep up with the other students, my struggling students were some of the school's funniest, most inventive, and most creative problem-solvers.

Then I had children of my own. My two children couldn't be more different from each other. When my son, Ian, was diagnosed with dyslexia, his doctor explained that, given how severe his dyslexia was, he must be brilliant to be doing as well as he was in school. Then, after evaluating me, he said, "The apple doesn't fall too far from the tree." What a thing to say, right? I'll never forget the doctor's words to me that day.

This little boy was doing puzzles designed for eight-year-olds when he was only three. He was constantly exploring how things worked and how they were put together. He was that kid we gave old appliances so he could take them apart and figure out how they worked. He was also the kid who was so behind in reading that teachers thought he had ADHD. His teachers told him he wasn't honors-level material when he wanted to take an honors English class. He saw the world with a different set of eyes from his peers and many adults.

I saw his brilliance. I made it my mission to teach him that (1) he was smart, and (2) he would have to learn how to learn so he could survive the flawed school system. Schools are based on a deficit model of skills instead of a gifts-mindset that focuses on student strengths.

Today Ian is an award-winning mechanical engineer working for one of the big three in the automotive industry. He has not only exceeded most of his teachers' expectations but also become a sought-after talent in his field. Throughout his career, Ian has been hand-selected by two different automotive companies to work on cutting-edge projects. In one role, he was chosen to design a high-performance race-car engine, showcasing his ability to push the boundaries of automotive technology. Currently, he's applying his innovative thinking to the development of hydrogen fuel technology, a crucial area for the future of sustainable transportation. Ian's success story demonstrates how his divergent thinking, seen as a challenge in school, has become his greatest asset in an engineering department that values creative problem-solving and groundbreaking ideas.

In today's fast-changing business world, embracing neurodiversity is vital. It's the right thing to do. It also gives your organization a strategic edge. It can help your business reach new heights. My journey has sparked a passion for fixing a problem that affects us all. It began with feeling different as a child. Then I saw my students' struggles. Ultimately, I needed to help my son see his worth and capabilities.

Neurodiversity is about unlocking untapped potential. Varied cognitive styles can drive innovation and success in your corporation. In a world obsessed with 'normalcy,' we value conformity over creativity. We risk stifling the differences in perspective that fuel progress. Our schools often reflect this mindset. They segregate students by perceived ability. Businesses frequently mirror this approach by only hiring people who fit their narrow definition of an ideal employee. Yet true breakthroughs occur through divergent thinking. They come from welcoming unconventional views.

Imagine a workplace where diverse cognitive styles are not just accepted but celebrated. Where diverse views enrich problem-solving and challenge the status quo. This leads to innovative solutions and competitive advantages. This is the power of neurodiversity—a power that is often overlooked yet holds the key to transformative success.

As a leader, your role is critical in shifting the narrative from a deficit mindset to a gifts-mindset. By harnessing the unique strengths of neurodivergent individuals, you can create an environment where all employees thrive. This will lead to a dynamic, forward-thinking organization. This isn't just about shedding outdated views. It's a step toward a future that values all employees' talents.

Join me in this mission to redefine success, not just for the few but for all. By championing neurodiversity, you will enhance the well-being of your workforce and position your company as a leader in innovation and inclusivity. Together, we can create a world where different minds drive extraordinary achievements.

Leveraging Neurodiversity: A Strategic Advantage for Business

Big tech companies have faced a skills gap for years, and the demand for talent in this industry has never stopped growing. So tech has been the perfect setting for the embrace of neurodivergent thinkers. Over the past decade, efforts to promote neurodiversity in the workplace have gathered steam, and companies have benefited.

Neurodiverse-friendly recruiting and hiring practices can benefit any company. The investment has yielded greater patenting, innovation, process improvement, efficiency, and creativity not only in technology but also in fields that include investment banking, insurance, the energy sector, skilled trades, and mortgage banking.

What can employees with dyslexia, autism, or dyspraxia, or those who are differently abled, bring to a company?

Adding divergent thinkers to the workplace may be a company's best investment to increase its competitive advantage.

Adding divergent thinkers to the workplace may be a company's best investment to increase its competitive advantage.

When my children turned sixteen, I had their aptitudes assessed at the Johnson O'Connor Research Foundation in Boston, Massachusetts. I'll never forget the words of the evaluator who assessed my son's aptitude. She said, "I've never seen an aptitude chart like yours. Your spatial intelligence is literally off the chart. You could be a successful surgeon, architect, or engineer with this profile. The only problem is that your ability to do clerical work is extremely low. Those are the skills necessary to do school."

> *She also said, "You work best in the middle of chaos. Make sure your roommate in college doesn't mind a messy room." I was stunned. I didn't know that was a thing! He works best in a mess.*

Divergent thinkers are different. They think differently, they learn differently, and they communicate differently. Instead of measuring divergent thinkers' value with a deficit model, focus on their gifts. Instead of a deficit mindset, consider a gifts-mindset instead.

Traits of ADHD

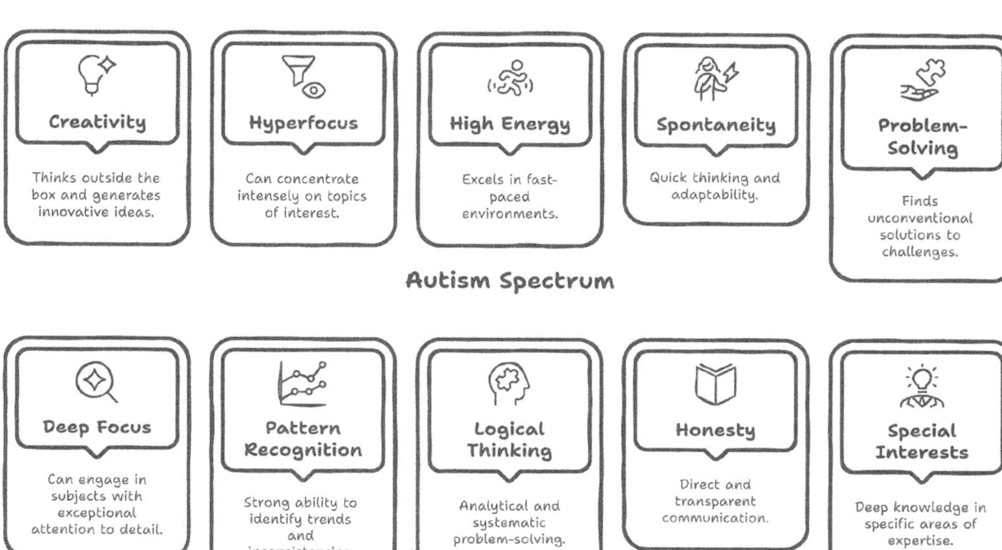

Dyscalculia

Dyslexia

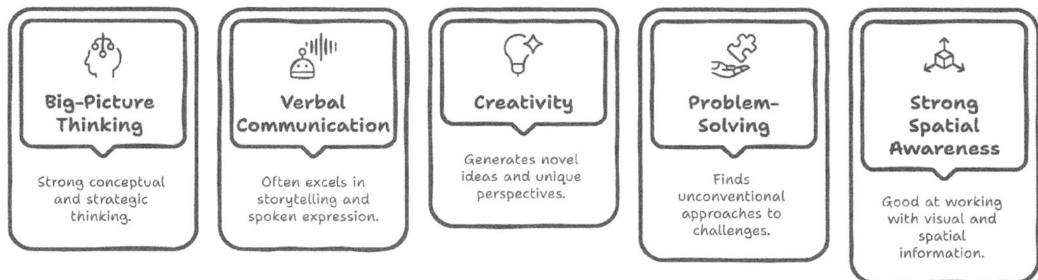

Figure 1.1A -· neurodivergent strengths chart

Dyspraxia

Creativity
Thinks divergently and innovates in problem-solving.

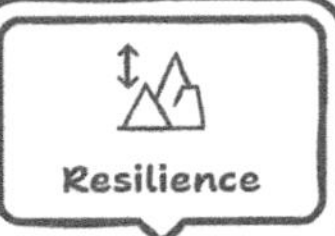
Resilience
Overcomes challenges with persistence.

Empathy
Strong ability to understand and connect with others.

Verbal Strengths
Often articulate and expressive in storytelling.

Strategic Thinking
Finds alternate ways to complete tasks.

Obsessive-Compulsive Disorder

Attention to Detail
Excels in precision and accuracy.

Strong Work Ethic
Commitment to completing tasks thoroughly.

High Standards
Produces high-quality work.

Reliability
Consistently follows through on tasks.

Pattern Recognition
Identifies trends and inconsistencies others may miss.

Tourette Syndrome

Quick Thinking
Reacts fast in dynamic situations.

Resilience
Develops strong coping mechanisms.

Creativity
Expresses thoughts in original and spontaneous ways.

Humor
Often uses wit to navigate social interactions.

Sensory Processing Differences

Heightened Awareness
Strong ability to notice details others overlook.

Creativity
Uses sensory experiences to inspire innovation.

Empathy
Deep understanding of sensory challenges in others.

Unique Perspectives
Approaches tasks in nontraditional ways.

Figure 1.1B - neurodivergent strengths chart

The Business Case for Hiring Neurodivergent Talent

Neurodivergent employees think in ways that bring a different level of talent and skill to the problem-solving process. For example, a person with dyslexia can be an advantage to a company that needs someone skilled in pattern recognition.

"Many people with these disorders have higher-than-average abilities; research shows that some conditions, including autism and dyslexia, can bestow special skills in pattern recognition, memory, or mathematics. Yet those affected often struggle to fit the profiles sought by prospective employers," said Robert D. Austin and Gary P. Pisano in a *Harvard Business Review* (HBR) article.

Neurodivergent team members challenge groupthink and the status quo. They bring a new perspective to process improvement, problem-solving, and innovation. They can see value and opportunity in areas that may otherwise be overlooked or put aside.

Unfortunately, unemployment among neurodivergent individuals at all levels of ability runs as high as 80 percent (and that was pre-pandemic). According to the Austin and Pisano report, those who manage to find employment are often underemployed, not fully using their talents.

What a loss for companies that would benefit from neurodiverse teams.

Neurodivergent employees think in ways that bring a different level of talent and skill to the problem-solving process.

Future-Proofing Your Workforce: The Strategic Advantage of Neurodiverse Teams

Innovation and creativity are the lifeblood of business. To get to both, you need different perspectives and ways of thinking. That is why companies hire consultants and agencies.

A more effective way for businesses to gain different perspectives and divergent thinking, though, is to hire a diverse team. Neurodiversity is just as important as other forms of diversity. A neurodivergent person's brain is wired differently. They experience the world differently from neurotypical people and often have different perspectives.

People with obsessive-compulsive disorder (OCD) or autism may be frustrated with systems or processes and, consequently, find ways to make them more efficient. People with sensory processing disorders may help workplaces rethink how they communicate to keep employees happy and increase productivity.

Recently, I spoke with Gregg Gregory on his podcast, *The Teamwork Advantage,* about the importance of neurodiverse teams. We discussed the challenges of neurodiversity in the workplace and its advantages.

So why is neurodiversity important in business environments?

Driving Innovation: The Neurodivergent Advantage

Some of the world's greatest minds are neurodivergent. Bill Gates recently identified as autistic. Richard Branson and Charles Schwab have dyslexia. All of them credit their neurodivergence for their success. It allowed them to see the world differently and approach problems from a different angle.

Did you know the late founder of Ikea, Ingvar Kamprad, was dyslexic? His dyslexia was the reason for the unique Swedish names of all their products. He struggled with inventory numbers, so he decided to name the products.

The corporate world often gets bogged down in "the ways things are done" and fails to acknowledge that there may be better ways to do things. All it takes is a little bit of frustration and determination to find a solution. For example, at one point many businesses shifted to an open-plan office layout to encourage collaboration and create a sense of team unity. At the time, a lot of data showed that the switch would positively affect employee productivity. However, many thought leaders and researchers have since come to realize that the challenges of these designs outweigh the benefits. Instead of adhering to rigid, one-size-fits-all solutions, it's time to embrace flexibility in workspace design.

I propose the concept of Inclusive Dynamic Workplace Design™ (IDWD), explained in chapter 2. This allows for multiple workspace options and thus supports employees' diverse needs and preferences.

Neurodivergence Leads Us to Rethink Talent

Each employee brings a unique set of strengths and weaknesses to their role. One may excel at presenting and public speaking but struggle with project management, while another may be a coding whiz but fall behind on admin work. It's time to shift our perspective and recognize that these differences are not shortcomings but unique attributes that contribute to a team's success.

Workplaces are already familiar with combining different disciplines and talents to create a product or finish a project. Marketing agencies will form small groups to create a campaign: Writers, designers, project managers, and lawyers all work on a new campaign to ensure that each aspect of the project is completed to the highest standard. It is unreasonable to expect one person to be able to research, write, design, *and* check a campaign for compliance.

People with OCD or those on the autism spectrum have shown remarkable talent, especially in technical fields such as software development. However, many have historically failed the traditional interview test because their behavior doesn't follow social protocols. Or worse, they are hired for their exceptional talent but leave when bullied or ostracized in their teams because people feel uncomfortable around them. Why? Because they are odd or quirky or don't make eye contact.

In reality, neurodiverse teams offer businesses an opportunity to rethink the way they do things. The scope of roles could be narrowed to better fit employees' talents. What if each job-related task was always done by the person who was the most talented at it? An IDWD approach would consider what works best for the employee or team in a given situation.

Neurodiverse teams offer businesses an opportunity to rethink the way they do things.

Would sales increase if a business always sent the salesperson that was most knowledgeable about the client? Would technology improve if the person doing the coding was the best at that specific coding language and kind of project? Instead of forcing employees to spread their efforts over various tasks, we could laser-focus them on getting the most out of their aptitudes.

Driving Innovation: Leveraging Neurodiversity for Market Leadership

Moving to neurodiverse teams offers a prime opportunity to rethink corporate culture. It forces businesses to recognize that no two employees are the same; therefore, a one-size-fits-all approach will not work. When you rework the standard operating procedures to get the most out of neurodivergent employees, it leads to getting the most out of all employees. A better way to support productivity and promote employee loyalty is IDWD, the opposite of one-size-fits-all!

How Top Companies Capitalize on Neurodiversity

Divergent thinkers have helped drive innovation and find radical solutions to challenging problems at firms such as SAP, one of the first companies to develop a neurodiversity program, along with Google, Microsoft, IBM, Hewlett Packard Enterprise, Ford, and others.

Accommodating the preferences of neurodiverse teams can drive significant and positive changes across the workforce. As Celia Daniels wrote in a Daivergent.com post, "Paying attention to the comfort of your employees, especially [neurodivergent] ones, will make your working environment better for your staff." The shift toward inclusivity can create a more optimistic and productive work environment.

At SAP, including divergent thinkers on teams has had a profound effect. "SAP teams who have colleagues with autism report a rise in patent applications, innovations in products, and an increase in management skills and empathy," said Chief Executive Christian Klein, according to a report in *The Conversation.* (Adams, 2020) This underscores the unique skills and contributions that neurodivergent individuals can bring to the workforce, fostering a sense of appreciation and respect for their potential.

> ***"SAP teams who have colleagues with autism report a rise in patent applications, innovations in products, and an increase in management skills and empathy."***
>
> ***~ Chief Executive Christian Klein***

Optimizing Talent Acquisition: Removing Barriers to Neurodivergent Talent

Customary hiring practices will almost always miss neurodivergent talent.

Trying to change this by hunting for more variety in candidates has been shown not to work. HBR said, "Many have taken that approach: Their managers still work top down from strategies to capabilities needed, translating those into organizational roles, job descriptions, and recruiting checklists. But two big problems cause them to miss neurodivergent talent." (Austin & Pisano, 2017c)

Those two problems are *traditional interviewing approaches* and a *desire for conformity.* These trouble spots are challenging for those on the autism spectrum.

Many people on the autism spectrum *do not* interview well. They may have trouble making eye contact or take the conversation off on tangents. Worse, they may have low self-confidence due to poor interview experiences in the past. The traditional interview is not an effective way to assess their capabilities. Companies recruiting neurodivergent talent must adjust their interview and selection process to be more inclusive.

Every one of us has unique talents that we bring to our work and our teams. Sometimes the best solutions evolve out of the divergent thinking fostered by neurodiversity in the workplace.

Shifting Paradigms: A New Approach to Talent Management

Historically, people have viewed neurodiversity from a deficit model point of view. Unfortunately, this is the prevailing view. While the world remains largely neuro-typical- centric, it's crucial to recognize that neurodivergent brains are merely the other side of the same human neurological coin. Both are integral parts of our diverse cognitive landscape.

To illustrate, consider this: Humans tend to categorize, sort, and normalize information. In short, we do this to facilitate our understanding of a complex world. This tendency to categorize makes things manageable so we can focus on what we need to do. Unfortunately, the approach fails us when we attempt to understand humans. We desperately want human interaction to be simple, but it isn't.

The Double-Edged Sword: Medicine and Mental Health Diagnoses

Medicine has done a fantastic job defining medical pathologies that can be addressed and cured. But how do we know when we have gone too far? Diagnosing neurological differences is a double-edged sword. On one hand, a diagnosis can open doors to support, accommodations, and vital resources allowing neurodivergent individuals to thrive. Accessing these supports can be challenging, if not impossible, in most countries without a formal label. On the other hand, we must question: At what point does labeling natural human variation as a "disorder" become excessive? There's a fine line between recognizing genuine challenges and pathologizing normal differences in human cognition and behavior. This balance is critical as we strive to create a more inclusive society that values neurodiversity while still providing necessary support.

To illustrate this concept, consider that as humans, we pride ourselves on being unique. We show compassion that counters the survival-of-the-fittest idea. We take care of one another, even to our detriment. We are charitable. We love and mourn in ways that aren't seen among other creatures. All this is clearest in families and small communities. However, as the group grows, people create divisions among themselves. This division happens when some interpersonal conflict can potentially threaten the group's status quo. The result is an us-versus-them mindset.

This situation can stabilize if the conflicting groups are well matched in number and strengths. However, it can become a vastly different situation when there is a clear social minority. Without a proper understanding of differences, this approach can cause harmless traits to be pathologized, and those possessing those traits become marginalized.

Asset-Based Talent Strategy: Moving from a Deficit Mindset to a Gifts-Mindset

This fact is evident if we consider the ideas behind the deficit mindset versus a gifts-mindset. As mentioned earlier, medical diagnoses are inherently based on a deficit mindset. (ANet Staff, n.d.).That's appropriate since medicine aims to heal a problem. When does this go too far, though?

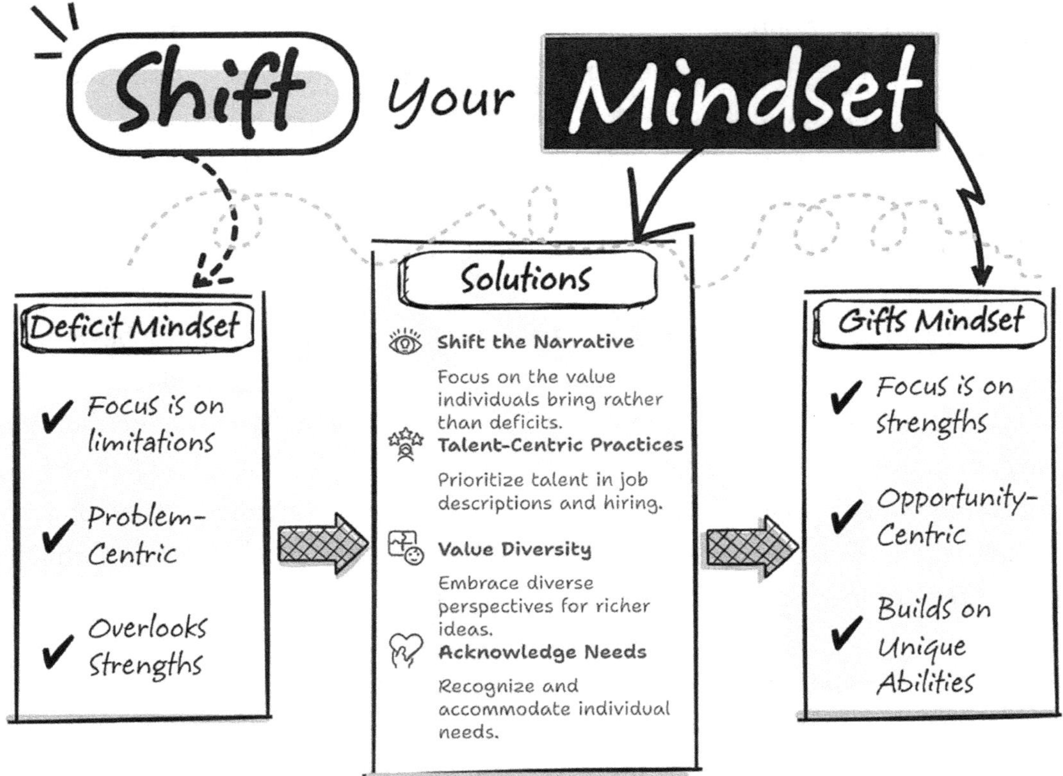

Do all aspects of a learning or sensory processing difference need to be viewed from a deficit point of view? No. They do not.

"In education, a **deficit mindset** is when teachers or school leaders focus on problems rather than potential." (ANet Staff, n.d.-a) I prefer a **gifts mindset** approach. A gifts mindset focuses on a person's strengths first and teaches how to utilize a learner's gifts while using specific strategies to overcome obstacles in maximizing talent.

We can extend learners' experiences to the modern workplace. How do employers view neurodiversity in the workplace? Does it seem too much effort to accommodate so much "deficit"? Suppose an employer views neurodiversity through the limiting view of the deficit mindset. In that case, it can seem like more effort than it's worth.

However, by shifting toward a gifts-mindset, organizations can unlock tremendous potential. Embracing neurodiversity isn't just about accommodation. It's about using unique strengths to drive innovation and productivity.

The Double Empathy Theory

Like so much of life, the viewpoint we choose matters. The double empathy theory purports that deficits in communication between autistics and non-autistics are a two-way street. In other words, the deficit in communication must be accounted for by both parties instead of laying the blame on the autistic alone. An extension of the theory holds that the problem is not precisely the pathology of a neurodivergent individual but rather the setting or the environment. Consider this:

The double empathy model "suggests that disability is more external circumstances that impact a person, and less a set of personal attributes. So, the person with ADHD is disabled by a busy, loud office apartment. They themselves are not 'the problem.'" (JazzHR, n.d.)

Recognizing that the entire problem does not belong to the autistic individual is a significant shift in mindset. It's a change that can lead to a more inclusive and understanding workplace.

Workplace Communication Breakdown

The manager interprets the employee's behavior as rudeness due to lack of small talk and eye-contact.

The employee feels frustrated by the manager's indirect communication style. [e.g., hinting ad deadlines instead of stating them clearly

Both parties experience a breakdown in effective communication.

What Both Could Change

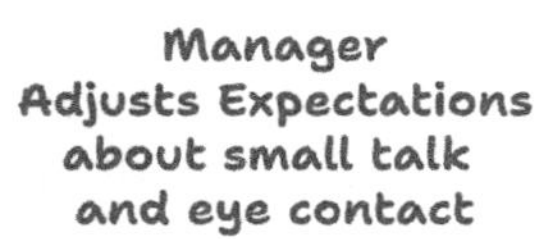

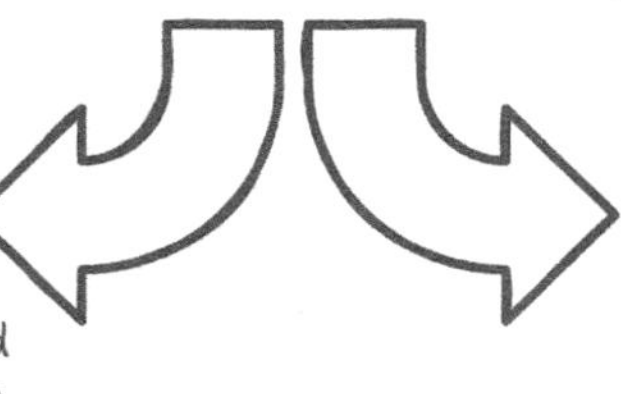

Manager Adjusts Expectations about small talk and eye contact

Focuses on work quality and task completion rather than social conventions.

Autistic Employee Adjusts Without Overcompensating

- Briefly engages in small talk if possible (e.g., "Hope your weekend was good")
- Uses alternative signals of engagement (e.g., nodding, paraphrasing).

How the Scenario Plays Out with These Changes

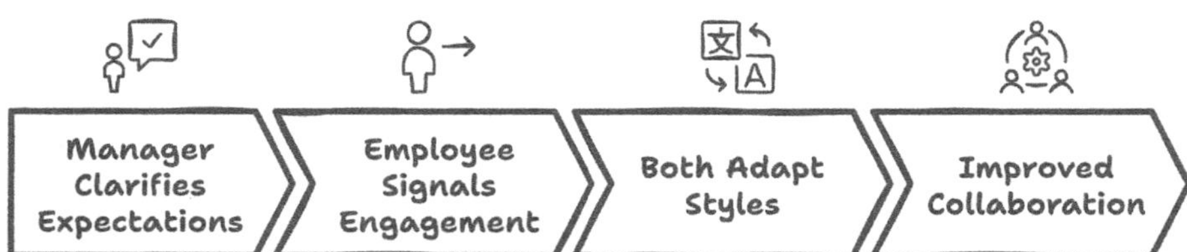

Be direct. Subtlety and hints are often missed.

Nod, paraphrase, or signal as is comfortable

Both parties adjust without forcing one to conform entirely to the other's style

Resulting in effective teamwork

How the Deficits Model Fails Us in the Workplace

Consider an octopus that ventures out of the water onto the seashore. Under such exceptional circumstances, the octopus can survive for a few minutes. However, its ability to thrive is limited by the environment. Does this mean the octopus has an inherent deficit or pathology? No, it's the environment that restricts its potential.

Okay, let's take a classroom example I have seen firsthand many times. Jayden is a first-grader who is doing exceptionally well in school. His parents were concerned because he had so much energy that he could barely sit still in kindergarten. In first grade, everything was coming together for Jayden. He was thriving. He loved his teacher.

Then, in second grade, everything changed. Jayden's teacher called home multiple times to complain that Jayden was distracted, bored, and exhibiting challenging behaviors. Finally, the second-grade teacher referred Jayden to special education for an evaluation. Jayden is now diagnosed and labeled. This is the same kid who thrived in first grade with a teacher who understood how he learned. Then he went to the second grade and had a different teacher who was less tolerant of Jayden's energy level and struggled to engage him in learning.

Is Jayden like the octopus?

Over the past four decades, countless stories and studies have shown how students who fail in one learning environment may thrive in a different one. So why are children pathologized?

They're pathologized because it's easier to blame the children or parents than to fix a broken system. The system is broken for many reasons; however, it starts by viewing children through a deficit model instead of a gifts-mindset. A gifts-mindset would focus on children's strengths instead of their deficits.

Environment plays a huge role in life, from microscopic life to plant life to, without a doubt, humans' ability to thrive. If the deficit point of view is maintained, accommodating neurodivergent talent in the workplace can seem impossible.

To create beneficial and kind classrooms and workspaces, we must replace the deficit mindset with a gifts-mindset. In schools, this is called Universal Design for Learning. In the workplace, it's called Inclusive Dynamic Workplace Design.

A key characteristic often associated with autism is difficulty in social interaction and communication. However, the double empathy model challenges us to reconsider this perspective. This theory suggests that communication challenges aren't solely the responsibility of autistic individuals. Instead, it proposes that the difficulty arises from both sides—autistic and non-autistic—struggling to understand and relate to each other's different ways of thinking and communicating.

While this might be uncomfortable, it deserves consideration. Consider marriage relationships; both parties hold some responsibility in a disagreement. It gets ugly when one party puts itself on a perfection pedestal and claims the other is always to blame.

In his article "The Double Empathy Problem," Dr. Damian Milton stated, "These issues are not due to autistic cognition alone, but a breakdown in reciprocity and mutual understanding that can happen between people with very different ways of experiencing the world."

Why Does This Change in Perspective Matter?

Imagine a world where we lead with reciprocity and mutual understanding. Is it possible? I'd like to believe it is for those who strive for it in their corner of the world, one human light at a time. Each of us has the power to make a difference, and it's through our individual actions that we can bring about this change.

We are experiencing a world where an us-versus-them mindset leads to striations and conflict. The result is chilling. It's tearing apart families, friendships, and countries. So how can we be the light? Let's start with inclusion: Workplaces, like classrooms, are based on an implicit hierarchy. The teacher can implicitly and unconsciously influence the classroom culture at the school. The same goes for management in the workplace.

We are experiencing a world where an us-versus-them mindset leads to striations and conflict. The result is chilling. It's tearing apart families, friendships, and countries.

What can management do? Work toward a company culture that includes IDWD. Not only does IDWD consider physical space, corporate policies, and options for individual employee success, but it also makes inclusion and equity the norm.

The Language of Neurodiversity: Terms and Definitions

In my work to help businesses and educational organizations develop and implement strategies that optimize learning and productivity in a neurodiverse world, I have come to realize that there is quite a bit of confusion and disagreement out there about the vocabulary we use to discuss neurodiversity and the neurodivergent community.

This lack of clarity came into focus during an interview with Ken Blackwell on his Insight at Work podcast. When he asked me to explain the difference between neurodivergent, neurodivergence, and neurodiverse, we discussed prejudice, intrinsic bias, and how we define normal. This conversation got me thinking about how our use of language influences both our individual and our collective sense of reality, particularly when it comes to how we see, interact with, and regard the people closest to us.

After all, these terms describe concepts that have only become available within the last thirty-five years or so.

When advocating for neurodiversity and inclusion, we must speak the same language. Intentionally choosing our words is one of the most impactful steps we can take toward creating the inclusive world we are striving for. There is some disagreement in the field over the language chosen as well as how it is used. Partly this is because, for many years, the term *neurodiverse* referred to adults with autism. There is also controversy over person-first versus identity-first language. I have chosen to take my definitions from the universities that define and research neurodiversity at work initiatives. I've also decided to respect the autistic community, which mostly (but not entirely) prefers identity-first language. Following are the definitions I will be using in this book.

Autist

Urban Dictionary states that this word, "has contemporary usage as a self-identifier and a term of endearment used online by individuals who self-identify as non-neurotypical."

Divergent Thinkers

I prefer to use this term to describe neurodivergent people. They are those whose ways of thinking diverge from the norm.

Inclusive Dynamic Workplace Design

IDWD is a holistic approach to workplace inclusivity. It focuses on how employers can adapt to support neurodivergent employees. This approach goes beyond the physical workspace to address learning design, psychological safety, diversity, inclusion, and workplace culture.

Critical components of IDWD include:

- Reprioritizing physical office space to accommodate new ways of working, such as creating a variety of spaces within the office for different types of work, designing employee workspaces for a hybrid environment, and ensuring a comfortable and safe environment.

- Ensuring employees have access to necessary tools and technologies, which includes creating a secure IT environment for both in-office and remote work, seamless file access for remote employees, and implementing reliable communication systems.
- Improving knowledge management and employee learning by providing resources that deliver information in multiple formats and prioritize accessibility. Learning Management Systems (LMS), workshops, and training that recognizes and supports each employee's unique skills and abilities yield the highest training return on investment (ROI).

The goal is to create flexible work environments that cut distractions, build collaborative teams, and promote innovation and focused productivity. Most accommodations benefit all employees, not just those who are neurodivergent. IDWD delivers an inclusive, human-centric workplace.

Gifted

Gifted individuals demonstrate exceptionally high levels of aptitude or competence in one or more areas. Gifted children perform at levels significantly beyond what is considered typical for their age. For example, a child can be gifted with high intelligence or exceptional musical, art, or math talent.

Identity-First Language versus Person-First Language

The identity-first language used in this book is a choice made out of respect for most autistic adults and many neurodivergents' preferences. A new rule emerging is if a diagnosis is typically regarded as a disease, then it's "a person with..." (person-first language), but if it's part of a person's "wiring" such as autism, then it's "autistic person." (identity-first language).

Masking

It's what neurodivergents do when they don't want others to know they are different. When a neurodivergent person is masking, they are hiding their neurodivergent traits or learning challenges from their peers, teachers, or co-workers.

Neurodevelopmental Condition

Neurodevelopmental conditions, usually called disorders, develop before birth, in infancy, or in early childhood. The term refers to cognition that develops differently from the norm. Examples are ADHD, autism, speech and language disorders, and Tourette's syndrome. This differs from mental illness. Note that these conditions are classified differently in various countries.

Neurodivergence

This general term describes the different manifestations of neurodivergent thinking in a neurodiverse world. It is the "state of being neurodivergent." For example, dyslexia and dyspraxia are specific types of neurodivergence.

Neurodivergent (ND)

This word describes an individual whose way of thinking is outside society's defined version of typical. Frequently, it is abbreviated as ND.
Many times, neurodivergent people will have a diagnosis or label you may recognize, like autism, dyslexia, or ADHD. Neurodivergent people are sometimes described as having a neurodevelopmental disorder. Their brain wiring is different from birth.

Neurodiverse

The term neurodiverse was coined in 1998 by Australian sociologist Judy Singer in a thesis published at the University of Technology in Sydney. Singer introduced the term as an alternative to deficit-based language, such as disorder. This word is pretty similar to neurodiversity but should be used as an adjective. You can say, for example, that your workplace is neurodiverse.

Neurodiversity

Judy Singer initially proposed the term neurodiversity to describe an emerging movement that includes people who are autistic or have a range of other conditions, such as ADHD, dyspraxia, dyslexia, and more. They are part of the endlessly different ways that human brains are wired. This term recognizes the natural variation in how human minds work. It includes people who are neurotypical as well as those who are neurodivergent. When I talk about promoting neurodiversity in the workplace, for example, I am referring to creating a diverse workforce representative of the broad spectrum of ways of thinking, processing information, communication, and learning that exist. Some employees may be "normal" or neurotypical, while others may have ADHD, dyslexia, autism, OCD, or dyspraxia. Neurodiversity, in this capacity, does not refer to any particular label or diagnosis but rather the concept of an environment where diverse minds coexist.

Neurodiversity at Work Initiatives

Neurodiversity at work initiatives encompass various programs aimed at supporting neurodivergent individuals in the workplace, recognizing their unique talents, and promoting inclusive employment practices. Two renowned initiatives are:

1. Neurodiversity at Work at Kennedy Krieger
2. Neurodiversity @ Work Employer Roundtable

Both underscore the value of embracing neurodiversity in the workplace, not just for the benefit of neurodivergent individuals but also for enriching organizational culture and performance. These initiatives demonstrate a growing recognition of the need to support neurodivergent talent through inclusive hiring practices, training, and community engagement.

Neurodiversity Movement

The neurodiversity movement is a social and advocacy movement that promotes the understanding and acceptance of neurological differences as natural and valuable variations in the human brain. This movement is grounded in the belief that neurological differences like autism, ADHD, dyslexia, and others are not defects or disorders that need to be cured or fixed but rather unique attributes that contribute to the natural variation of human experience.

Neuroinclusive

Neuroinclusive refers to practices, environments, or philosophies that actively include and accommodate people of all neurological types. Being neuroinclusive means acknowledging that there is no one "right" way of thinking, learning, or behaving. A workplace culture that is neuroinclusive makes a concerted effort to respect and accommodate diverse neurological conditions within society.

Neurominority

This term refers to specific groups of individuals who can be grouped based on the shared characteristics of their neurodivergence. What is interesting to note here is that the neurodivergence such a group shares is often discriminated against. You could say that autistic people are a sizable neurominority. People with OCD are also a neuro- minority, with many individuals choosing to take dramatic measures to blend in with their neurotypical counterparts to avoid judgments and misunderstanding. This effort to hide neurodivergence is an example of masking. If individuals are unsuccessful, they are frequently discriminated against and socially excluded.

Neurotypical (NT)

Neurotypical people are what society would generally deem to be "normal." They are often abbreviated as NT.

In Summary

I choose to align with definitions that do not focus on disorders or label atypical cognitive function as a mental illness or disorder. After decades of working with neurodivergents, I understand all too well the damage those classifications can cause because of stigma and stereotypes.

On the other hand, I realize that we must be careful not to promote a view that neurodivergence needs no accommodations or services. Labels exist because a diagnosis or label is required to get needed services. It's a double-edged sword!

People involved with neurodiversity at work initiatives have been working for a long time to create consistency in the correct usage of the words I've described above. When we can accurately describe the world around us and the people that inhabit it, we can develop the collective mentality necessary for a world free of discrimination.

A Word about Diagnoses and Labels

One thing I want to touch upon when I talk about the language of neurodiversity is the concept of neurodivergence as a disorder. The neurodiversity movement clarifies that individual neurodivergence does not equate to a neurological disorder. That word, *disorder,* fundamentally implies that something is wrong with a person.

I suppose this is really at the heart of the issue. While neurodivergence does not need fixing, accommodations and support may be necessary. In some circumstances, such as brain changes that may be the result of a physical illness or trauma, they may need to be treated medically. Other times, different brain wiring can cause significant challenges that require accommodation and support. Some of the backlash against the neurodiversity movement is because neurodivergence, especially autism, is painted with a broad brush that minimizes the needs of neurodivergent children and adults who are more challenged and, therefore, need significant support. There is a danger that government support of individuals with more significant needs will be denied or minimized if we don't acknowledge the entirety of the spectrum.

As an educator who understands how the system works, I am greatly concerned about this. It's essential to focus on people's strengths, but it's also important not to deny services to individuals with significant needs. In the United States, the reason that neurodivergence is considered a disability and designated as such in the *Diagnostic and Statistical Manual of Mental Disorders* (DSM) is that for money to be appropriated for specialized training and supports, a student must be labeled and identified as disabled or otherwise health-impaired to get any services in schools.

Neurodivergent People Do Not Need to Be Fixed

There is no ideal kind of mind. There is no right or wrong. The spectrum of human cognitive patterns is just as valuable as the tapestry of human culture.

Unfortunately, many divergent thinkers have grown up defined by the labels placed upon them. These labels often carry stereotypes, misconceptions, and outright discrimination. While diagnosis and labels can be helpful and, at times, necessary tools, they just as often create mental roadblocks for the neurotypical person. This can lead to subtle and not-so-subtle discrimination against the divergent thinkers of the world.

Mitigating Labels and Bias: Strategies for Equitable Career Advancement

I strongly dislike labels. I'm putting that right out there so I can explain why. When I was a teacher, I understood the advantages and disadvantages of labeling students. Labeling can be much more problematic in adulthood, especially in the workplace.

With neurodiversity at work initiatives being embraced in companies worldwide, labeling seems to be in vogue, at least in the executive suite. At the employee level, it's not nearly so popular. Most employees who were labeled in school with learning disabilities do everything possible to hide those labels in their adult lives.

Yet it seems that many companies want to fly the banner and shout out to the world that they are embracing neurodiversity. In their efforts to do so, they are embracing labels to identify and classify neurodivergent workers and new hires. While this can be helpful when educating neurotypical employees and managers about neurodivergent conditions, in many cases, companies are:

- Struggling to get the labels right.

- Unwittingly creating a subgroup in the workspace that may not appreciate being put out on display.
- Oblivious to the neurodivergent thinkers who have been hiding in their ranks for decades.

The Power of a Word

Words aren't just placeholders. They determine what we see and, therefore, influence our mental set—which in turn influences our response to situations and people. This is why we must be careful before labeling a person as either neurodivergent or neurotypical. Even when you're poised to take steps forward in a neurodiversity at work initiative, sometimes it's necessary to take a step back to sort these dynamics out. And to be honest, there is still a lot of controversy over these labels.

Some gifted people are furious that the *gifted* label is being used interchangeably with autistic. Not all people in the autism spectrum are gifted, and not all gifted people are in the autism spectrum.

There's also controversy over whether we should say *autistic people* or *people with autism.* Then we have the challenge of understanding that neurodiversity includes divergent thinkers who may not be autistic. They might have dyspraxia, OCD, dyslexia, ADHD, and more.

Wait! They might not even have a diagnosed cognitive issue!

I've never really liked the label *neurodivergent.* I prefer *divergent thinker,* even though neurodivergent is the more accurate definition. But think about the word neurodiversity: *neuro-diversity.* Different patterns of thinking. Unique ways brains process information. It is about divergent thinking.

Unfortunately, this terminology is being increasingly used as a generic label that assumes all neurodivergent people are autistic.

In the admirable move toward creating a more inclusive, rounded, innovative workforce, companies may unwittingly be doing more harm than good by using labels that create assumptions in the minds of their neurotypical workers.

And what will divergent thinkers do if they believe they'll be labeled and treated differently from their peers?

They may shrink into the shadows. They may worry that their peers and managers will ignore or marginalize them. Or worse, they could be laid off and have trouble finding another job because of a label their employer decided would be great for the company.

Workers have reason to worry. An October 2020 survey of United Kingdom managers by The Institute of Leadership found that half of those leaders would not hire a neurodivergent person (The Institute of Leadership, 2020). "Most employers are scared to hire neurodivergent people as they only calculate the risks based on the deficits of the condition," said Claire Smith, CEO of Autistic Nottingham, about the report. (Hanson, 2024)

How do you think this deficit mindset affects neurodivergent employees? Many of them are already painfully aware of prejudice. They experience it in every aspect of their life. Even worse is the feeling that their peers socially exclude them, something The Institute of Leadership report also noted. Labeling isn't going to help them in this case.

It's essential to be informed about these concerns before jumping on the neurodiversity bandwagon and haphazardly applying labels to neurodivergent employees or calling them out to their peers.

Companies must develop a solid strategy for implementing programs that genuinely support neurodivergent employees and divergent thinkers rather than just following a fad.

Embracing the Language of Inclusivity

If you want to dig a little deeper into the specifics of the vocabulary of neurodiversity, look up Nick Walker of *neurocosmopolitanism.com.*

Chances are, whether you know it or not, you have neurodivergent people in your life. If you want to do your part to create a more inclusive world for them and everybody, try to learn and embrace the vocabulary of neurodiversity.

Chapter One Reflection Questions

1. How can embracing neurodiversity give a strategic advantage to businesses? Provide examples from the chapter.
2. What is the difference between a deficit mindset and a gifts-mindset when approaching neurodiversity? How might adopting a gifts-mindset change workplace dynamics?
3. How does the double empathy theory challenge conventional views on communication difficulties between autistic and non-autistic individuals?
4. Discuss the importance of language in shaping perceptions of neurodiversity. How can careful word choice contribute to a more inclusive environment?
5. What are some potential challenges companies might face when implementing neurodiversity initiatives? How can these be addressed?
6. Reflect on the statement: "Neurodivergent people do not need to be fixed." What implications does this have for workplace policies and practices?
7. How can organizations balance the need for diagnoses and labels (to provide necessary accommodations) with the potential negative impacts of labeling employees?
8. Based on the information provided in the chapter, what steps could a company take to create a more neuroinclusive workplace culture?

Optimizing Workplace Design for Peak Performance and Inclusion

At the beginning of this century, one of the hottest trends in office design, at least at dotcoms, where companies all vied to look like they were on the cutting edge of trends, was creating a "loosened up" workplace. (Villalon, n.d.). Companies wanted to attract younger employees with lots of energy and creativity, so dress codes were relaxed. Recreation centers were added that offered video game consoles, nap centers, and meditation rooms. Larger companies added perks like a massage studio, fully stocked kitchens, and even beer and wine.

My conversation with Sam, a neurodivergent individual, revealed a stark contrast with the loosened-up-workplace trend. For her, the open office plan of the past two decades was not an appealing trend, but a source of discomfort and distress.

She explained, "The thing is, I never cared about any of those freebies. I liked the updated dress code because it was realistic. But all those extra perks were distractions I could not stand."

Sam pointed out that the problem was not the perks themselves, but their haphazard implementation. Many workplaces added these perks as an afterthought, creating a cluttered, noisy, and unpredictable environment. This, she explained, could be distressing for people who need structure.

Sam added, "I once walked out in the middle of a job interview because they insisted on conducting it right next to their indoor skateboard ramp! I'm sure they thought it would make them seem really cool or whatever. But it was this huge, noisy thing right next to my head! I freaked out and just left. The woman leading the interview had to come out to the parking lot and give me my backpack because I'd left it there when I ran out."

Regrettably, similar experiences are all too common among neurodivergent individuals in the workforce. They often bear the brunt of policies and procedures designed to enhance efficiency or general productivity, without due consideration for the diverse needs of the workforce. This underscores the pressing need for IDWD, a solution that cannot be delayed.

Don't Leave Out the Human Equation in Office Design

It's estimated that 17 to 33 percent of American adults in the workplace are neurodivergent, according to a recent *Journal of the American Medical Association* article (High Lantern Group, 2024). That range is so wide because many diagnoses are underreported in the workplace, and employees are often, understandably, unwilling to disclose their neurodivergence.

Neurodivergent disorders include learning challenges like dyslexia, dyspraxia, or dysgraphia. They include mental health challenges like depression, anxiety, and OCD. Developmental disabilities such as autism spectrum disorder and ADHD also fall under the neurodivergent umbrella.

It's estimated that 17 to 33 percent of American adults in the workplace are neurodivergent.

DWD is helpful for companies that need flexibility as they grow. It's a practical design approach in the post-pandemic working world, where hybrid work is here to stay. A workplace implementing IDWD can, for example, enable a company to lease a smaller office space and rotate its workers between the office and home using a modified hot-desk system. An office plan is only helpful if it properly accommodates all employees.

IDWD goes beyond the physical workspace environment. It includes flexibility in learning design and is attentive to psychological safety, diversity, and inclusion. It addresses workplace culture and the physical environment.

Key Components of IDWD

Dynamic workplaces need to address these three key elements (Sharma, 2021):

1. Reprioritizing the physical office space and configuring it to address new ways of working.
2. Ensuring employees can access the tools and technologies needed to accomplish their assignments.
3. Leveling up knowledge management and employee learning.

When implemented thoughtfully, these three elements benefit the entire company and can be of the most significant benefit to neurodivergent team members. Let's break them down.

Traditional Workplace Design

Pros	Cons
Encourages collaboration	Increased noise
Innovation potential	Distractions
Social interaction	Fixed seating
Recreational spaces	One-size-fits-all
Structured environment	Lack of flexibility

Three Steps for Reprioritizing Office Space

1. Create a variety of spaces within the office. The old "many cubicles plus one conference room" office setup isn't conducive to concentration or collaboration. A significant element of IDWD is having spaces for employees to do deep work, interspersed with areas where teams can collaborate and people can freely socialize.
2. Design employee workspaces to accommodate a hybrid environment. Remote work was here long before the pandemic. Office space should include consideration that a percentage of your workforce is at home for part (or all) of the week.
3. Create a comfortable, safe environment. Spend a little more on ergonomic chairs and desks. Make sure workers can access their files quickly through a robust network. Designate quiet areas so employees can concentrate. Also, consider a calm, sensory-soothing space free of fluorescent lights and noisy distractors. Furnish it with comfortable seating options with soft fabrics and focus tools.

Tools and Technologies That Increase Productivity

1. Engage with your chief information officer (CIO) to create a secure IT environment for in-office and remote work. All employees need the hardware and software to perform at their best. (That can mean investing in pricier, industry-standard software like Adobe and Microsoft products.)
2. Ensure that remote employees can access their files and virtual workspaces seamlessly. Reduce the hoops they must jump through and implement a single sign-on policy across the company.
3. Implement a reliable, secure videoconferencing system that can be accessed in the office and remotely without a problem.

4. Implement secure, reliable telephony. An office phone is still an essential tool for employees. For many reasons, employees are best not using their personal phones for work calls. Some workers are more comfortable communicating by phone, while others, whether neurodivergent or neurotypical, prefer text or email. And those who work with clients must have a phone. Today's voice over internet protocol (VoIP) softphones have a range of features, including text messaging, video calls, integration with email and calendar, and more.

Knowledge Management

1. Provide employees with a Learning Management System (LMS). This digital platform streamlines both mandatory workplace training requirements and ongoing professional development, allowing employees to access learning materials from anywhere while tracking their progress.

2. Learn about your employees' skills and abilities. Neurodivergent individuals have so much to offer to companies, but often, they're stuck in a job that requires few skills and has no opportunity for growth. Train managers to recognize and support employees' knowledge and skills and to help them set and achieve personal career goals.

Incorporating Neurodiversity into IDWD

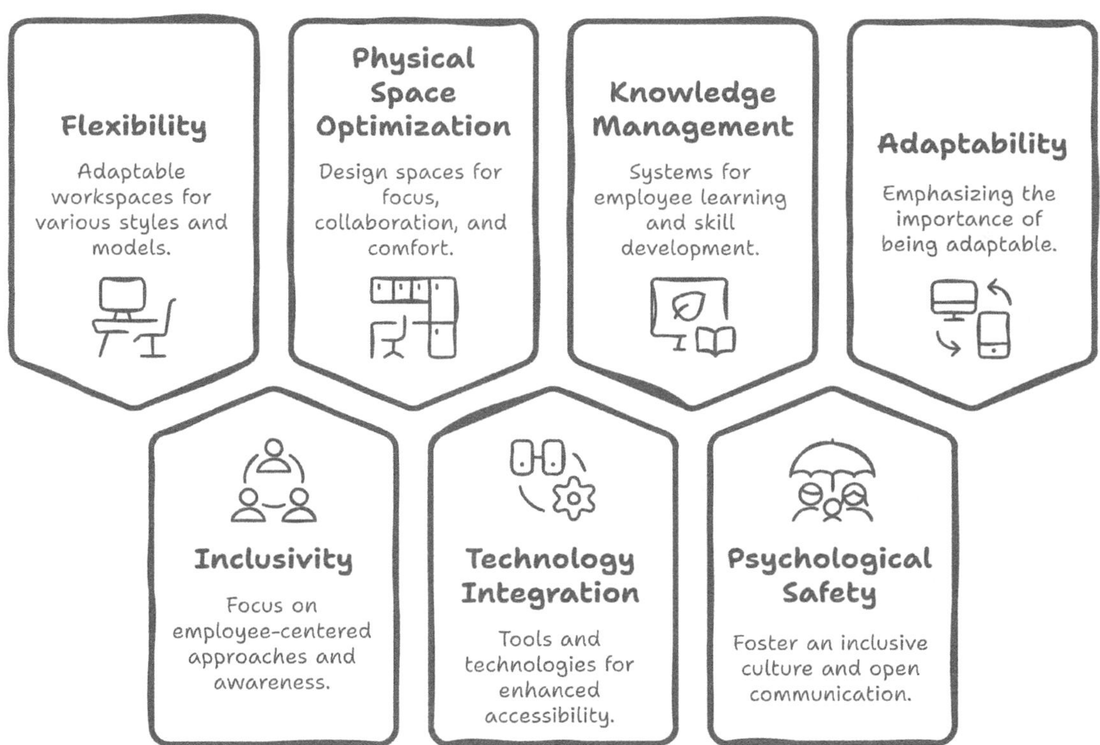

Let's return to what doesn't work for neurodivergent workers or any of your workers: Thoughtless planning, snap decisions, and a lack of commitment to adequately implement an office plan don't only hurt your bottom line. They hurt your employees, too.

In the office, neurodivergent employees need an environment where they can focus and minimize distractions. (Gain, n.d.) In an open-plan office, this may mean accommodating employees with a cubicle with higher sides than other employees' desks. (Shepherd, 2022).It may also mean creating a rest space with low light and few stimuli (skip the music, video games, TV, or clutter) where any employee can go and take a break.

Neurodivergent employees can often focus better in a hybrid environment, where they spend part of their workweek at the office and the other part working from home. For example, a company can reimburse employees for ergonomic desks and chairs, decorations, and items that enable them to focus. Options could include freestanding screens to help partition off their home office work area, which is helpful in small apartments and when they must share a work area with their spouse or roommate.

I understand that companies may feel these are extra expenses they don't need to reimburse. However, to support remote workers effectively, companies could offer a curated selection of work necessities such as desks, chairs, and focus aids. This approach ensures that company funds are used appropriately for work-related items. Additionally, remote workers could be given a modest stipend for minor office supplies or decor to personalize their workspace. Consider how much corporations save now that they are selling their office buildings to move toward remote work. Using a portion of those savings to support remote employees through targeted offerings can increase productivity and job satisfaction.

This chapter provides an introduction and a way to start thinking about your company's office design. With such a large, often unknown, quantity of neurodivergent individuals in the workforce, updating your office to support neurodiversity can help the entire team succeed. You don't necessarily have to make considerable changes to the existing office design; consider making changes with empathy for the employees who drive the company's overall success.

IDWD goes beyond the physical workspace environment. It includes flexibility in learning design and is attentive to psychological safety, diversity, and inclusion.

Neurodiversity-Friendly and Psychologically Safe Workplace Assessment

This assessment helps you determine how welcoming and supportive your workplace is of all types of thinkers and workers, including those whose brains may work differently from what's considered "typical."

Instructions:

Please base your answers on what you've seen and experienced in the company or organization for which you currently work.

For each question, place the appropriate number in the space provided. Choose the answer that best fits *your* experience.

Possible answers, and values, are:

0—I'm not sure
1—No, this doesn't happen
2—This happens sometimes
3—Yes, this always happens

Questions:

Job Postings and Applications

___ Does your company use clear, straightforward, language in job postings?

Example of unclear language: "We need a rockstar ninja coder who thrives in a fast-paced, high-energy environment!"

Example of clear language: "We're looking for a skilled programmer who can work well on team projects and meet deadlines."

Interview Process

___ Does your company offer different ways for job candidates to show their skills beyond just talking?

Example: Allow candidates to do a small project, show a portfolio of past work, or take a skills test instead of just having a conversational interview.

Workspace Options

___ Does your company provide different types of work areas to suit various needs?

Example: Are there quiet spaces for focused work, areas for collaboration, or the option to use noise-canceling headphones?

Flexible Work Arrangements

___ Can employees choose when and where they work, if their job allows it?

Example: Employees can work from home some days, or choose to start earlier or later in the day.

Clear Communication of Expectations

___ Does your company clearly explain what's expected of employees in their roles?

Example: Provide written job descriptions, clear project goals, and regular check-ins to discuss progress and challenges.

Feedback and Performance Reviews

___ Is feedback provided in a way that's clear, specific, and focused on the work rather than personal, or personality, traits?

Example of unclear language: "You did a good job, but try to be more dynamic."

Example of clear language: "Your report was well organized and met the deadline. Next time, include more data visuals to make it even stronger."

Mental Health Support

___ Does your company or organization offer resources to support employee mental health and well-being?

Example: Is access to counseling services, mental health days off, or stress management workshops provided?

Accommodations and Adjustments

___ Is it easy for employees to request changes that would help them work better?

Example: Could an employee ask for a different type of chair, a standing desk, or adjusted lighting without a complicated process?

Training on Neurodiversity

___ Does your company provide training about different ways people think, learn, and communicate?

Example: Are there workshops that teach about various thinking styles, communication preferences, and how to work effectively on diverse teams?

Respect for Different Communication Styles

___ Do people respect that not everyone communicates the same way?

Example: Is it widely understood that some people may prefer written communication over verbal, or may need more time to process information during meetings.

Conflict Resolution

___ Is there a clear, fair way to handle disagreements or misunderstandings?

Example: Is there a process by which both sides can explain their perspective, then turn to a neutral person to find common ground and resolution?

Encouraging Different Ideas

___ Does your company or organization welcome and consider ideas from all employees, regardless of their position or how they express themselves?

Example: Are there suggestion boxes, open forums, or regular meetings where everyone is encouraged to share their thoughts?

Inclusive Company Events

___ Are social events and team-building activities designed to be comfortable for everyone?

Example: Is there a mix of high-energy and low-key options, with some activities that don't involve alcohol?

Awareness and Celebration of Differences

___ Does your company or organization actively recognize and appreciate different ways of thinking and working?

Example: Do you host events or share information about neurodiversity, or highlighting the unique strengths of different thinking styles?

Continuous Improvement

___ Are employees regularly asked for feedback about how to make the workplace better for everyone?

Example: Are there anonymous surveys, suggestion boxes, or open discussions about how to improve the work environment?

Scoring:

To score your assessment, add the total of all your responses together. Enter your response total below.

Your total: ___________

If you scored:	**Then:**
45–36	Your organization is doing well in creating an inclusive environment.
35–24	Your organization has some good practices but can still improve.

23–12	Your organization needs to focus more on inclusivity and psychological safety.
11–0	Your organization should prioritize making significant changes to become more inclusive.

Next Steps:

Look at the areas where you answered 0, 1, or 2.

These are areas of opportunity to make your workplace more welcoming and supportive for all types of thinkers and workers.

Consider discussing these findings with your company's leadership to develop an action plan for improvement.

Chapter Two Reflection Questions

1. How does Inclusive Dynamic Workplace Design differ from traditional office design approaches? What are its key components?
2. Discuss the potential benefits and challenges of implementing IDWD in a company transitioning to a hybrid work model.
3. How can the creation of diverse spaces within an office (such as deep work areas, collaboration zones, and quiet spaces) benefit both neurodivergent and neurotypical employees?
4. Analyze the importance of proper tools and technologies in creating an inclusive workplace. How do these elements support neurodivergent employees specifically?
5. Consider the story of Sam's experience with the loosened-up-workplace trend. What does this anecdote reveal about the potential pitfalls of office design that doesn't consider neurodiversity?
6. How might companies balance the need for an engaging work environment with the sensory needs of neurodivergent employees?
7. Discuss the potential benefits and challenges of supporting remote work setups for neurodivergent employees. How might this impact company policies and budgets?
8. Reflect on the statement: "Updating your office to support neurodiversity can help the entire team succeed." How might implementing IDWD principles benefit all employees, not just those who are neurodivergent?

Building a High-Performance Culture through Neurodiversity

Why would an initiative designed to support neurodivergent employees fail some of them? Such initiatives can fail miserably or be successful beyond our expectations!

Much research has been done on the competitive advantages of diversity in terms of race, ethnicity, gender, sexual orientation, and socioeconomic status. In most workplaces, the company culture has already been adapted to include people of all types, gender preferences, colors, and creeds.

The natural variation in how our brains work is an aspect of human difference that most companies have not yet learned to fully embrace and integrate. Interest in building capacity for neurodiversity in the workplace is based on evidence that neurodiversity also gives companies a competitive advantage. That's true, but only when it's done right. It could also be a complete failure that leaves damaging fallout—the human kind—in its wake.

The natural variation in how our brains work is an aspect of human difference that most companies have not yet learned to fully embrace and integrate.

I asked Gord Sherwood, founder of The Human Intelligence Factor, "What is the key to successfully implementing a neurodiversity at work initiative in the workplace?" He explained, "That's a big question. With a lot of big answers. Is it complex? Of course. Can it be accomplished? Absolutely!"

He continued, "First, the people leading the programs need to understand how to lay the groundwork and know when the organization is ready to move forward. As the programs advance, [the leaders] need to understand the dynamics at play. They need to anticipate misalignment and know how to turn it into opportunities—often exceptionally good ones."

A Long Time Ago in a Land Far Away, This Happened...

My former school district, with all the best intentions, implemented an initiative to include students with learning disabilities in general education classrooms. The move was met with anger, frustration, and resistance. Why?

The groundwork for the initiative was not done ahead of time. We were unprepared for the mandated inclusion initiative. The benefits of placing students with learning disabilities in classes previously considered beyond their capabilities weren't immediately apparent to us. This marked the beginning of our journey to understand and embrace neurodiversity in education.

At the time, we failed to recognize that inclusion not only didn't hinder other students but actually benefited them. Without the internet at our disposal, we lacked easy access to information and research on inclusive education. We were essentially navigating uncharted territory. We were proceeding with caution in an unfamiliar landscape.

Diversity initiatives are frequently introduced to organizations without adequate training and preparation. The idea is brought to the table and is developed into an initiative. Then hiring and supporting a diverse workforce fail somewhere between conception and implementation.

Fortunately, in my story, our initiative was overwhelmingly successful because of the determination, persistence, and dedication of the people assigned to the challenge. That experience taught me a lot about moving forward with neurodiversity at work initiatives.

Good Intentions with No Groundwork Leads to Failure

Creating processes that make it easier to hire, train, and develop people who are divergent thinkers can be a win-win for the company and the divergent thinker. However, it is fundamental that these processes be well thought out and implemented in a way that considers the very people they are designed to support.

Not so long ago, I published an article about this topic. I was thrilled when the article was shared on LinkedIn and a robust discussion started in the comments. One commenter, in particular, caught my attention.

He was a neurodivergent person who did not have a pleasant experience in one of these programs and was angry and hurt. His ordeal was validated and echoed by others who also identified as neurodivergent. Their comments revealed that not all neurodiversity at work initiatives succeed, which gave me pause. Someone who is neurodivergent had a terrible experience in a program that was developed specifically for people on the spectrum. Coming face-to-face with this reality reminded me that we must proceed cautiously.

If we're going to do this work, we need to do it right. We need to proceed thoughtfully and with sensitivity. We must leave our ego behind and listen to neurodivergent thinkers' concerns.

To successfully lay the groundwork for a neurodiversity in the workplace initiative, we must incorporate the neurodivergent perspective.

What must we consider to ensure that *all* parties reap the benefits of a neurodiversity at work initiative? What is the "neurodivergent perspective"?

Some of the concerns I've gleaned through reader comments and conversations with neurodivergent thinkers are (in their own words):

> *"Hiring neurodivergent people is great, but not developing the right environment for us to succeed sets us up for failure before we can even begin to showcase our strengths."*
>
> *"At recruitment, accommodation or support is often poor. Not intentionally, but often because staff have few reference points. There are often few sources for guidance beyond rigid standard policies."*
>
> *"Once employed, there's often a gap in support. It's usually up to the individual to take the lead. How many feel comfortable doing that when they join an organization?"*
>
> *"Please don't try to put us in a box with a label. It feels patronizing to some of us. Celebrate our divergent thinking without making assumptions about us. Companies need to avoid the pitfalls of labeling and categorizing people because that is not the intent of increasing neurodiversity in the workplace."*

Creating processes that make it easier to hire, train, and develop people who are divergent thinkers can be a win-win for the company and the divergent thinker.

How to Respond to These Concerns

Creating an environment that nurtures success for neurodivergent workers is made easy through simple strategies that can make a huge difference.

- **Promote new ways of communication:** Discard the old my-way-or-the-highway attitude that practically defined the corporate workplace just a few decades ago. Instead, management and supervisors could promote empathetic, "nonviolent" communication methods, including active listening training. Respect individual employees' preferences and allow them to communicate in the ways that feel most comfortable for them.
- **Promote a cultural shift in the workplace:** As we move forward with neurodiversity, employees and managers must be given the opportunity and training that will inspire a change in their perspective. This shift can't be forced. It must come from the standpoint that there is much to be gained, personally and professionally.
- **Promote psychologically safe workplaces:** All employees will be more effective when the workplace culture fosters safety: for the open expression of ideas, for differences in work styles, for different learning and communication preferences, and for diversity.

There's much to be gained by welcoming neurodivergent thinkers into the workplace. However, the initiative may fail despite our best intentions if we don't do the groundwork first.

A poorly implemented initiative may become a poor experience for the team and, worse, a horrific experience for the neurodivergent employee.

The repercussions of a failed initiative can be devastating. For divergent thinkers, who have often experienced years of unemployment, underemployment, being let go from companies, or not even getting in the door because they don't interview well—a bad experience with a poorly planned initiative for inclusion can have a tremendously detrimental effect.

Have You Ever Planted a Garden?

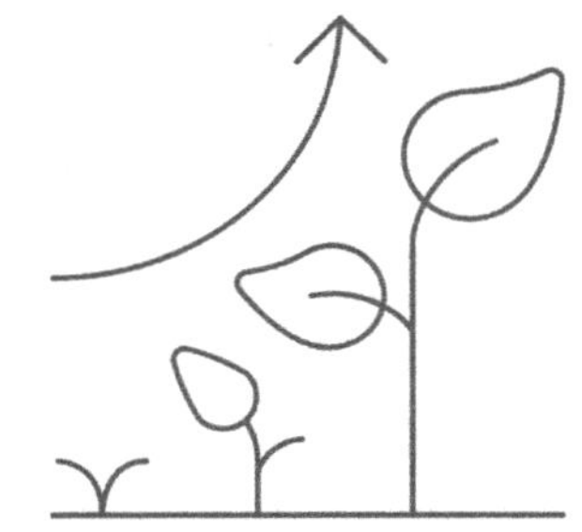

Cultivating Neurodiversity for Growth

- Companies must approach implementing a neurodiversity program like a gardener starting a new garden on untilled land.
- If we don't add the right fertilizer to the soil, if we don't till the ground first, if we don't do the work to prepare the soil for the seeds, they probably won't grow. They'll die.
- It's the same concept when we introduce initiatives into our companies. When an initiative involves changes at a team level, it can be emotionally charged. The idea will face pushback because people often resist what they don't understand.
- We have to prepare the soil first.
- Then, once the seeds are planted, we can't just walk away and expect them to grow. They need water, sunlight, and fertilizer in the right amounts. We must watch those plants and adjust the environment to optimize their growth. Without regular monitoring and care, the plants will wither and die. If that happens, we don't blame the plants for dying; rather, we realize the environment did not support the garden's growth.
- Our neurodiversity at work initiatives will fail if we don't take the time to lay the groundwork through carefully planned baby steps. Our employees will thrive if we adjust the environment to support employee growth, just as plants do in the right environmental conditions.

Our neurodiversity at work initiatives will fail if we don't take the time to lay the groundwork through carefully planned baby steps. Our employees will thrive if we adjust the environment to support employee growth, just as plants do in the right environmental conditions.

Promote Inclusivity while Avoiding Stigma and Discrimination

Fostering understanding and promoting inclusion are essential components of organizational culture. When you can physically see someone's differences (in their skin color, age, gender, and so on), it is easier to be conscientious and mindful of avoiding using labels or falling back on stereotypes.

Neurodivergence is different because you most likely cannot visually identify any particular person as being neurodivergent or not. But here's the thing: The reality is that most companies have neurodivergent thinkers already in their ranks. You don't see them. The overwhelming majority of those employees are in hiding. They are invisible and unlabeled. And most of them prefer it that way. Considering the misconceptions, labels, and stigma they encounter daily, many divergent thinkers feel safer hiding in the shadows.

Popular culture, through music, film, and social media, has created a romanticized view of autistic people. Examples include Sheldon Cooper from *The Big Bang Theory,* Max Braverman from *Parenthood,* Dr. Shaun Murphy of *The Good Doctor,* Sam Gardner of *Atypical,* and Adam Raki of *Adam.*

This romanticized view has created an unfortunate stereotype of the nuances and behaviors of people with autism. A misunderstanding surrounding an autistic person's capabilities can lead to managerial expectations that negatively influence performance rating results. Similarly, most people expect a person with Tourette's syndrome to spontaneously yell out vulgarities or a person with dyslexia to shy away from reading.

The truth is, no two ND persons are the same.

All people are complex.

Regarding neurodivergents, it's vital to remember that a diagnostic label does not represent the entirety of a person's personality and abilities. Because of this, it's essential not to make assumptions based on stereotypes. Misinformation or conflicting information about neurocognitive differences often causes people to draw incorrect conclusions about how to accommodate neurodivergent peers. Conclusions are usually based on minimal knowledge frequently gleaned from pop-culture stereotypes.

On the job, NDs often rely on coping mechanisms they've learned over their lifetime to avoid the stigma and discrimination of co-workers. When they successfully do this, their difference becomes invisible. Making their difference invisible is called masking, and for the divergent thinker, it can be exhausting.

While this may ease social assimilation, the downside is that they often hide their brilliance. They fear their unorthodox solutions and creative ideas will be rejected. Usually, they already have been.

The takeaway here is to understand that neurodivergence already exists in your company.

Seven out of ten neurodivergent workers have faced discrimination in the workplace. Seventy-three percent do not disclose their condition or diagnostic labels because of their fear of discrimination. (Cooper et al., 2018)

Yet JPMorgan, Google, SAP, Ford, and Ultranauts are trailblazers in the corporate inclusion of neurodiversity. James Mahoney, executive director and head of Autism at Work for JPMorgan Chase, said in an official statement, "Many autistic people are brilliant people—highly educated, highly capable, detail-oriented, yet unemployed," adding, "I firmly believe that companies could always benefit from having employees who see things in an unconventional way, which is something to remember any time an individual on the spectrum is seeking a job." (Mahoney, 2017)

Be Aware of Unintentional Discrimination

Be aware of stereotypes. A misunderstanding surrounding an autistic person's capabilities can lead to managerial expectations that negatively influence performance rating results. Keep tabs on productivity and performance ratings so biases don't creep in unwittingly.

Although well meaning, some team leaders may, intentionally or not, base their decisions and accommodations on assumptions and stereotypes fueled by popular culture. Consequently, attempts to support neurodivergent employees may not be what the individual needs to function at optimal productivity. In some cases, uninformed attempts to support divergent thinkers may even be discriminatory.

Discrimination in the workplace may occur directly or indirectly and may lead to harassment and victimization. Direct discrimination occurs when a neurodivergent person is treated negatively compared with other workers. Indirect discrimination occurs when a policy or practice presented as neutral puts neurodivergent employees at a disadvantage.

When the needs of these employees are not given proper consideration, indirect discrimination occurs. Examples include:

- Not making accessibility options available during presentations or meetings.
- Refusing a request to provide a quiet, distraction-free space to work in a department with an open office environment.
- Dismissing an ND's concerns about privacy, security, or anxiety by insisting on the status quo.
- Pressuring neurodivergent employees to generate creative ideas on the spot without considering their need for processing time or alternative brainstorming methods.

Discrimination may take the form of harassment, such as when colleagues violate one's dignity or are hostile, degrading, or offensive toward the ND individual. Thomas Armstrong, the author of *The Power of Neurodiversity,* maintains that employers unintentionally exclude or discard notable talent in neurodivergent people. Stereotypes and stigma surrounding neurodivergence create more limitations than the divergent cognitive function itself.

Educate Yourself and Your Employees

Some of the best ways to avoid stigma while implementing neurodiversity at work initiatives at work include:

- Taking the time to research all types of neurodivergence.
- Learning the appropriate terms and context of use to prevent indirect labeling or discrimination at work.
- Consulting with experts in neurodivergence when establishing procedures and promoting inclusive culture. Ask what works and what doesn't.
- Establishing protocols for communication that foster psychological safety for all employees, including neurodiverse teams.

A great example of an inclusive policy that avoids stigma comes from Ultranauts, a software testing company. In their organization, all new employees, whether neuro-divergent or neurotypical, create a personal profile called a Biodex. This contains twenty-eight data points about each individual, including their preferred communication channels, and is used to guide team interactions. By having everyone complete a Biodex, Ultranauts normalizes the sharing of personal work preferences and accommodations, fostering a more inclusive environment. (KeepingTABS, 2018)

This approach honors neurodiversity, prevents indirect discrimination, and encourages every new employee to feel recognized and supported by the company without setting anyone up for misunderstandings or harassment.

Provide Appropriate Training

There are nuances we must understand when working with NDs that aren't typically covered in standard workplace training. For example, it's crucial to comprehend how literal NDs may be; you might need to keep the sarcasm in check.

Also, overstimulation is a known trigger for many autistic people, making office banter, sarcasm, or harassment difficult and (sometimes unbearable) to cope with. In Inclusive Dynamic Workplace Design™, a workplace may have a zero-tolerance policy to ensure a safe and welcoming environment for autistic people. Again, a policy such as this benefits everyone. Not only will people who are neurodivergent benefit from a psychologically safe environment, but so will employees who have a history of being marginalized, abused, or put down for their learning difficulties. This need is not exclusive to people who are autistic. The need for a psychologically safe working environment applies to all employees.

Make sure all impacted staff have the opportunity to learn about appropriate accommodations and options for effective and flexible communication. Remember—look beyond the social constructs of "normal" and focus instead on the skills and benefits each new hire would provide the organization.

Training should equip leaders to identify and address organizational issues that could impact their ND colleagues.

Appreciate Weird Ideas

The day you have zero weird ideas will probably be a bad day for your company. Don't immediately throw out ideas because they seem strange. Your team may have just come up with something brilliant.

This new attitude may require a culture shift in your company or on specific teams. As a neurodivergent myself, I cannot tell you how many times my weird idea was put down, dismissed, or laughed at publicly in the workplace or at board meetings where I've been a member. When that happened, I learned very quickly to stop contributing my ideas.

Several years ago, I proposed an idea to boost our company's success, and my supervisor angrily dismissed it as folly. Ironically, as he was leaving the company, he admitted, "I remember when you suggested that we do x, y, and z to get ahead of our competition.

I disagreed with you then. I now realize you were right." Unfortunately, his realization came too late for the company and its employees. They missed their window of opportunity to stay ahead of the trend, which would ultimately have a profound and negative impact on their success.

Build a Company Culture That Embraces Different Thinkers

> ***"Neurodiversity is the diversity of human brains and minds, the infinite variation in neurocognitive functioning within our species"***
> ***—Dr. Nick Walker***

Several factors influence our opinions of other groups, as well as how we interact with them:

- Our social culture, or way of seeing things, imprinted in our youth.
- Our real-time experiences, if any, played out in social interactions.
- Opinions expressed by role models and other social influencers.

In the workplace, these factors often come together with a predictable result.
We hire people like ourselves.

According to Kimberly Giles, a Forbes Councils member, in a 2018 article titled "Why You Mistakenly Hire People Just Like You," this is an outward sign of unconscious and favorable bias toward people of the same race, education level, economic status, and values as the decision-maker. (Giles, 2018) This bias results in an organization that is comfortable with its behavior.

Changes to the status quo may provoke hostility toward behavior or ideas that challenge the collective version of normal. Countless women, LGBTs, minorities, and neurodivergent thinkers have buckled under the weight of this type of status quo, eventually leaving and taking their talent elsewhere. Suppose a company's culture is such that minds are entrenched with how things should be and ready to repel nonconformists. In that case, the culture will be a severe obstacle to the success of the neurodiversity at work initiative.

If we include this wealth of neurodiversity in every aspect of our organization's functioning, however, everyone wins. Imagine the benefits of moving beyond allowing neurodiversity to exist in small pockets and into embracing it in every aspect of company culture.

Leaders who have done their research understand that this process begins by accepting that all humans are different. It's the richness of our differences that makes our teams unique and successful.

Great, enduring works of art succeed because of the rich detail that inspires fresh views on life. Just as art can invite us to think about the world differently, so can including divergent thinkers in our lives and workspaces.

Divergent thinking is like an artist's unique rendering of an idea.

It's encouraging that many forward-thinking companies recognize the value of varied cognitive styles and thinking patterns in their workforce. Whether the motivation for these initiatives is altruistic or financial doesn't matter. The groundwork needs to be the same. Companies must start by focusing on company culture to be inclusive in recruiting and hiring.

Rethinking Systems

One of the first things a company can work on is creating a culture that supports neurodiversity by rethinking the systems under which the company currently operates.

As previously mentioned, divergent thinkers who are extremely capable of doing a specific job often don't get hired because they are not enough like those doing the hiring.

Susan Van Klink, chief revenue and diversity officer at Grokker, proposes reorienting hiring practices to bring out everybody's best. (Van Klink, 2021). This would counter the human tendency to hire people who fit our preconceived notions about the ideal employee.

Job interviews traditionally measure candidates' ability to make small talk and put on a friendly face. They often focus on surface impressions rather than skills crucial for the job the candidate will perform.

The traditional approach does not favor socially awkward, neurologically diverse people who might otherwise have the skills to solve problems, exhibit creativity, and demonstrate what they know. A better option to approach interviews would be to focus on practical skills tests that eliminate unconscious bias. Unconscious bias disproportionately affects people with autism or poverty, for example.

Aside from the hiring process and guidelines for promotion, what other workplace systems might be fraught with hidden biases? Does the way things are done in your workplace support neurodiversity and promote inclusion? Or do those systems promote masking and shame?

Check Your Expectations

The best way to explain this is with a real-life example. My son, who had a language-based disability, was told he should not be doing as well as he was in English class. The assumption was that if he had this disability, he couldn't do well in English.

His teachers were wrong.

When he used strategies to overcome his language disability, he could write exceptionally well. However, his performance was viewed with skepticism. Some teachers refused to believe he belonged in an honors- level English class.

Again, they were wrong.

They could not overcome their subconscious stereotype: To them, a student with a language disability didn't belong in an honors English class.

Finally, he got an English teacher who did not share this prejudice. And guess what? He got an A in English.

Unfortunately, this same paradigm often exists in the workplace. When we know that a worker has a neurodivergent condition, our expectations of and for them will be tainted by our assumptions of their capabilities.

When managers and supervisors do not burden their workers with limiting thoughts and expectations, those workers are free to work to the best of their abilities.

Know Your Why

When thinking about creating an inclusive company culture, it might not seem necessary to reflect on your motives. But those motives will shape every policy change you implement as part of your inclusion strategy.

Reflect on your motivation for participation in a neurodiversity at work initiative. Is it to wave a neurodiversity banner as part of your company's marketing strategy? Is it because it's good PR?

Or is it because you believe in the power of divergent thought?

Maybe it's a practical matter, and you're having trouble filling positions, and you've heard that autistic people make great coders.

Be honest. The initiative's success depends on the company's motivation, which directly influences the company's culture.

Promote a Culture of Safety

One of my clients shared this powerful story that illustrates the importance of creating a safe workplace for all employees, especially those who are neurodivergent:

"I shared a cube pod with Cathy, who sat across the aisle from me, with two guys in front and two behind. Cathy was on a different team from the rest of us. She struggled with social skills, often talking loudly and abruptly, and was generally difficult to communicate with. I later realized she was probably sitting in the middle of my team because her own team couldn't stand having her around.

"Cathy was a coder, and quite frequently her supervisor and another woman would come to her desk to give her instructions and feedback. Their treatment of her was outrageous, rude, unkind, and vicious.

"One day when Cathy was out of the office, I stood up in the aisle, caught the guys' attention, and asked them if they were hearing what I was hearing and if they were bothered by it. They said yes, and one guy actually said it bothered him so much he had to put his headphones on. I told them that as witnesses, we had a moral obligation to do something about the situation. Since it was her supervisor who was torturing her, I offered to call HR but I needed their assurance that they would back me up if HR called them.

"They agreed, and after I called HR and explained that Cathy's tormentors were creating a hostile environment for all within earshot, the guys all got calls and confirmed my story. HR took immediate action, and within days Cathy's supervisor came to my desk to apologize. I told her that she needed to find a way to communicate her project needs to Cathy in a courteous and respectful manner.

"After this event, Cathy's personality evened out and we became good office buddies. It hurt my soul to think that she had been through twenty or thirty years of torture working with people who wouldn't take the time or effort to ease her into their work group."

This story powerfully demonstrates the critical importance of promoting a culture of safety in the workplace. By speaking up against mistreatment and creating an environment where such behavior is not tolerated, we can dramatically improve the work experience for neurodivergent employees. It shows how a safe workplace isn't about just physical safety, but also emotional and psychological well-being. When employees feel secure enough to be themselves and are protected from harassment or bullying, it can lead to improved relationships, increased productivity, and a more positive work environment for everyone. This culture of safety is especially crucial for neurodivergent individuals who may struggle with social interactions or communication, ensuring they have the support and respect they need to thrive in their roles.

> ***By speaking up against mistreatment and creating an environment where such behavior is not tolerated, we can dramatically improve the work experience for neurodivergent employees.***

The one non-negotiable for creating an inclusive workplace is zero tolerance for treating people like outsiders, which often leads to exclusion and other forms of workplace bullying. A welcoming and psychologically safe work environment must be a core value in a company that embraces neurodiversity in the workplace. (Fitzell, n.d.).

I'll discuss the details of creating a psychologically safe workplace later in this book, but it's worth mentioning for now.

For an inclusive workplace to thrive, company policy must support safety for the open expression of ideas, differences in work styles, and different learning and communication preferences.

Invest the Time to Implement Neurodiversity Thoughtfully

None of these steps can be implemented overnight. This is just the beginning. As we grow as human beings and as our company cultures evolve, we will welcome employees with a broader range of life perspectives, experiences, and competencies. Customizing work environments to meet individuals' preferences, abilities, and goals will become commonplace. Understand that these customizations don't reduce but rather enhance the quality of the work individuals and teams produce

.

It's a journey, and it's worth it. Each of us is unique. Most of us want to be valued for the unique skills that make us the high-performing employees we are capable of being. This is achieved when we understand, accept, and embrace neurodiversity in the workplace.

Each of us is unique. Most of us want to be valued for the unique skills that make us the high-performing employees we are capable of being.

Create a Workforce Where Employees Can Ask for Help When They Need It

I Had to Do It Myself

As a young woman, I was fierce about wanting to be independent. And that meant I didn't like asking for help for anything. I had an old beater of a car that I was able to buy with my own money: a 1968 Chevy Nova. Oh, did I love that car! I wanted to be able to take care of it myself. I wanted to know how to change tires, change the oil, and do all the basic maintenance myself.

One summer day after work, I got into grubby clothes, put on some work gloves, got a big pan, and went outside. I got under the car, unscrewed the oil plug, and let it drip into the pan. I was so proud of myself.

When the oil stopped flowing, I lifted the hood again, pulled out the dipstick, and looked at it. The engine was still full of oil!

Oh no, what had I done?

With a sinking heart, I moved over to the transmission fluid cap, unscrewed it, and pulled out the dipstick. Guess what I had drained instead: all the transmission fluid.

I had two new problems: I didn't have any transmission fluid. And I was nowhere near a store.

I couldn't drive a car without transmission fluid, so I had to ask for help. This was an upsetting realization because my father was the only person home at three o'clock in the afternoon. I didn't want to ask him for help, as I was trying to be independent, but I had no choice.

So I called my dad. He listened as I explained my problem. Then he said he'd be over in half an hour to take me to the store to get more transmission fluid and stay with me while I replaced the oil. He wanted to be available in case I needed him again.

I felt so humiliated to call him for help, and I still felt that way when he drove up. But the moment I got into the car and we started driving, I realized something. My dad was so happy to be able to help me. He was in his element. He told me he was proud of me for trying to change the oil myself. He didn't care that I emptied the wrong tank. He said that was part of learning.

My mistake became a bonding experience with my dad that I still remember.

> *An hour earlier, I wouldn't have let that moment happen because I felt I had to be independent and do things for myself. I didn't want to ask for help. Yet making an effort, making a mistake, and asking for help became a rewarding growth experience.*

This personal experience taught me a valuable lesson that applies equally in the professional world. Just as I learned that asking for help could lead to growth and connection, employees need to understand that seeking assistance in the workplace is not a sign of weakness but a path to learning and improvement. However, fostering an environment where people feel comfortable asking for help requires intentional effort from leadership.

Having the Confidence to Ask for Help

This lesson from my personal life resonates strongly with my conversations with clients about their employees' reluctance to ask for help. In the workplace, this hesitation can have significant consequences.

When an employee doesn't want to ask for help, it costs the company money and possibly customers.

All this could be avoided if employees felt comfortable and confident about asking for help. There is probably someone in the workspace who would be thrilled to be able to help and grateful for the opportunity to share their knowledge (just like my dad).

If an employee doesn't feel safe seeking help, they won't ask for it. They won't give that other teammate a chance to step up and solve a problem before it's too late.

Encouraging Employees to Speak Up

Asking how to best support your team members shouldn't be limited to neurodivergent individuals. Getting to know your entire team and understanding how to bring out the best in each individual should be a universal practice. This approach fosters an inclusive environment where everyone feels valued and empowered to contribute their unique strengths.

One simple change that can make a massive difference in creating an inclusive work environment is normalizing open communication about where talents lie and what people need to do their best work. The language around neurodivergence often focuses on a deficit, but just like neurotypical people, neurodivergent people have strengths and weaknesses.

For instance, people with dyslexia often excel in interpersonal skills, making them valuable assets in team leadership or sales roles. However, many organizations inadvertently create barriers for these talented individuals. Consider Learning Management Systems (LMS), which require salespeople to complete text-heavy modules and quizzes to learn about new products. Such practices can disadvantage dyslexic employees, potentially leading to the loss of top sales talent.

Imagine the positive impact if dyslexic employees felt comfortable requesting alternative assessment formats. This scenario underscores the importance of creating an environment where employees can openly discuss their needs and leverage their talents effectively.

By fostering such an inclusive culture, companies can tap into the full potential of their diverse workforce, leading to increased innovation, employee engagement, and overall productivity.

When you have an environment where people feel comfortable expressing their needs, you have an environment where you don't have to guess how to get the best out of your team. They will tell you. People feel comfortable saying they struggle in loud environments and prefer hybrid working or working from home. People feel comfortable telling you they forget instructions quickly, so having notes gives them something to refer to when they forget.

Normalize Expressing Needs

Creating a company culture where employees feel comfortable asking for help as soon as it's needed is crucial. Here are some strategies to foster such an environment:

- **Cultivate a safe, judgment-free workplace:** Eliminate stigma and create an atmosphere where employees feel secure expressing their needs.
- **Implement an open-door policy:** Actively encourage employees to approach leadership with work-related concerns. Make it clear that uncertainty is not a weakness but a natural part of growth and learning.
- **Identify and leverage team strengths:** Get to know your team's individual talents. This knowledge allows you to efficiently match employees who need help with those best equipped to provide it.
- **Practice empathy and humility:** Set aside ego and pride. Remember that showing vulnerability can be challenging for employees, and respond with understanding and support.
- **Facilitate team communication:** Encourage employees to share their skills and experiences with each other. This fosters a collaborative environment where team members feel comfortable working together and know who to approach for specific expertise.

Implementing these strategies creates a culture that values open communication, mutual support, and continuous learning. This approach not only improves individual performance but also enhances overall team efficiency and innovation.

Put Yourself in Their Shoes

Imagine you are an entry-level employee just starting your new job. How might they look for the help they need when they need it?
They might:

- Seek out co-workers they feel confident speaking to.

- Build supportive relationships with teammates they resonate with.
- Need to feel free to admit they don't know how to do everything.

When employees work in a supportive environment and are encouraged to build meaningful connections with their co-workers, they are more likely to seek help when they need it. Knowing they can ask for the help they need will skyrocket their confidence and performance. That's a win for your company, the team, and the employee.

Now ask yourself: Does your workplace culture allow for and encourage workers to resolve situations by proactively seeking assistance?

Workplace Bullying Exists

Although there are laws to protect employees, the dark side of human nature often prevails. Unfortunately, workplace bullying usually goes unreported out of fear of retaliation. A proactive approach is required when it comes to neurodiversity and protecting a person's psychological safety at work.

It Can Happen Anywhere

One of the most profound experiences I've had with work-based bullying occurred at a local hospital. I was presenting training for nursing staff on the topic, and approximately thirty people were in attendance.

About an hour into the training, a nurse approached me and apologized that she had to leave. A doctor had called her out of the session, demanding that she return to work. The training organizer later confided in me that the doctor who called that nurse back to work was known to harass the nurses with whom he worked.

It was because of him that she was in the session.

That same client later suggested that I change the name of my workshop. She explained that the title "workplace bullying" was too much of a red flag. If a nurse attended, people wondered who was bullying them. Attending was a risk for someone whose psychological safety at work was being compromised. She felt a title that did not include the word bullying would have better attendance.

This experience taught me several important lessons:

- **Bullying can occur in any workplace:** Even in professional environments like hospitals, where you might expect a higher standard of behavior, bullying can still be a significant issue.
- **Power dynamics play a role in workplace bullying:** The fact that a doctor was able to pull a nurse out of an anti-bullying training session demonstrates how power imbalances can contribute to bullying behavior.
- **Stigma surrounding bullying persists:** The suggestion to change the workshop title indicates that there's still a stigma attached to admitting that you're being bullied, even in a professional setting.
- **Seeking help can be risky:** The concern that attending a bullying workshop might identify someone as a victim highlights the complex dynamics and potential risks involved in addressing workplace bullying.
- **Institutional support is crucial:** The hospital's decision to offer the workshop shows an awareness of the issue, but the incident during the session suggests that more comprehensive, systemic changes may be needed to truly address the problem.
- **Bullying affects productivity and well-being:** The nurse being pulled out of an important training session demonstrates how bullying behaviors can disrupt work and potentially impact patient care in a healthcare setting.

- **Addressing bullying requires sensitivity:** The suggestion to change the workshop title indicates that addressing workplace bullying requires careful consideration of how to approach the topic without further endangering those who are already vulnerable.

This story illustrates the complexity of workplace bullying and the challenges of effectively addressing it, even in professional environments where such behavior should not be tolerated.

Seven Ways to Prevent Bullying in a Neurodiversity at Work Initiative

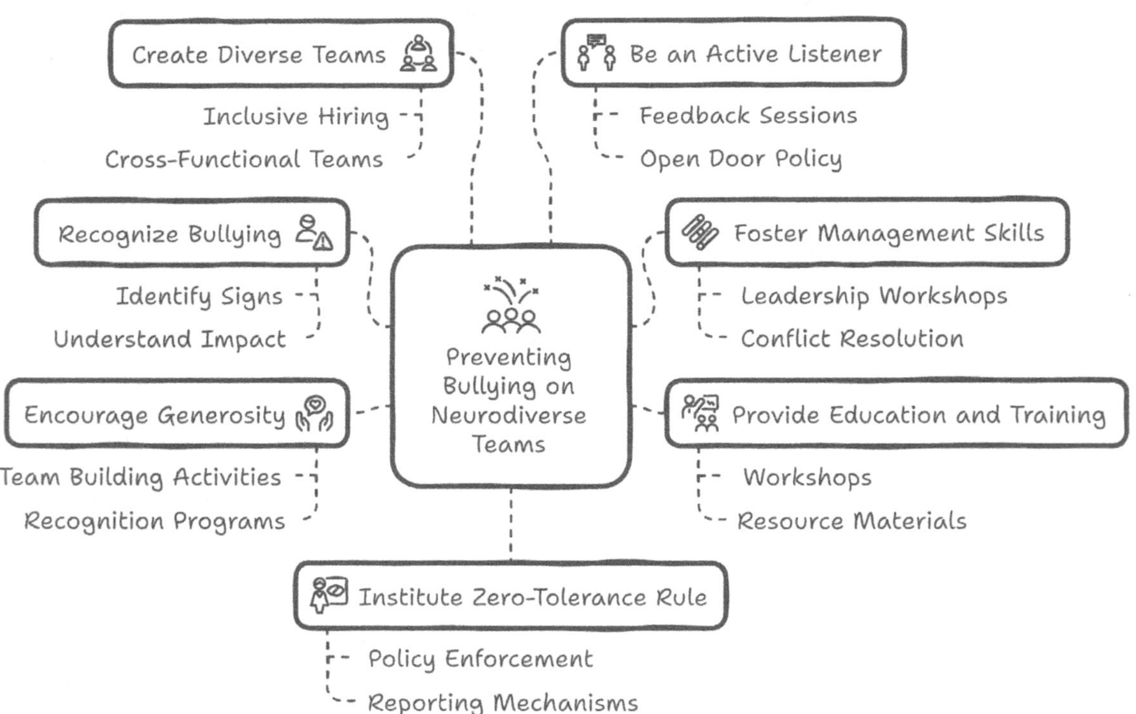

Enhancing Performance and Reducing Risk: Creating Psychological Safety for Neurodivergent Talent

Fostering psychological safety for neurodivergent employees not only mitigates legal and reputational risks but also drives innovation, reduces turnover, and enhances overall productivity. This section outlines evidence-based strategies to create an inclusive environment that maximizes the potential of all employees.

As the workforce becomes increasingly diverse, it's crucial to understand the unique challenges faced by neurodivergent employees. A *New York Times* article by Jane Gross highlighted how the social gap widens for individuals with autism as they age, presenting new challenges in the workplace. (Gross, 2005) To harness the full potential of neurodivergent talent and create a more productive work environment, consider the following strategies.

Creating a Culture of Safety

To gain the maximum benefit for all employee talent and foster a workplace culture that nurtures neurodiversity, consider the following statements:

1. **Cultivate understanding, not judgment.** *Business impact:* Reduced conflict, increased innovation. *Action:* The first step companies can take to promote a safety culture in their workplace is to understand neurodivergent individuals. Everyone has unique abilities. Sadly, these capabilities are often obscured by the fact that socially neurodivergent people often behave differently than the status quo. Discourage intolerant behavior toward those with different communication styles or thought processes.

2. **Move beyond labels.** *Business impact:* Improved talent retention, enhanced creativity. *Action:* It is important to note that not all neurodivergent workers agree that they have a disability. (Neurodiversity in the Workplace - Thinking Differently at Work Toolkit, 2018)

Why is this important? Labels can trigger a host of negative emotions that build up through childhood. They may provoke defensiveness or feelings of insecurity on the job. On the other hand, a workplace culture that embraces divergent thinking and different personalities *without labeling* creates an environment for all employees to thrive.

The reality is that we all are unique individuals who bring our individual strengths to the job. Fostering a space where neurodivergent talent is well understood without judgment will create a safe space for all employees to open up and share their expertise.

3. **Invest in education and training.** *Business impact:* Reduced workplace conflicts, improved team collaboration. *Action:* Conduct regular seminars to educate employees about the value of divergent thinking for the organization's success.

   One of the major underlying causes of abuse and bullying in the workplace is a simple lack of understanding of people who are different. Although some people are intentionally mean, the most common cause of bullying or microaggression in the workplace is *ignorance.*

   Without understanding neurodiversity, many employees think of their neurodivergent co-workers as peculiar and strange. Most often, people believe that these co-workers have mental health issues. (Neurodiversity In the Workplace, – Thinking Differently at Work Toolkit, 2018) This misconception can lead to conflict, which can lead to misguided solutions that do nothing to foster a productive working environment.

   Training on how neurocognition differs in neurodivergent people supports the understanding and appreciation of divergent thinkers and their unique talents and abilities.

4. **Adopt a gifts-mindset**. *Business impact*: Increased productivity, improved employee engagement. *Action:* Focus on individual strengths rather than perceived deficits. This approach contributes directly to the bottom line while protecting psychological safety.

5. **Set up a support team.** *Business impact:* Reduced turnover, improved employee satisfaction. *Action*: Create a non-judgmental support team for addressing concerns, particularly microaggressions and harassment. Ensure confidentiality and fair follow-up processes.

   A thorough and justifiable system should be in place to investigate situations. Incident reports should be evaluated in a reasonable and comprehensive manner. Having a support team will create a safe environment where neurodivergent employees feel heard and protected.

   Employees need to know that this support system exists and, most important, how to access it.

6. **Implement and enforce clear rules and policies.** *Business impact:* Reduced legal risks, improved company culture. *Action:* Company culture is defined by action or inaction, not policy.

   Though rules and policies may be set on paper, implementation is sometimes lacking. Without proper implementation and the periodic reevaluation of anti-bullying policies, all your efforts will be in vain. All employees need to know what the company's values are and what behaviors are expected from them.

   It is crucial that these policies are consistently enforced. The consequences of breaking anti-bullying rules should be clearly stated so that employees know exactly what will happen if they engage in bullying acts.

   By implementing these strategies, we're not just creating a more inclusive workplace—we're unleashing the full potential of human creativity and innovation. The investment in fostering psychological safety for all employees pays dividends in productivity and reduced turnover.

At the heart of every policy and procedure are people—unique individuals with hopes, fears, and immense potential. By creating an environment where every employee feels valued and understood, we're not just building a better workplace; we're shaping a more compassionate and productive world.

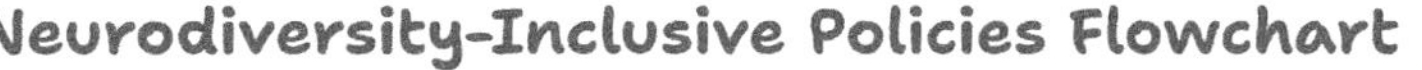

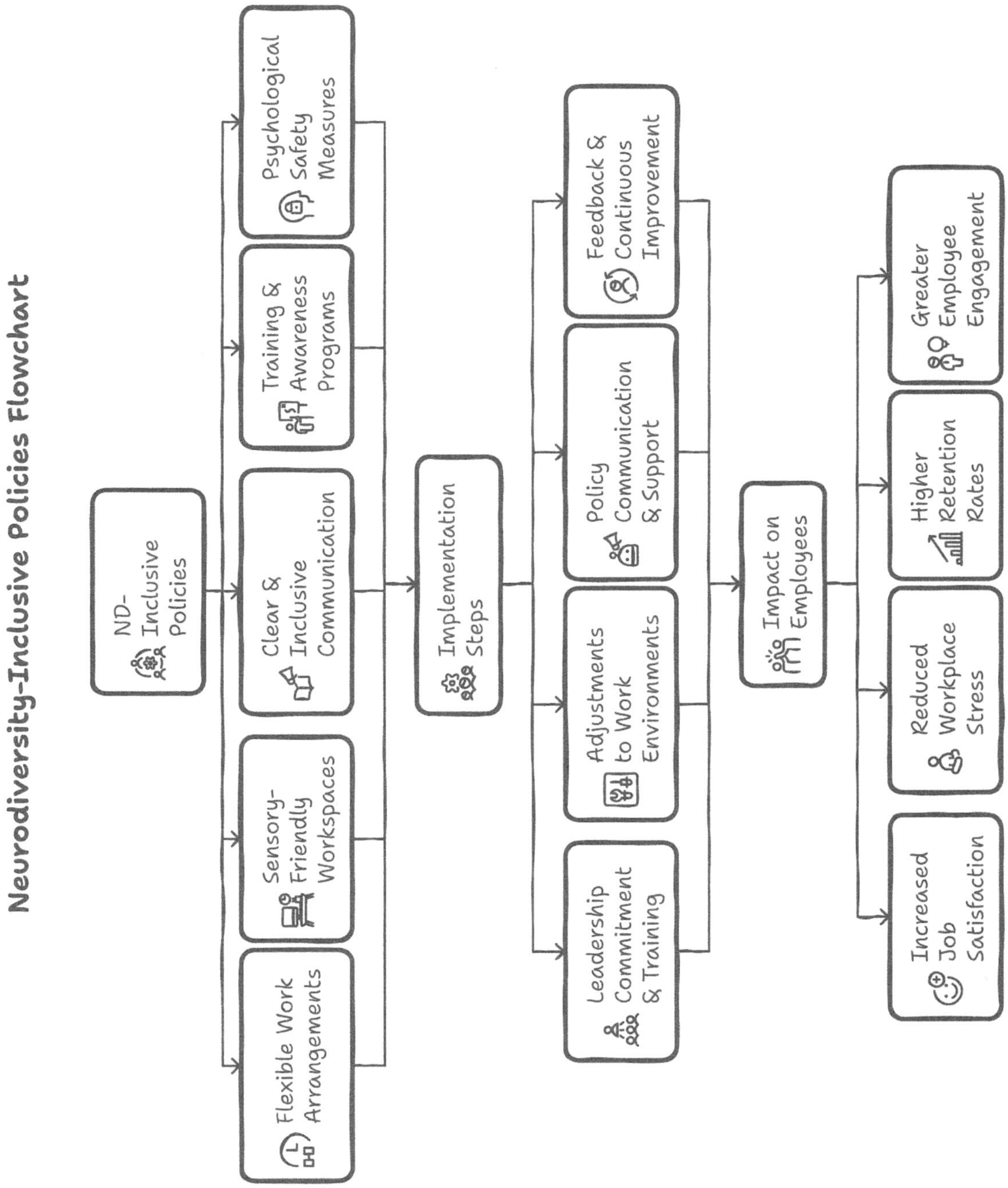
Neurodiversity-Inclusive Policies Flowchart
ND-Inclusive Policies
Flexible Work Arrangements
Sensory-Friendly Workspaces
Clear & Inclusive Communication
Training & Awareness Programs
Psychological Safety Measures
Implementation Steps
Leadership Commitment & Training
Adjustments to Work Environments
Policy Communication & Support
Feedback & Continuous Improvement
Impact on Employees
Increased Job Satisfaction
Reduced Workplace Stress
Higher Retention Rates
Greater Employee Engagement

How to Foster Trust and Authenticity in Neurodiverse Teams

There are many different ways that human brains work.

Anyone who has ever worked with another human knows that great things can evolve when we approach conversations, problems, or ways of being in the world differently. Yet while wisdom unfolds when people with differently wired brains collaborate, there is also a chance of friction. Some friction can spur better problem-solving, yet it can sometimes interfere with cohesive teamwork.

Individual Success versus Team Success

Employees naturally seek to grow in their careers. Because opportunities for recognition, professional reward, and promotion are limited, competition can cause conflict among team members. The potential for conflict is especially likely when a team member stands out as nonconformist, intense, and talented. However, at the same time, most individuals realize that working together is integral to achieving a company's overall business goals. Managers also recognize that the company can only succeed if everyone works together.

Neurodiversity in Workplace Teams

A lack of knowledge about neurodiversity can lead some to believe that neurodivergent individuals may not be team players or may potentially pose a risk to team cohesiveness.

Imagine that you are on a team that has been working to solve a complex problem. Most of the team feels strongly about a proposal that a seasoned, well-respected team lead recommended. Just when everyone sees a resolution in sight, one team member passionately shares a solution that is so unconventional, it seems destined to fail. Add to that scenario that the team member constantly rubs others the wrong way because of their quirky behavior. They interrupt, argue to make their point, and lack finesse. In the moment, it doesn't matter to the rest of the team that the proposed solution may deserve their consideration. And on some level, this team member's divergent ideas threaten competitive team members looking to win the boss's favor.

People tend to lack trust in those who are different from themselves. Human nature is often suspicious of what isn't easily understood. As leaders, our challenge is to create and nurture teams that work well together despite their differences.

Teamwork in the Neurodiverse Workplace

Teamwork isn't about people getting along and liking each other. It's about team members working together for the success of the organization.

In very general terms, the following are five characteristics of effective teams (Ingram et al., 1997) :

1. A unitary mindset among team members—working toward the same result.
2. Recognizing one another's strengths and allowing team members to do what they do best.
3. Holding one another accountable for achieving successful results.
4. Trusting your team members.
5. Effective communication.

These five factors work together to create an effective team that produces results. To do this, all team members must be aware of and buy into the results they are working to achieve.

This buy-in calls for effective communication and group-wide awareness of each person's strengths. Recognizing one another's strengths allows team members to give each other the freedom to get on with their tasks without feeling watched or judged, which may hamper morale, self-esteem, and overall success.

When team members trust each other, they also look out for each other's success, find ways to support each other, and move toward the team's end goal. A culture of genuine "How's it going?" and "Anything I can do to help?" contributes to team and individual success while reinforcing the quality of trust within the team.

Divergent Thinking in the Workplace

This is where neurodiversity comes in. All the characteristics that make up an effective team also help to create a successful neurodiverse workplace.
How so?

Many neurodivergent thinkers do their best when there is a clear goal and purpose. You probably think we all need a clear goal and purpose when working on a team. This is true, and because of how neurodivergent brains are wired, they need it more. Divergent thinkers thrive when they are made aware of the big picture, their place in it, and why their work is essential. Having a clear purpose helps to create the emotional buy-in required for success.

Atypical thinkers are aware of what they are good at and painfully aware of their weaknesses. Therefore, allowing employees to use their expertise and show what they can do is essential. Give them the autonomy to be successful.

For example, in the scenario above, ask the team member with the nonconformist solution to research the remedy, present pros and cons, and flesh out the idea rather than dismiss their concept because it's inconvenient. Allowing them to elaborate on their vision and present at the next meeting builds confidence in that team member and strengthens the whole team.

Acceptance of our differences can lead to excellent results if there is awareness and trust.

"Diversity practices and inclusion interact to foster a trusting climate and employee engagement." (Downey et al., 2015)

A culture of trust and safety where all members work together to help one another fill the gaps allows teams to complete their mission successfully. While one person may be able to hyperfocus and complete intense, high-concentration tasks, another may be able to think creatively and link unrelated facts to find unique solutions.

Both individuals contribute to the team's goals and play a crucial role in team success. Cognitive skills and strengths from all employees are celebrated. Creativity, pattern recognition, visual-spatial thinking, and resilience are all characteristics of neurodiverse thinkers. Linear thinking gets consistent results, is predictable, process-oriented, and time-tested. Teams need both types of thinkers to achieve maximum results. In the animal kingdom, we call this symbiosis and mutualism.

Cognitive Skills and Strengths

Hyperfocus

Ability to immerse in complex tasks for extended periods. Ideal for roles requiring problem-solving, coding, research, and analytics.

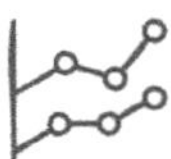

Pattern Recognition

Quickly identifies trends, inconsistencies, and unique connections. Strength in finance, cybersecurity, AI, and scientific research.

Creative Thinking

Generates out-of-the-box solutions and innovative ideas. Strong in marketing, design, and strategic planning.

Attention to Detail

Excels in quality control, auditing, compliance, and precision-based work. Reduces errors and enhances process efficiency.

Visual-Spatial Thinking

Exceptional at conceptualizing structures, maps, and processes. Excels in engineering, architecture, and logistics.

Analytical Problem-Solving

Uses structured approaches to break down challenges and find optimal solutions. Ideal for IT, mathematics, and operations management.

Emotional Intelligence

Strong in understanding diverse perspectives, conflict resolution, and team dynamics. Enhances HR, leadership, and customer relations.

Resilience

Excels in navigating uncertainty and responding effectively to change. Key asset in entrepreneurship, crisis management, and fast-paced industries.

A culture of trust and safety where all members work together to help one another fill the gaps allows teams to complete their mission successfully.

Did you know that zebras and ostriches have a symbiotic relationship?

"Zebra and ostriches look out for each other. Zebras have a great sense of smell and hearing but poor eyesight. While the ostrich has great vision but not great hearing or smell. They often travel together and warn each other when danger is coming. Each animal benefits from the strength of the other animal. This relationship keeps them safe from lions on the hunt." (*Zebra and Ostrich – Symbiotic Relationships,* n.d.)

Effective Communication Builds Trust

Effective communication is critical to the success of neurodiverse teams.

Atypical thinkers understand and process communication differently from the norm; innuendo, implied meaning, inside jokes, and sarcasm can be missed or misinterpreted. Without awareness of this, misunderstandings are bound to happen. Receiving mixed messages makes the neurodivergent team members look like they are being difficult or ignoring instructions.

This confusion over real meanings is why some feel that neurodivergent employees aren't team players. Setting up a culture of clear communication serves everyone in a neurodiverse workplace. It leads to more accountability and builds trust among team members.

Creating strong, cohesive, trusting teams promotes authenticity. An authentic team working with purpose toward the same goal makes your company future-proof, flexible, and innovative.

It's a win-win for everyone, regardless of differences.

Allow Employees the Freedom to Be Themselves

The way we manage employees, the way systems and structures are organized, and our day-to-day interactions all need to be reexamined to create a genuinely inclusive workplace for all workers.

I firmly believe that company culture is the most critical factor for creating a safe space for neurodivergence in the workplace.

When I talk about "safe space," I am obviously talking about physical safety, but I am also referring to psychological safety. I want you to dig a little deeper and think about safe spaces in a way that you may not have before.

I want to talk about a safe space as being a place where neurodivergent workers are safe to be themselves.

I have a colleague, Amanda, who has struggled with her divergent thinking in the professional realm.

Amanda was thrilled when her manager recognized how her OCD need for perfection interfered with her ability to meet deadlines. Instead of taking a punitive approach, this manager was creative. He worked with her to devise a solution that helped her meet her goals while allowing her to lower her standards of absolute perfection.

This manager wasn't hung up on labels, and he wasn't bound to a strict review process. He was conscientious and respectful. He wanted to help Amanda meet her goals while respecting her unique working style. She was allowed and even encouraged to be herself.

She was supported in working in the way that came naturally to her.

The Fundamental Questions

Having the right systems is a great place to start for any company that wants to support divergent thinkers in its workplace. However, creating the safe environment I'm proposing requires an honest assessment of your organization's culture.

Take the time to honestly assess the potential roadblocks to a safe workspace.

Chapter Three Reflection Questions

1. Discuss the potential challenges and benefits of implementing a neurodiversity initiative in a workplace. How can organizations ensure these initiatives don't inadvertently lead to discrimination or stigmatization?
2. What are some practical ways to create a psychologically safe environment for neurodivergent employees? How might this impact overall workplace productivity?
3. How can managers and team leaders foster trust and authenticity in neurodiverse teams? Provide specific strategies based on the chapter's content.
4. Reflect on the story about Amanda and her manager. How does this example demonstrate effective leadership in a neurodiverse workplace? What lessons can be drawn from this approach?
5. Discuss the concept of "masking" in the context of neurodiversity in the workplace. What are the potential negative impacts of this practice, and how can organizations create an environment where masking is less necessary?
6. How might the traditional hiring and promotion processes in companies inadvertently disadvantage neurodivergent individuals? Suggest ways these processes could be modified to be more inclusive.
7. Analyze the five characteristics of effective teams mentioned in the chapter. How might these need to be adapted or reinterpreted in the context of neurodiverse teams?

8. Reflect on the statement: "Teamwork isn't about people getting along and liking each other. It's about team members working together for the success of the organization." How does this perspective apply to managing neurodiverse teams?
9. What are some practical ways to create a psychologically safe environment for neurodivergent employees? How might this impact overall workplace productivity?

Neurodivergent Women at Work

As we explore neurodiversity in the workplace, it's crucial to address the unique challenges and opportunities faced by neurodivergent women. This intersection of neurodiversity and gender adds another layer of complexity to the professional landscape, one that has been historically overlooked but is increasingly relevant in our quest for truly inclusive workplaces.

Throughout this book, we've examined how neurodiversity can benefit organizations and individuals alike. Now we turn our attention to a specific subset of the neurodivergent population—women—whose experiences often differ significantly from those of their male counterparts due to societal expectations and ingrained biases.

We understand that businesses exist to make money. So naturally, an employer wants people who can best contribute to that goal. From the start of the Industrial Revolution, the ideal employee had no "hindrances" in helping the company meet its goals. As such, types of work were divided along gender lines. This pattern is evident even today. Thankfully, the needs of society in the 1700s are not the needs of today. Further, current issues need innovative, out-of-the-box solutions, so a cookie-cutter "ideal" doesn't have to exist for many roles.

The stats regarding employment rates for ND women are frighteningly low, and not for the reasons you think. Consider the following:

- Humans still, subconsciously, at least, prefer sameness when employing others, which translates into a favorable bias for neurotypicality, whiteness, maleness, and other things traditionally deemed "normal" in the workplace. This natural human inclination results in a bias toward team-player personalities and those naturally comfortable in social settings. This tendency excludes many neurodivergent women.
- Neurodiversity is often unheard of or misunderstood. So management makes assumptions without accurate knowledge of this group of people and simply runs with them.

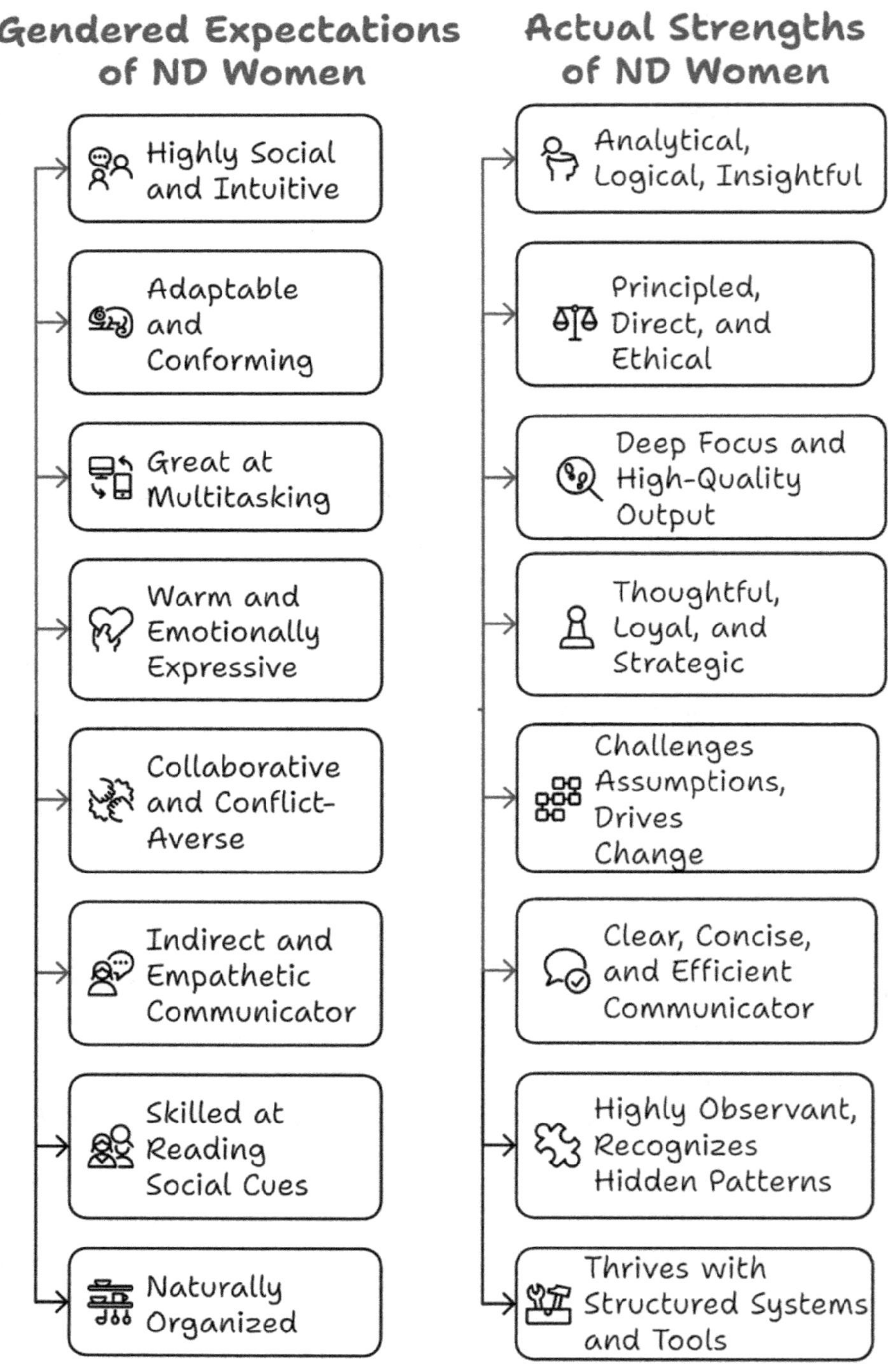
Gendered Expectations of ND Women
Highly Social and Intuitive
Adaptable and Conforming
Great at Multitasking
Warm and Emotionally Expressive
Collaborative and Conflict-Averse
Indirect and Empathetic Communicator
Skilled at Reading Social Cues
Naturally Organized
Actual Strengths of ND Women
Analytical, Logical, Insightful
Principled, Direct, and Ethical
Deep Focus and High-Quality Output
Thoughtful, Loyal, and Strategic
Challenges Assumptions, Drives Change
Clear, Concise, and Efficient Communicator
Highly Observant, Recognizes Hidden Patterns
Thrives with Structured Systems and Tools

- Workplace gender inequality is still a thing. The unconscious idea that women are less suited to specific roles exists, and it comes through even more strongly when neurodivergent traits are apparent.
- Sadly, mental illness and mental differences are still taboo, and many aren't yet able to see beyond a diagnosis, labeling others with it when there isn't a need to do so.

These facts converge into a situation affecting 15 to 20 percent of the population. That's significant.

Embracing neurodiversity, particularly among women, isn't just about compliance or social responsibility—it's a strategic imperative for businesses aiming to maintain a competitive edge. In today's rapidly evolving market, cognitive diversity is a key driver of innovation, problem-solving, and adaptability. By tapping into the unique perspectives and skills of neurodivergent women, companies can unlock new sources of creativity and efficiency. The question isn't whether the effort is worth it but whether your organization can afford to overlook this valuable talent pool. To fully appreciate the potential impact, let's explore the distinct strengths and insights that neurodivergent women bring to the table.

Embracing neurodiversity, particularly among women, isn't just about compliance or social responsibility—it's a strategic imperative for businesses aiming to maintain a competitive edge.

Who Are We?

Neurodiversity encompasses autism, ADHD, Tourette's, dyslexia, dyspraxia, dyscalculia, and other mental health expressions. Many of us know what these conditions may "look" like. Still, that idea is typically based on what we see on television—a form of media where the male representation of these conditions dominates.

According to Dori Zener's 2019 article "Journey to Diagnosis for Women with Autism," autistic females are less likely to be diagnosed at an age where appropriate support can be put in place. If a medical professional sees them, they are often misdiagnosed as having anxiety, depression, or bipolar disorder.(Zener, n.d.)

The same applies to ADHD. Try to find media representations of dyslexic celebrities and business leaders. Chances are, they are male.

Recently, to ensure that my keynote on the topic of neurodiversity at work included successful neurodivergent women of color, I spent five hours combing the web to find representation that was self-disclosed and well known. I avoid using examples that others have diagnosed from afar. I was shocked that examples were not easier to find. The only neurodivergent woman of color I found who openly discussed her diagnosis is artist Morgan Harper Nichols. If you do a search on YouTube for her name and the keyword *autism,* you should find the video where she discusses her diagnosis and the impact it had on her life.

As is common in medical research, neurodiversity has been studied using mainly male sample groups. Consequently, the diagnostic tools designed based on these studies favor diagnosis in males rather than females; thus, females are diagnosed less. All of this reinforces the false paradigm that neurodivergence is predominantly male.

Males tend to externalize their distress through disruptive behavior or violence, while females are more likely to turn inward, resulting in psychosomatic symptoms, self-harm behaviors, and anxiety. This tendency is well known and is mirrored in the manifestation of clinical depression and suicidality in men versus women. (Hiller et al., 2014; Solomon et al., 2012)

What to Do (and Not Do) When Your Employee Reveals Their Neurodivergence

If a neurodivergent employee at work discloses that they are neurodivergent, here are some helpful things to know:

- Their diagnosis will likely take you by surprise. Try not to react with statements like, "Oh! No way you are autistic! You don't [fill in the blank—flap, have poor eye contact, et cetera]." They're likely been invalidated in this way their entire life. When an employee has the courage to disclose their neurodivergence, immediately dismissing what they are saying undermines their truth.
- Don't presume anything.
- Don't reference pop-culture examples of neurodiversity. They're often wildly inaccurate, one-sided representations from a neurotypical perspective only. Never say, "So you're like...[fill in the blank—Rain Man, Sheldon, the Good Doctor, what have you]."
- Listen with an open mind.
- Ask them about previous work experiences and how you can best support them.
- Understand that disclosing a diagnosis involves a lot of risk, and they are taking a significant risk by being open about it.
- Get to know the strengths and weaknesses of their type of neurodiversity and then ask what their lived experience has been.
- Don't pathologize their symptoms if they experience difficulties. Respect them instead. No one is perfect, and room for grace is always appropriate.
- Please do not talk about their disclosure to other employees.
- Discuss appropriate workplace accommodations and keep an open mind.
- Be patient with yourself and with them.
- Depending on their diversity, be aware that some tasks and obligations might be more difficult or tiring for your neurodivergent employee than others.

What Neurodivergent Women Want You to Know

Challenges Faced by Neurodivergent Women in the Workplace

Office Politics
Struggles with navigating office politics limit professional growth.

Bias in Hiring
Preferences for neurotypical candidates lead to bias in hiring and promotion.

Communication Differences
Different communication styles can be misinterpreted.

Gender Inequality
Gender biases are magnified for neurodivergent women in the workplace.

Masking and Burnout
Constant masking leads to exhaustion and burnout.

Misunderstanding
Misconceptions about neurodiversity lead to stigma and lack of support.

- If we don't appear neurodivergent to you, it doesn't mean we aren't. Masking is extremely common; we've developed it as a survival mechanism.
- We know what we are capable of, and we also know what we cannot do. Please don't underestimate our abilities.
- Know that many neurodivergent women don't comply with society's idea of what a woman "should" be. Don't draw conclusions based on normative standards. I can't tell you how many times in my life I've been told I act more like a man than a woman. Unfortunately, most people, especially men, don't consider that a good thing.
- We don't use our differences as an excuse for special treatment, so try to bear that in mind when we do things differently.
- We learn differently from others. As such, our career path may look different from the usual.
- We may ask many questions or request clarification in writing more often than expected. There may be several reasons for this. But none of them are because we are stupid or are trying to be annoying.

  This is another point that has been challenging for me at work and in personal relationships. I've learned to warn people that I ask questions not to challenge but to better understand the why and how of what I'm being asked to do. So often, this questioning is read as resistance. Take a step back and hold your judgment. This person may be working to meet expectations and do an excellent job.
- We might struggle to speak up in social situations or be heard and understood in meetings. Our colleagues can often miss our ideas because of that. Try to be conscious of this tendency.
- We often have an offbeat sense of humor. Try not to let it offend you.
- Any unexpected bluntness from us isn't malicious.

This bluntness causes so many misunderstandings! It's exhausting to try to make what needs to be said soft and pretty, like a lady should say it. I've spent a lifetime reframing what I need to say so that it doesn't offend, especially in writing. If the person I'm talking with is from the West Coast USA, I tell them I'm a New Englander, so I'm direct. Then they may give me a pass!

- We are likely oblivious to office politics and may never be proficient in reading the room for trouble spots.
- Our facial expressions might be complex to read. Just know that it's not deliberate. We are probably just concentrating hard.

  In professional settings, I've often found myself intensely focused on processing information during meetings or discussions. Unfortunately, my concentrated expression has frequently been misinterpreted as anger or displeasure. This common misunderstanding isn't unique to neurodivergent individuals but can be particularly pronounced for us. The phenomenon even has a colloquial term: *resting [fill-in-the-blank] face.* For neurodivergent women in the workplace, such misinterpretations can lead to unwarranted negative perceptions and impact professional relationships.

In an interview with neurodivergent women on neurodiverging.com, Lauren Melissa, autistic advocate and creator of AutieTips, had this to say:

"We do have struggles, but we also have so much to offer. We are inherently valuable in a society that needs out-of-the-box thinking and innovation to overcome the complex issues we face. Not autistics face, but society as a whole face."

It's that last bit from Lauren that makes the point. Modern society as a whole has unique and complex challenges and needs. The one-size-fits-all, best-practice, rigid thinking that defined work in the last century is outdated. There is no blueprint for tackling society's challenges. Success requires that we embrace the complexity and draw upon the full range of human insights and capabilities to work toward solutions.

How to Support ND Women in the Workplace ... and Elsewhere

Career coach Jorun Bork wrote the article "5 Ways to Empower Neurodivergent Women in the Workplace" and includes this gem on neurodiversity:

"Assume that all employees are neurodivergent to create an inclusive culture. Don't assume that everyone would feel comfortable switching desks or not find the lights too bright. Then, if an employee is neurodivergent and you check in with them regarding the seating allocation and the environment, they will feel more supported."

Chapter Four Reflection Questions

1. How might societal expectations and ingrained biases affect neurodivergent women in the workplace differently from their male counterparts?
2. Analyze the impact of male-dominated research and diagnostic tools on the recognition and support of neurodivergent women. How might this affect workplace inclusion?
3. Reflect on the statement: "We know what we are capable of, and we also know what we cannot do." How can managers balance supporting neurodivergent women's strengths while accommodating their challenges?
4. Discuss the concept of masking in the context of neurodivergent women in the workplace. What are its potential impacts on employee well-being and performance?
5. How might traditional expectations of workplace communication and social interaction disadvantage neurodivergent women? What strategies could be implemented to create a more inclusive environment?
6. Based on the information provided in the chapter, what specific steps could organizations take to better support and empower neurodivergent women in the workplace?

Neurodiversity: HR's Competitive Edge in Talent Management

Everybody varies a little from the definition of the "standard" human. Some of us are tall. Some of us are short. Some of us are right-handed. Some of us are left-handed (unless you are a baby boomer and went to Catholic school). Do those things matter? Not. It gets more complicated, however, when we factor in cultural differences and distinct ways of doing things.

Every manager or business owner knows they must look past superficial differences and concentrate on choosing the right people for the right job. This understanding is the key to unlocking the potential of a diverse workforce.

While workplace inclusion isn't new, the value of neurodivergent perspectives has only recently been recognized. Research showing how different cognitive styles can fill skill gaps on our teams has deepened our understanding of what genuine inclusion means. When we examine the status quo through a contrarian lens, we may realize that we often hire people who reinforce our existing paradigms, unintentionally creating skill gaps that diminish our workforce's productivity.

Every manager or business owner knows they must look past superficial differences and concentrate on choosing the right people for the right job.

Different People Think Differently

The prefix neuro- refers to the nerves transmitting electrochemical signals through our bodies and brains. These signals regulate our neurological processing, patterns of thought, and behavior, which are deeply influenced by and embedded into our collective culture. However, from time to time, atypical patterns of processing emerge also. Think of these as different ways brains are wired.

Optimizing Workplace Roles for Neurodivergent Employees

Underutilized potential

Employees have strengths but lack role alignment.

Low Strength Recognition

Misaligned roles

Roles do not match employees' recognized strengths.

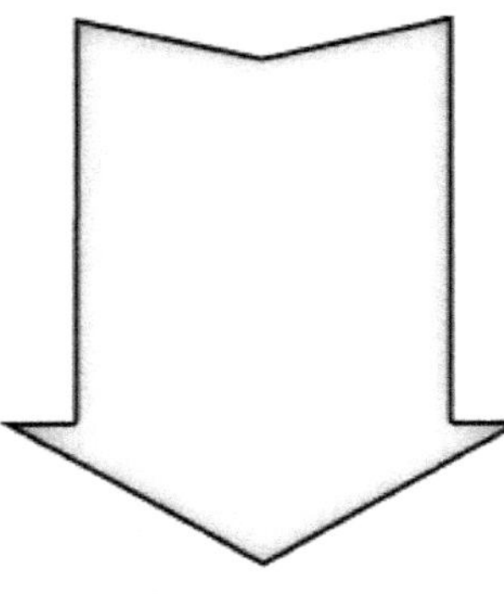

High productivity team

Team excels by aligning strengths with roles effectively.

High Strength Recognition

Recognized strengths

Strengths are acknowledged but not aligned with roles.

These varied thinking patterns open up new possibilities for creativity in every field. They shrug off the usual way of doing things and find new ways to achieve their objectives. In the workplace, it is easy to accept their slightly left-of-center behavior when they increase the team's productivity.

However, neurodiversity sometimes reveals itself in differences that go beyond the reach of the socially "normal." When unconventional behavior presents itself, people get confined into tidy boxes that help a neurotypical society deal with differences.

As I explained in chapter 1, these boxes are often labeled, usually with the diagnostic terminology medical professionals use to categorize divergent thinkers so they can get help. Without a diagnosis that appears in the DSM-5, insurance and other entities are unlikely to pay for or provide support and services. Consequently, neurodevelopmental differences fall under mental disorders and are stigmatized.

So the labels are necessary, especially in the school-aged years, for students to get the support they need. Unfortunately, those same labels often condemn neurodivergent individuals to the slow lane of life, and that's not fair or ethical.

It's a significant loss to the world, because neurodivergent people do not have an intellectual disability. Sometimes, a person will have both neurodivergence as well as an intellectual disability (ID). However, ID is a separate diagnosis.

NDs' thoughts may follow different paths, but their intelligence, personhood, and potential to live rich, meaningful lives remain intact. Understandably, seeing past the socially awkward behavior of people who learn differently can be challenging. Nonetheless, embracing diversity in all its forms is about learning to look beyond our differences and recognize strengths instead of deficits. By reframing this perspective, we shift from a deficit mindset to a gifts-mindset, appreciating the unique contributions of neurodivergent individuals.

Neurodivergent thinkers are not asking for favors. They certainly don't want to use the diagnosis that has followed them since childhood to ask for special treatment. They want to claim their right to reach their full potential in the workforce.

Embracing neurodiversity in the workplace will require some adjustments. The bonus is that if you adopt these adjustments with the mentality that they are for everybody, the result will be a richer, more productive, and more all-around positive experience for the entire workforce. Remember, *you are not performing an act of charity when hiring neurodivergent employees.* You are nurturing the depth of talent on your team.

Neurodivergent people, including those with autism and dyslexia, may have exceptional pattern recognition, memory, or mathematics skills. These strengths help businesses sharpen their problem-solving skills and become more innovative. The research on successful neurodiverse teams backs this up! (Austin & Pisano, 2017a) Yet many NDs, especially autistic adults, can only get low-skilled jobs that do not take advantage of their full potential.

The bonus is that if you adopt these adjustments with the mentality that they are for everybody, the result will be a richer, more productive, and more all-around positive experience for the entire workforce.

As discussed, company culture has a colossal influence on an organization's group dynamics. Consequently, successful neurodiversity at work initiatives start by aligning workplace culture with values that accept and support divergent thinkers. Implementing a neurodiversity at work initiative in a company without preparing the culture would be akin to planting a garden without preparing the soil first.

So let's look at the logistical aspects of making neurodiversity happen in your workplace. Let's start with the most basic. How do you get divergent thinkers through the door and onto your teams?

How can your company tap into this underutilized resource of human talent?

It all starts with how you hire.

Implementing a neurodiversity at work initiative in a company without preparing the culture would be akin to planting a garden without preparing the soil first.

Is Unconscious Bias Stopping You from Hiring a Neurodiverse Team?

How Do You Overcome Unconscious Bias When Interviewing to Hire a Neurodiverse Team?

Your company is ready to promote neurodiversity—great! The only problem is that you aren't hiring neurodivergent candidates.

Difficulty recruiting and hiring neurodivergent talent is a common scenario. It happens because hiring practices favor neurotypical people. A talk of mine about the unconscious bias surrounding neurodivergence was recently nominated for a Virtual Speakers Hall of Fame Award. It got me thinking a bit more about how unconscious bias keeps neurodivergent people from being hired, even when a company is motivated to employ neurodivergent people.

Difficulty recruiting and hiring neurodivergent talent is a common scenario. It happens because hiring practices favor neurotypical people.

What Is Unconscious Bias?

Unconscious bias is preconceived notions about what people may be like based on a single attribute. It often comprises stereotypes, experiences, and things we have heard. Even if we consider ourselves open-minded, we can still have unconscious bias.

I have spent thirty years working with neurodivergent people, and I'm neurodivergent myself. A few years ago, I was asked to give a keynote address to the Down Syndrome Guild of Dallas. Usually, when I give talks like this, I share vignettes of famous neurodivergent people. You'd be surprised at how many celebrities there are with OCD, autism, ADHD, dyslexia, and the like. It got me wondering if there are any celebrities with Down syndrome.

I did a Google search, and I'm ashamed to admit that I wasn't expecting to find any results. Imagine my surprise when Google returned results for well-known artists, musicians, models, and actors with Down syndrome!

Unconscious bias caused me to underestimate the abilities of people with Down syndrome. If I can fall victim to unconscious bias after decades of working with neurodivergence, then it's understandable that unconscious bias may impact people involved in the hiring process. We all have preconceptions of which we are unaware.

How Does Unconscious Bias Affect the Hiring Process?

Unconscious bias doesn't just affect how we view someone when we know they have neurodivergence but can also affect how we see their neurodivergent behaviors.

Let's say you're interviewing someone who barely makes eye contact throughout the job interview. Your impression of this behavior might be that they lack confidence or are socially awkward, traits that would knock them out of the running for the position. The interviewer might even feel uncomfortable with the lack of eye contact and decide not to proceed with the candidate. However, the candidate may not lack confidence or be unfit for the job. Instead, they could be autistic and struggle with eye contact. Do they have the skills to do the job for which they are being interviewed? Unless the job they are applying for is customer- or vendor-facing, does eye contact matter?

Unconscious bias doesn't just affect how we view someone when we know they have neurodivergence but can also affect how we see their neurodivergent behaviors.

Many companies use artificial intelligence (AI) technology to screen résumés so they can create a shortlist to make the hiring process more efficient. The AI is programmed to reject résumés based on guidelines that would automatically rule out some groups of neurodivergent people. For example, someone with dyslexia may be ruled out due to spelling errors in their résumé.

During the pandemic, many companies asked candidates to complete assessments and online tests while being recorded by AI to prevent cheating. People with ADHD or dyslexia are often ruled out during these assessments because of how their eyes move around the screen. Autistic candidates may also be ruled out during this process due to facial expressions or behavior that falls outside expected norms. While AI makes hiring more efficient, it also makes hiring practices less inclusive, forcing candidates to disclose their neurodivergence and seek accommodations.

Unconscious biases could prevent you from hiring fantastic employees and bringing in fresh perspectives when building a neurodiverse team. Next time you catch yourself making an assumption, I challenge you to question it.

Stereotypes in Neurodivergent Hiring: When Exceptional Is the Expectation

For all the acceptance that neurodivergence has received, including workplace initiatives to recruit and train neurodivergent talent, we still have a long way to go to attain equity and full inclusion. Stereotypes still impact hiring patterns, and hiring practices are standardized around these stereotypes.

I am guilty of espousing the idea that neurodiversity is a competitive advantage. I've quoted corporate studies confirming that having neurodiverse teams fuels innovation.

I also believe that each human has unique gifts that can be described as superpowers. Yet there is much concern about a "superpower" stereotype emerging in the world of neurodiversity. This superpower descriptor is most common when considering those on the autism spectrum. It's time that concerns about stereotyping people with autism and other neurodivergence are brought into the open for discussion.

I am guilty of espousing the idea that neurodiversity is a competitive advantage.

When neurodiversity hiring initiatives are pitched and accepted, there's often an assumption that candidates will primarily be people with autism, and that those candidates will be savants and nothing less. Furthermore, it is frequently believed that neurodivergent hires will assimilate into a neurotypical working environment that is not friendly to neurodiversity. They must also exceed all expectations while exhibiting capabilities that may be deemed beyond human.

This superhuman expectation is particularly pronounced in the approach of many corporate workplaces toward autism. Our natural tendency to embrace stereotypes about people different from us hamstrings hiring initiatives. Today, despite the high demand for workers in every industry, 75 to 85 percent of adults with autism are unemployed globally, a number that hasn't moved since the last major studies were published in 2017. (Heasman & Gillespie, 2019) A 2021 study by the United Kingdom's Office of National Statistics found that people with autism experience some of the highest unemployment rates in that country. (Sparkes et al., n.d.) It's crucial that we redefine our approach to neurodiversity in corporate workplaces to ensure a more inclusive and equitable treatment of all individuals.

At a time when tech billionaires celebrate their forays into outer space, we would do well to consider what the idealization of successful autistic outliers has done to the big picture of neurodivergence and those who live with it. More than one autistic colleague has implored me not to use high-profile entrepreneurs and celebrated academics as examples of neurodivergent success. Stereotypes that set the expectation that neurodivergents are supposed to be savants or genius outliers are detrimental and affect their sense of self-worth. At its worst, the phenomenon results in what is known as autism masking (Draaisma, 2009; Pearson & Rose, 2021), a coping mechanism that can, over time, seriously affect mental and physical health.

Each human has unique gifts that can be described as superpowers.

What Can Be Considered an Acceptable Presentation of Neurodivergence, and What Cannot?

Organizations trying to define this may make arbitrary decisions. Yet when decision-making doesn't include neurodivergent people in the discussion circle, the result is that standards are set so that presumed exceptional attributes become the norm. Often corporate narratives are rooted in societal misconceptions. They tend to tokenize inclusion.

Well-respected platforms often depict neurodivergence as a competitive advantage using arguments based on on neurodivergent employees' extraordinary mathematical abilities or software development skills. However, this tendency to focus on superpowers sets unrealistic expectations and can be damaging. Instead of fostering an equitable space, these narratives distort the truth. They lead people to see a traditionally othered community as a privileged one with superpowers. This blatant denial of reality not only creates a façade of inclusion and equity in corporate workplaces but also perpetuates harmful stereotypes.

Much of the stereotyping and idolization of superpowers among autistic individuals stem from the images portrayed in pop culture. (Draaisma, 2009)

These stereotypes originated with movies like *Rain Man,* one of the first films to attempt to shed light on neurodivergence. While *Rain Man* may have been revolutionary in presenting a subject as sensitive and tricky as autism on screen, the movie still fell short, relying on the main character's savant syndrome to move the plot along.

But that was thirty years ago. Perhaps society's perceptions have changed. Let's look at the past decade of neurodivergent representation in the media. The most prominent ND individual portrayed in pop culture may be Sheldon Cooper, the physics prodigy with above-and-beyond intelligence embodied in a white male celebrated as eccentric. His quirky demeanor is played for laughs in *The Big Bang Theory* and its spin-off, *Young Sheldon.* More recently, *The Good Doctor* featured a main character who is an autistic savant solving medical dilemmas.

Is neurodivergence only legitimized when there is an exceptional talent?

Revamping Our Hiring Practices

Generalizing the entire neurodivergent populace under one umbrella does little to remove the stereotypes that guide most HR decisions. Hiring practices that see the neurodivergent picture in black and white alone leave neurodivergent candidates with the same recurring issue; to be inducted into a neurotypical society, they need to successfully camouflage their neurodivergence (masking, or autistic masking) or somehow transform into savants with extraordinary capabilities.

Pop culture paints images of neurodivergence that promote extraordinary abilities as the only acceptable form of talent in the neurodivergent community. This critique of savant syndrome does not advocate for lower hiring expectations. Instead, it's a call for awareness. Be aware of stereotypes that do not serve organizations that seek to build a diverse, equitable, and inclusive workplace.

Pop culture paints images of neurodivergence that promote extraordinary abilities as the only acceptable form of talent in the neurodivergent community.

Inclusive Hiring: How to Revamp Your Company's Recruitment and Interviewing Processes

A neurodiverse workforce is born from the people you bring onto your team. If you want to tap into the talent and potential of divergent thinkers, decision-makers need to intentionally hire more neurodivergent employees. To do this, taking a long, hard look at your company's recruitment, hiring, and interviewing practices is essential. There are ways to make recruiting and hiring procedures more neurodivergent-friendly.

Option 1: Create a Dedicated Hiring Stream Explicitly Focused on Recruiting Neurodivergent Workers

Large corporations frequently set up a separate hiring stream to attract ND talent. Alternatively, they may partner with a private company that provides this service as an outside hirer. Some consider this a form of affirmative action because it is a program set up and designated *exclusively* for ND workers.

This option requires individuals to disclose their neurodivergent condition to participate in the specialized hiring stream. Still, it allows them immediate access to accommodations throughout the hiring and onboarding process.

An excellent example of this type of dedicated recruitment and hiring program is the Autism at Work Program, initially created by tech giant SAP and now partnering with more than thirty corporations. (Woo, 2019) Workers apply to the company through the program instead of the standard HR department. And instead of applying for a specific posted job, interested individuals describe the type of work they seek. When their stated skills, desired type of work, and job availability match, they are invited to continue through the interview process. If hired, their onboarding and training will be individually determined by their unique needs. Additional support is provided through an on-the-job mentor or dedicated support person until the new employee fully acclimates to their role.

The entire process, from start to finish, is fully adapted for inclusion. The needs of ND individuals are considered every step of the way. HR professionals in these programs are highly trained and specialized in working with ND workers.

The major downside to implementing a dedicated recruitment and hiring program is that it requires a fair amount of resources. You are creating an entirely new division within your HR department or hiring one as an outside contractor!

However, it's important to consider that this type of dedicated hiring stream may unintentionally create a situation where job applicants feel compelled to disclose their neurodivergent condition. This brings us back to our earlier discussion about the potential complexities surrounding labels and diagnoses in the workplace.

Because participation in this type of hiring program requires full disclosure, some ND individuals may be hesitant to participate. This type of hiring program may have the unintended consequence of discouraging divergent thinkers from applying.

Think about it...suppose your access to a job opportunity was dependent on you outing yourself and your ND condition after a lifetime of masking and trying to put a diagnostic label behind you. In that case, you might decide you'd prefer to look elsewhere.

This is why I am a big fan of my next suggestion.

Option 2: Revamp Existing Recruitment, Hiring, and Interviewing Processes to Be More Inclusive for Neurodivergent Workers

Only some businesses can afford to create or contract an exclusive department dedicated to hiring ND workers.

Fortunately, having a program like Autism at Work is *not* a prerequisite to becoming an inclusive, neurodiverse workplace.

Most accommodations can easily be implemented into your existing recruitment, interviewing, and hiring processes. The Inclusive Dynamic Workplace Design™ changes I suggest are simple, cost-effective, and highly impactful. (Employer Assistance and Resource Network on Disability Inclusion, n.d.)

An added benefit is that neurodivergent individuals do not need to reveal a diagnosis to be considered for a job. Job postings are accessible, interview processes are nondiscriminatory, and *everyone* has a fair chance to prove their capabilities for any given role.

Simple Steps to Create Neurodivergent-Inclusive Recruiting, Hiring, and Interviewing Processes

ND-Friendly Job Description Elements

Use this checklist to ensure that job descriptions are inclusive, accessible, and supportive of neurodivergent applicants, helping attract diverse talent.

- ☐ **Clear, Jargon-Free Language** – Use simple, direct wording (e.g., avoid vague terms like "rockstar" or "fast-paced").
- ☐ **Essential vs. Preferred Requirements** – Clearly distinguish must-have qualifications from nice-to-have skills.
- ☐ **Concrete Job Duties** – Provide specific, detailed expectations rather than broad or ambiguous descriptions.
- ☐ **Alternative Communication Options** – Allow for applications in various formats (e.g., written, video, or skills-based submissions).
- ☐ **Skills-Based Emphasis** – Focus on the candidate's abilities rather than subjective qualities like "strong interpersonal skills" unless truly essential.
- ☐ **Predictable Interview Process** – Outline the hiring steps clearly, including interview format, number of rounds, and expectations.
- ☐ **Sensory and Environmental Considerations** – If applicable, mention workplace flexibility, remote options, or accommodations like quiet spaces.
- ☐ **Supportive Workplace Culture** – Highlight inclusivity efforts, mentorship programs, and accommodations for neurodivergent employees.
- ☐ **Flexibility in Work Styles** – Acknowledge different ways of working, including structured workflows, flexible deadlines, or assistive tools.

Source: Neurodiversity in the Workplace: Maximizing Success through Inclusive Dynamic Workplace Design™ by Susan Gingras Fitzell, M.Ed., CSP

Revamp Job Postings

Standard job descriptions are usually typed-out text documents. Consider creating an audio file or a short video that provides all the same information. Distribute these together, allowing interested job candidates the freedom to choose which format works best for them to receive the information they need about your open position.

Revamp Job Descriptions

Make sure the job requirements posted reflect the job you need to be done. Avoid personality or character descriptions. Are soft skills like "good ability to work in a team" or "strong communication skills" crucial to the role, or do they exist just to maintain workplace culture?

Ditch AI Screening Tools

While AI can undeniably make our lives easier (I *love* talk-to-type technology with predictive text), it can also underscore the intrinsic bias in the data it operates on. Eliminate AI screening tools that claim to measure a person's soft skills or analyze facial expressions during screening processes. A highly trained, conscientious professional is more effective when hiring a neurodiverse workforce.

Ditch Traditional Interviews

Arrange to meet potential job candidates outside the traditional interview. Consider adopting a meet-up process where potential employees are encouraged to interact and complete tasks in a group or individually (depending on the role you are hiring for). You could also organize a meeting to review candidates' portfolios, put them to work on a test project, or have them complete a skills assessment.

Specialisterne, a European consultancy company with a significant percentage of its employees on the spectrum, has a groundbreaking approach to the interview alternative, which it calls a "hangout." In an informal environment, job candidates can discuss and demonstrate their skills with hiring managers in a low-stress atmosphere. Candidates who make an impression move into the next round of training.

Partner with Advocacy Groups

Reach out to groups such as Teaching the Autism Community Trades (TACT) or NeuroTalent Works, among many others, to build relationships with the neurodivergent community. (Bernick, 2022) Publish your career opportunities in their job listings and ask them to recommend talent. Better yet, consider creating a cooperative relationship that could result in collaborative projects between the ND community and your business, mutually benefiting both!

When you revamp your company's recruitment, hiring, and interviewing processes to be more inclusive of neurodivergence, you support the creation of a genuinely neurodiverse workforce. Whether through clearly stated hiring goals and quotas or by creating more accessible job opportunities, bringing new neurodivergent employees onto your team will supercharge your crew's creativity, problem-solving capacity, and productivity.

The steps I've outlined above require a change in perspective and some ingenuity if they're to work for your organization. These simple adjustments will demonstrate your company's commitment to fostering a workplace that welcomes different viewpoints and experiences.

Say Goodbye to the Traditional Interview

Traditional screening practices, like the sit-down interview, value skills that neurotypicals usually possess. Hiring managers and HR look for workers who seem capable of being a team player, have good communication skills, show confidence, and demonstrate the ability to subconsciously mirror the interviewer. Most important, a potential job candidate should show the essential life skill of knowing what not to say.

Neurodivergent candidates without these skills may never make it through the first interview phase.

I've interviewed many autistic employees in the process of authoring informed articles. One of them, Maria, was frustrated by her interview experiences. This is her story:

"It's a mini performance. It's like acting for thirty minutes to an hour and hoping I get all the lines right, even when my script doesn't resonate with me. In all the jobs I've interviewed for, it always felt like I had to act.

"I would have preferred an opportunity to demonstrate my skills, perhaps using a simulation, a game, or a case study. Once, I landed a job that I wanted. When I got to work, many of my peers were surprised at the high level of my work. I was even awarded for it. But what I could do wasn't apparent in the interview, as I later found out.

"I would take the entire day off from my current job when interviewing because it was so stressful. I remember migraines after one particular interview. But surprisingly, that was a job I actually managed to secure."

As the above demonstrates, many neurodivergents struggle with interviewing procedures. Many autistic job candidates, for example, struggle with eye contact, have difficulty determining rank and status, and are honest to a fault. People with ADHD may miss what the interviewer says because they are worried about what to say next. People with dyslexia may perform poorly on interview assessments, not because they don't have the required skills but because they have difficulty reading text under pressure and with time constraints.

Hiring managers need to reverse this trend. To diversify the talent pool, it's time to opt for screening processes that value cognitive divergence.

A study co-authored by Margaret Neale at Stanford Graduate School of Business found unconscious bias that favored neurotypical candidates over neurodivergent applicants:

"Due to our tendency to be swayed by displays of overt confidence, we may be reinforcing an already unfair social hierarchy. When overconfident people from upper-class backgrounds walk into a job interview or are vying for a leadership role, they have an immediate advantage, the researchers say. We can't help but fall for their bravado, endowing them with greater talent and skills than they, in fact, possess."(Binns, 2020)

Overconfidence is not something neurodivergents typically possess, so there's an inherent disadvantage there.

Further, Jessica Stillman's article "Yale Researcher to Bosses: Science Proves Job Interviews Are Useless"(Stillman, 2017) illuminates why clinging to standard interview practices is illogical and not in an employer's best interests. Interviewing methods could benefit from a revamp to become more inclusive of neurodivergent candidates.

Apprenticeship as an Alternative Hiring Strategy for a Neurodiverse Workforce

There's one approach to neurodivergent hiring that has not received much notice in the United States: apprenticeships. Data from the United Kingdom (HM Government, 2020), where renewed interest in apprenticeships has spurred relevant research, indicates that 89 percent of employers said that apprenticeships helped companies develop skills pertinent to their organization. Over 74 percent of employers believed that apprenticeships helped them improve productivity and the quality of their product or service.

I remember a time when teens who weren't into academics and preferred to work with their hands had the option of becoming an apprentice. Starting in secondary school or after graduation, they worked side by side with a plumber, electrician, carpenter, or the like. They learned the trade hands-on. These opportunities are almost nonexistent today. Now they must (usually) go to a tech school. More school! One out of five apprentices may be neurodivergent. Consequently, it's essential to discover and maximize their strengths. (Kirby, 2021).

Most corporate learning initiatives reap minimal engagement and success because they are canned learning modules that do not consider individual learning preferences.

Any two individuals with neurodivergent attributes have different combinations of strengths. For example, one person with dyslexia may have predominant challenges with spelling and another with reading comprehension. The first person may also have difficulties communicating verbally, and the second person may have additional challenges relating to ADHD traits such as time management. Consequently, their training and support must be tailored to meet their needs.

If that seems daunting, consider that this is true of over 50 percent of your workers, whether identified as neurodivergent or not! Most corporate learning initiatives reap minimal engagement and success because they are canned learning modules that do not consider individual learning preferences. When individualized options for learning and training are provided, *all* employees benefit, which means the company benefits from its corporate learning investment.

One of the challenges both companies and apprentice candidates face is the lack of confidence that often evolves during the school years for neurodivergent adults. Most were labeled learning-disabled during their school years. Some were labeled lazy, slow, or unmotivated. Sadly, because schools operate with a deficit mindset instead of a gifts-mindset, neurodivergent students go through the school years believing they are not intelligent. This reality exists even though many are not only smart but also talented in unique ways. They just don't learn and thrive the way schools dictate learning should happen.

So for apprenticeship programs to have the best chance of success, the workplace culture must embrace varied approaches to thinking, learning, and problem-solving.

"Apprentices who received support over the three-month period increased in confidence by 14% on average, and their motivation increased by 16% on average. Crucially, learners who did not have identified learning needs and, therefore, did not receive support experienced no increase in confidence or motivation over the same period." (Cecile, 2020)

This study is critical because, as previous scientific research has revealed, "Measures of confidence have the highest correlation with academic achievement." (Sanchez-Ruiz et al., 2016).

Seven companies that have established tech apprenticeships for professionals from diverse backgrounds stand out:

1. IBM Apprenticeship program
2. Google tech apprenticeship program
3. AirBnB Connect Software Engineering Apprenticeship
4. Accenture Apprenticeship Program
5. LinkedIn: REACH engineering apprenticeship program
6. Microsoft Leap apprenticeship program
7. Pinterest Apprenticeship Program

What can companies do to facilitate successful apprenticeships?

World Bank has listed three ways companies can successfully implement apprenticeships (Datta et al., 2020) :

1. Create a consortium where businesses can collaborate to design apprenticeship programs. For instance, in France, Sodexo, a food service enterprise; Adecco Group, a staffing firm; Accor, a hospitality company; and Korian,

a nursing facility company, collaborated to establish an apprenticeship training center that focuses on culinary arts.

2. Work with local universities and colleges. In Costa Rica, Intel is leveraging a student-worker model to recruit students part-time so they can gain work experience.
3. Introduce work contracts and certifications. A contract guarantees fair wages for all, while certification injects elements of formality into the experience. In the Republic of Benin, craftspeople partnered with the local government to secure government-issued certificates for apprentices. Every apprentice completes a practical and supervised exam from the local trade association when they graduate from the program.

Skill-Based Interviews for Apprenticeships

When screening candidates for apprenticeships, interviewers need to customize the interview process to meet the needs of neurodivergent candidates. Here are steps that companies can take to embrace this process:

- Provide clear instructions for locating assessment tools. One way to do that is to enhance instructions with visual cues or icons.
- Clarify expectations of the interview process. Lack of clarity causes increased anxiety and undermines a candidate's ability to prepare appropriately for the interview experience. Let the candidate know what interviewees should expect, the length and format of the interview, and the items the candidate should bring. Examples might include portfolios with work samples, a résumé copy, a pen, a notebook, and the like.
- Ensure that the candidate has information about whom they will meet with and how to contact them in an emergency.
- Secure a suitable interview space that is quiet and devoid of distractions.

- Ensure that the online application portal does not assess web page navigation instead of job skills. If the user interface is unfriendly, skilled candidates may be lost—not because they are not viable but because they can't navigate the web portal properly.

During my years as a teacher, I observed a similar issue with many test questions and instructions. Poorly worded questions or unclear instructions often led students (and even myself) to misinterpret what was being asked or required. The root of the problem wasn't the neurodivergent individual's ability or skill, but rather the creator's failure to design tests (or web pages) in a way that accommodates different thinking styles.

The mindset of both candidates and employers differs in apprenticeship programs compared with traditional hiring. There's an inherent expectation that training is necessary, and that growth will take time. This expectation isn't always present in conventional hiring practices, where candidates are often quickly onboarded and expected to perform with minimal support or training. This approach frequently fails, resulting in high costs for the employer. Apprenticeships, by contrast, tend to be more successful. Most important, employees who start through an apprenticeship program are more likely to stay and grow with the company.

The mindset of both candidates and employers differs in apprenticeship programs compared with traditional hiring.

Onboarding Neurodivergent Workers

Once you've hired your new talent, it's time to integrate them into the team. I've identified three broad principles that provide a starting point for building strong working relationships with ND talent from day one.

But before I proceed, I need you to accept that inclusion is a two-way street. The neurodivergent team members and their neurotypical colleagues need to make mutual and complementary adjustments to their mindsets regarding neurodiversity and what it means to work together.

This mindset is part of the larger company culture but is greatly influenced by the onboarding process for *all* new employees. I suggest incorporating these principles into standard company procedure through Inclusive Dynamic Workplace Design.

Improve the Onboarding Experience of New Employees

Often, new employees are given a short orientation and an extensive employee handbook. They are expected to figure out the rest on their own, but the unwritten workplace rules are often complicated. Employers can help smooth that transition with a few simple changes to the onboarding process. Provide information about job expectations in advance and make it available in different formats. Highlight "obvious" aspects such as expected working hours, typical break times, dress code, social events, and communication channels. (CIPD & Ouptimize, 2018)

Ask for Input

Simple questionnaires during the onboarding process that ask about workplace preferences can be invaluable. Include preferred location and workspace design, accommodation requests, and technology requirements. Tech requirements might include speech-to-text and text-to-speech as well as video speed controllers that adjust the rate of speed for content being listened to. Repeat the survey on an annual basis for all employees.

Often, employees are reticent to disclose learning differences to employers. Questionnaires about workplace preferences and accommodations allow employees to ask for their preferences without requiring disclosure. Providing these questionnaires to all employees allows for a better work experience for all. (Volpone et al., 2022)

Focus on Strengths

Typical workplace feedback focuses on areas of weakness: the deficit model. Employee personal development plans often skew heavily toward working on areas where the employee struggles the most. However, research suggests that this is not the most effective way to get the best out of employees. The opposite seems to be more effective. A strengths-based approach to task and employee management is correlated with better productivity. Research has shown that strengthening skill areas is more effective than working on skill deficits. (CIPD, 2018)

Dynamic Workspace Design

Designing inclusive workspaces helps level the playing field for adults with learning differences. Considering the sensory environment is critical. Allowing for flexible workspace arrangements, such as quiet spaces, comfortable lighting, and low-traffic areas, is reasonable and easy to implement in many workplace environments. (Wille & Sajous-Brady, 2018)

SEE CHAPTER 8 FOR HOW TO CREATE A SENSORY ROOM.

H3: Mentoring

Ongoing mentoring for neurodivergent employees is a positive way to provide continuous informal feedback and on-the-job training. Mentors are also available to address concerns as they arise instead of waiting for a bigger problem. Mentoring programs, with mentors trained to support neurodivergent employees, provide ongoing informal support to help those with learning differences close some of the gaps that would otherwise be difficult to overcome.

Reverse Mentoring

Reverse mentoring programs have recently become popular to bridge the gap between senior and junior staff members in organizations. They can also harness the often overlooked talents of neurodivergent employees. (Kaše et al., 2019) These employees often bring heightened creative thinking, identification of complexpatterns, and advanced technological skills. By leveraging employees' strengths with learning differences, organizations can help close the skills gap, foster crucial networking relationships, and improve retention and employee loyalty.

Support Circles

Support circles are designed with a broader scope in mind than one-on-one mentoring. They help new employees meet others within the organization and provide support during the crucial adjustment phase. For more experienced employees, support circles provide information, feedback, and a sounding board for navigating new challenges in the workplace. They can also be agents for change within a workplace setting.

Allow Team Members to Adapt Without Having to Ask

Provide all employees with the option of noise-canceling headphones, balance balls to sit on, and other sensory objects or accommodations. Don't force social interactions. Create "chill spaces" that are available to employees throughout the day. Make accommodations freely available to everybody in the workplace to create a productive work environment.

When bringing on new talent, proactively explain that these options are freely available. Ensure that the newcomers understand they are free to take advantage of all these accommodations without any formal review process.

Be Flexible during Group Sessions

Every team member has different interpersonal skills and strategies for influencing group thought. Allow space for everybody to make their unique contribution in a way that is comfortable for them. Use adaptive technologies such as voice-to-text tools for note taking, or video recording as an alternative to note taking. Permit extra time; interaction is a process, and team meetings may take longer.

Again, this type of flexibility is good for every person on your team, whether they are ND or NT. Every new hire should have their options clearly laid out so they understand they are free to work in the manner that best suits them.

About Rules and Expectations

As mentioned previously, many autistic adults have unique behavioral characteristics that sometimes seem unacceptable, strange, or blunt. Adjustments need to be made for each autistic employee to ensure these behaviors don't end up causing problems in the workplace.

Nonetheless, that doesn't mean autistic employees can do and say whatever they wish without consequences; there still need to be workplace expectations in place. Clear, explicit, and concise rules and expectations are fundamental when setting norms for neurodiverse teams. Some of the basic rules and expectations you put in place might even be things other team members take for granted (mainly unwritten rules). So write them down and be blunt and straightforward. These may include:

- Unacceptable language and words (you can't say f*#k, s*!t, et cetera).
- Inappropriate behaviors (touching others, removing clothing, and the like).
- Start and finish times, lunch break times and lengths (remember, if you set a specific time, the employee may not be able to be flexible around these times without notice).

You might think some of these are basic commonsense workplace or societal rules, but often, autistic people miss these nuances of life. Once they're explained, they become almost embedded in future conduct and behaviors.

The key here is to work individually with each autistic employee to ensure they have all the information they need to fit into a workplace successfully or for the workplace to adjust to suit their needs. Performance management plans that can be used for all employees can effectively create the right expectations.

These simple adjustments can help avoid HR complaints and other issues with autistic employees.

Role and Performance

Clear expectations for a role and detailed instructions are essential, even if you think they're obvious. Someone with autism spectrum disorder (ASD) may not interpret them the same way you do. This is especially important if the role involves their special interest. Without clear guidance, you could end up with wasted time, too much information, or the employee going in an unintended direction. Some simple things you can do include:

- Don't assume instructions are clear. Be concise and explain in detail exactly what you want from them. (If you ask for a list of cat breeds, for instance, don't assume you will end up with a short list of domestic cats. You may get a list of every species and subspecies of feline on earth—this can waste everyone's time.)
- Write down your expectations and instructions. Be as clear and detailed as possible.
- Ask the employee to clarify what they think the role is and what they should be doing. Let them read your instructions a day or two before the required start time. Providing instructions in advance is an easy way to ensure everyone is on track.

Even after you've clarified the role and performance expectations, if you still have performance issues with a neurodivergent employee, don't assume it's because they aren't good enough. Stop and think: Is there a simple adjustment we can make as an organization to fix this? Often, working with the employee on a quick fix can solve the problem.

However, be cautious about using formal performance improvement plans (PIPs) for autistic employees. These plans can be challenging for autistic individuals to understand and navigate, especially if there's inconsistency in messages from HR and management. PIPs often lead to the employee leaving the company, which may not be the best outcome for anyone involved. Instead, consider a more collaborative approach:

- Have open, clear conversations with the employee about specific challenges they're facing.
- Work together to identify potential accommodations or adjustments.
- Provide consistent, direct feedback on progress and areas for improvement.
- If necessary, consider whether the current role is the best fit for the employee's skills and strengths.

Remember, the goal is to support the employee's success, whether that's in their current role or potentially in a different position that better aligns with their abilities. Sometimes a different work environment might ultimately be better for the employee. However, before reaching that conclusion, make sure you've exhausted all options for support and accommodation within your organization.

Encourage Newcomers to Share Their Communication and Learning Preferences with the Group

Encourage transparency in the workplace through interactive discussion, carried out in each worker's preferred communication style. Some people might prefer phone calls, others email, and others a voice messaging app.

Let each individual express their preference, and as a team respect it.

The same goes true for learning preferences. While one person may need one-on-one mentoring, another may be fine with an online or video tutorial.

Allow everybody to naturally exchange information and get to know one another for the unique individuals they are.

New and existing workers will naturally grow in their understanding of how best to communicate with their teammates. Things will go easier once they understand the differences and subtle (or not-so-subtle) nuances of their neurodivergent co-workers.

Strive for Equity

There's a crucial difference between equality and equity in the workplace. This difference represents the evolution in thinking that has taken place in employment as different minorities make themselves heard in the workplace.

Consider these definitions:

Equality: Treating everyone the same way, often assuming that everyone starts on an equal footing or with the same opportunities.

Equity: Working toward fair outcomes for people or groups by treating them in ways that address their unique advantages or barriers. (Catalyst, 2019)

I've spent my entire career explaining the difference between equality and equity. Add to that the misconceptions about what it means to be fair. What's fair? What is equal? If some people have poor eyesight and need glasses to see, does fair or equal mean that everyone must wear glasses?

You might think this is a ridiculous analogy. On the contrary, it's a simple analogy that explains the issue well. Provide those who need glasses with glasses. Those who don't need glasses would not be forced to wear them. That's equity.

While measures to work toward fair outcomes based on gender and race have made great strides, the same cannot be said for groups in the neurodivergent space. So what do the phrases "working toward fair outcomes" and "their unique advantages or barriers" mean?

A person's unique advantages and barriers must be identified and respected to work toward fair outcomes. This worldview encompasses curiosity and acceptance of the whole human being.

In Malcolm Gladwell's book *Outliers,* the backstories of geniuses are shared. As a society, we love success stories. They inspire us to believe anything is possible if we put our minds to it. In truth, modern-day geniuses, tech tycoons, and billionaires often achieved success not only by their wits but because of favorable circumstances. Sometimes they were in the right place at the right time to take advantage of a life-changing opportunity. Gladwell explains that even birth month and year influence the extent of success, and we aren't talking about astrology here! Aptitude alone is not a predictor of success.

Aptitude and favorable circumstances are predictors of success.

Neurodivergent workers have traditionally faced less-than-ideal circumstances in the workforce. This might be due to context, environment, culture, or a combination of all of the above.

But given what we know now, why not do everything we can to create the favorable circumstances necessary to support every worker's success in an equitable workplace?

Seek Out the ND Perspective

A fundamental way to create an equitable work environment and successful neurodiversity at work initiative is to *include neurodivergent voices* at the table when establishing policies, procedures, and processes. This is a non-negotiable.

They'll help guide you in creating neurodivergent-friendly recruitment and interview practices and provide invaluable perspective as you work toward creating a workplace culture that normalizes accommodations. You'll begin to embrace a whole-person view of employees.

Conscientious Support for the Neurodivergent Employee *After* Hiring

After hiring and transitioning your new ND worker into the workplace, continued interest from HR can ensure that they can perform at their best. Staying in touch and checking in with employees after onboarding is critical. Neurodivergent people are dynamic creatures, like everyone else, and their needs can vary as time passes.

For example, even in a supportive environment, people with a neurodivergent condition may find themselves masking. This is quite common with female autistics, who mask more than men and in more elaborate ways, especially if the environment isn't inclusive. (Hull et al., 2017) This can lead to stress, anxiety, exhaustion, and even burnout.

Neurodivergent people are dynamic creatures, like everyone else, and their needs can vary as time passes.

That's a high price to pay for both the employer and the employee. However, companies can mitigate this risk by showing an honest and sincere interest in the employee's success.

When communicating with neurodivergent workers, be straightforward and avoid subtext, nuances, and unspoken social cues.

Subtle, indirect, or implied communication is difficult for the neurodivergent. Most autistics are very literal. They don't understand nuance or sarcasm. This is often true of other neurodivergent thinkers, too. In addition, an autistic employee may err by being too direct with peers and supervisors.

I understand this pain. I am a neurodivergent who is dyslexic, has ADHD, and has auditory processing disorder. Recently, I have had to come to terms with the realization that I'm also autistic. Some people love how these traits make me unique. In other cases, they've created conflict not only in the workplace but in personal relationships. It's been a lifelong battle.

Neurodivergent employees may not notice subtle cues used by others in their attempt to soften constructive criticism or feedback. These communication differences often lead to misunderstandings, and consequently, instructions may not be followed.

How Approachable Is HR?

It's critical to make sure neurodivergent employees feel safe to approach HR. When a person has an issue at work, it's often after much angst and deliberation that they find their way to HR to get help. It's even more difficult for the neurodivergents who don't want to be labeled as needy, whiny, attention-seeking, or worse by their colleagues.

To maximize their perceived availability and approachability, HR could take the initiative to schedule regular check-ins with openly ND employees to share how things are going without fear of repercussions.

Normalize Accommodations

Pre-2020 work-from-home arrangements were the exception, not the norm. The world has flipped since then, and work from home has become the norm for many professions. Can we extend the benefits of remote work for the greater good?

Pre-pandemic, managers were groomed to assure compliance with standards by having employees on-site and visible. Now, we have almost two years of experience managing employees remotely. When circumstances demanded it, companies were able to adjust work environments to meet individual needs. The cost of doing so is usually minimal, and the payoff is much more significant.

When "accommodations" become the norm, and the company culture embraces the flexibility necessary to allow employees to meet their needs to obtain maximum productivity, everybody wins.

Consider Some Quick-Win Accommodations

Let Employees Manage Their Sensory Needs

If someone needs to sit in a dimly lit work area, use noise-canceling headphones, or wear more comfortable clothing to be more productive, that's a win! Give them the go-ahead to do what works best for them. Doing so is a critical component of Inclusive Dynamic Workplace Design.

Be Flexible about Communication Preferences

As noted above, communication can make or break an individual or team's success. Often, neurodivergents are labeled as hard to communicate with or hard to read. This will most likely happen if only one communication style is "allowed."

Learn how your employees prefer to communicate. Do they prefer email? Telephone? Text messaging? Apps like Slack, Asana, or other tech options? It's essential to establish a channel of communication that is comfortable for all employees and team members.

For example, an autistic colleague, Sandra, a freelancer, had a client who insisted on using email to track work. The "who-said-what-and-when" problem arose many times. When Sandra suggested Google Docs as a collaboration tool, the idea was rejected. The client proposed that email be used with changes denoted in different-colored text. Each collaborator used a different color. This cumbersome approach didn't work, either, and misunderstandings continued.

A project that could have been completed quickly with multiple collaborators failed because of the client's unwillingness to be flexible in how changes were communicated. When working with neurodivergents (and neurotypical employees), consider tapping into the abundance of tools available to streamline and track communications. This approach can benefit everyone, not just divergent thinkers.

Consider Moving toward Flexible Scheduling

Flexibility in work hours can help neurodivergents avoid anxiety. It may also help all employees make the best use of their workday. Some people work best in the evening, some in the early morning, and some in a typical nine-to-five schedule. Sometimes flexible hours are impractical; however, when companies communicate with vendors or teammates worldwide, the nine-to-five days are often impractical.

Flexibility in work hours can help neurodivergents avoid anxiety. It may also help all employees make the best use of their workday.

Employees will typically take advantage of flexible work hours when offered, as long as they trust that managers won't judge them unfairly for taking advantage of these policies.

A flexible work schedule not only supports neurodivergent employees with autism or ADHD but would also support families that need that flexibility to care for children, people who are night owls and not at their best in the morning, and people who hyperfocus and may work a twelve- to fourteen-hour day then need to rest part of the next day. This is a policy change that benefits all your employees. It is critical, however, for the success of some.

Take a Whole-Person View of Employees

"Neurodiversity programs induce companies and their leaders to adopt a style of management that emphasizes placing each person in a context that maximizes her or his contributions." —Austin and Pisano, *Harvard Business Review* (Austin & Pisano, 2017b)

Why take the time to do this? With some neurodivergent employees, it absolutely will take time. I understand that this is one of the objections to implementing neurodiversity at work initiatives.

Here's a fact: Whether we are neurotypical or atypical, how our individual brains work defines who we are. Living things flourish when placed in a context that's best for their individual makeup.

I mentioned the time it can take to consider individual employees. One of my clients retorted, "You can't do that for four thousand employees!"

I realize that employers need to make a profit. Time is money. Yet pursuing profit can cause organizations to ignore the human need to be treated *humanely,* with consideration and care. The outdated, hard-line approach to managing by the numbers is most likely fueling the "great resignation" we are currently seeing in the United States. Dismissing the needs, goals, and concerns of employees costs companies in turnover and a substantial loss of corporate knowledge. A profit-first approach is no longer sustainable. Everyone has something, some quirk, that makes them a little different.

Not accommodating these differences and screening out those deemed "different" prevents a company from innovating and growing.

Dress Codes and Uniforms

Sensory issues may cause some fabrics or textures to be uncomfortable or even intolerable for many of your team members. This could be as mild as your team member feeling a little squirmy and pulling at their uniform throughout the day or as bad as your team member feeling like they need to rip their uniform off immediately when they get home.

Remember how everyone loved working from home at the start of the pandemic because they could wear leggings? While leggings are not an option in many industries, that doesn't mean your team can't be comfortable when they are at work. Most corporate offices have a dress code to give their employees options, but flexibility can be achieved even if you have a uniform. Give your team the ability to choose among different fabrics. Some may prefer a soft cotton T-shirt; some may prefer a polo. It is not just your neurodivergent team members who will be grateful for a bit of choice.

Create a Clear Career Path

Many autistic people struggle with transitions and can become confused or frustrated when tasked with responsibilities outside their comfort zone. Many don't deal well if they're assigned to a project that does not have clear instructions and timelines. Some employees, whether autistic, neurodivergent, or neurotypical, may want to map out their projects or tasks and get feedback or approval before they continue.

Although it may seem supportive to tell them you have confidence in them and you don't need to approve their plan of action before they start, that might backfire. They may need reassurance that they're on the right track before they continue, and not having that reassurance may cause great anxiety. If they highly value efficiency, they may also feel that they could be wasting their time because they don't know for certain if their work is going to meet expectations.

Don't Rely on Pop Culture

I've said it once, but I will say it again: Everyone hates being stereotyped, and the lesser known a minority group is, the more damage a stereotype can do. Stereotypes make for great entertainment to the detriment of society. Unfortunately, we see media depictions of minority groups as reality. Most of this conditioning of our attitudes and beliefs regarding minorities is subconscious.

The entertainment world knows exactly how to play into human psychology to win over viewers and increase profits. Consider that *The Big Bang Theory* was a hugely successful show depicting an eccentric genius, Sheldon Cooper. It was never stated that he was autistic; however, it was implied. For years, viewers were fed a steady diet of stereotypes about autistics, nerds, geeks, and neurodivergents for the sole purpose of getting laughs and gaining viewers.

Everyone hates being stereotyped, and the lesser known a minority group is, the more damage a stereotype can do.

How do we undo our reliance on pop culture to reshape our views of neurodivergents? Manny, one of my clients with ADHD, explained, "Let's start here: Neurotypes aren't adjectives. Saying that you 'feel bipolar today' or that you're 'being so ADD' or saying, 'he's so OCD' isn't okay."

Autistics aren't all mathematical savants and geeks. They aren't all male. And most autistics will state that they don't want to be "fixed." References to *Rain Man*, Sheldon Cooper, or Dr. Shaun Murphy aren't okay. Making assumptions about how Tourette's syndrome manifests or using the word bipolar to describe bad behavior isn't appropriate.

Neurodivergent people are tired of shouting to deaf ears, "Not all of us are like that!" Purging the pop-culture depiction of neurodiversity in corporate culture is an essential early step for HR to enact. The best strategy? Get a go-to person.

Get a Neurodivergent Go-To Expert in HR

A go-to person (or a few) should ideally be someone who deeply understands neurodivergent experiences through personal experience or extensive knowledge and empathy. While many neurodivergent employees, particularly autistics, are justifiably tired of neurotypical people speaking for them, the most important qualities for this role are genuine understanding, active listening, and effective advocacy.
This person could be:

- An officially diagnosed neurodivergent individual.
- Someone who self-identifies as neurodivergent without a formal diagnosis.
- A neurotypical ally with a strong track record of supporting and accurately representing neurodivergent perspectives.

The key is that this person must have earned the trust and respect of the neurodivergent community within the organization through their actions, empathy, and commitment to genuine representation.

This person can serve as an ally or neutral third party when matters get prickly, allowing the employees to feel more comfortable expressing themselves. In addition, HR and management can consult with the go-to person to bounce off ideas and verify how the company handles matters related to neurodivergent employees.

A Message to HR from a Neurodivergent Employee

Neurodivergent people have spent a large part of their lives coming up with an array of ways to cope with the challenges they face. Some have used their challenges and coping mechanisms to their advantage, though this isn't the norm. The fact that some neurodivergents are successful demonstrates at least four things: They are creative. They work hard. They have tenacity, and they foster innovation.

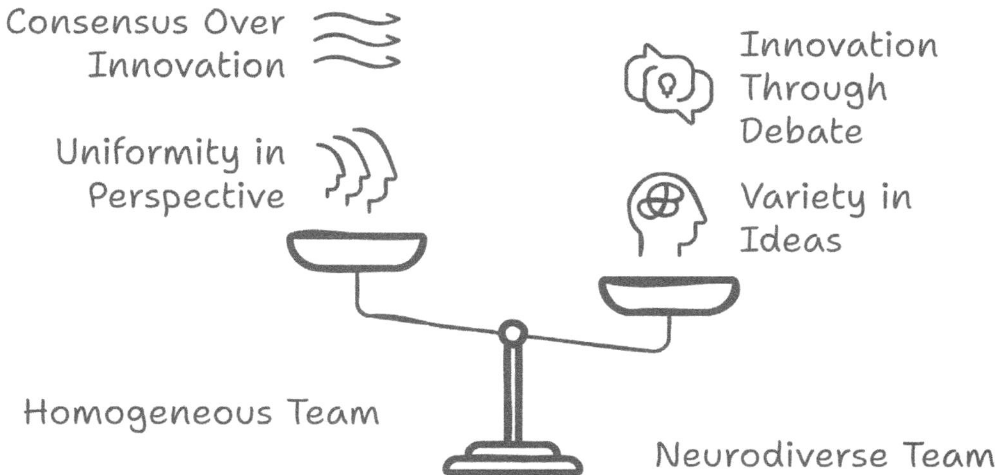

As we've already discussed, traditional interview techniques often favor those who interview well—individuals who are confident about their abilities and know how to charm the interviewer. However, these techniques and their unwritten "rules" can systematically filter out neurodivergent candidates. While ND individuals may not tick all the expected boxes, they can add new and valuable ones: honesty, hard work, out-of-the-box thinking, and much more. By recognizing this, we can create a more inclusive hiring process that captures a wider range of talents and perspectives.

We live in a world where diversity exists in all areas of life. Diversity can be a significant strengthening factor. Think of biodiversity, cultural diversity, racial diversity, and gut microbial diversity. All these areas benefit from the differences at play. Therefore, if businesses are to flourish, neurodiversity and the values that come with it are impossible to ignore.

When a company adopts this philosophy into its culture, and HR takes the steps to translate culture into action, everyone wins.

Signed, your neurodivergent employee

Chapter Five Reflection Questions

1. How might traditional hiring practices unintentionally exclude neurodivergent candidates? What changes could be implemented to make the recruitment process more inclusive?
2. Discuss the potential benefits and challenges of implementing an apprenticeship program for neurodivergent individuals in your organization.
3. How can unconscious biases affect the hiring and integration of neurodivergent employees? What strategies can be used to mitigate these biases?
4. Analyze the concept of "superhuman expectations" for neurodivergent employees. How might this stereotype impact both the individuals and the workplace culture?
5. Consider the differences between equality and equity in the workplace. How can organizations strive for equity when supporting neurodivergent employees?
6. What are some practical ways to create a more inclusive onboarding process for neurodivergent employees? How might these changes benefit all new hires?
7. How can organizations balance the need for structure and flexibility when accommodating neurodivergent employees? Provide specific examples based on the chapter's content.
8. Reflect on the suggestion to have a neurodivergent go-to expert in HR. What qualities should this person possess, and how might their role benefit the organization?
9. How can companies move beyond pop-culture stereotypes of neurodivergence to create a more accurate and inclusive understanding of neurodivergent employees?

Effective Leadership Strategies for Neurodivergent Teams

Management is an active and ongoing process. Every team leader aims to create an environment where all employees flourish and unwrap their potential. When workers are empowered to use their entire spectrum of gifts, they are better positioned to advance company objectives while simultaneously achieving their personal goals.

However, adjusting to the individual personalities that make up the rich tapestry of life can require some intentional strategy. In this sense, there's no significant difference in managing neurodivergent people. However, we must acknowledge that they think differently and have unique ways of processing information. (Forbes Councils Member, 2021)

Following are some strategies to support you when managing neurodivergent employees.

> ***Every team leader aims to create an environment where all employees flourish and unwrap their potential.***

Understand the Breadth and Depth of Neurodiversity

Set your preconceptions aside. Neurodivergent people share your humanity, even though their conscious and subconscious processes may unfold in ways you are unfamiliar with.

Strategies

- **Educate yourself:** Read books, articles, and research papers about neurodiversity to gain a deeper understanding.
- **Attend workshops:** Participate in workshops and seminars on neurodiversity to learn from experts.
- **Engage in conversations:** Talk with neurodivergent individuals to hear their experiences and perspectives firsthand.

Reach Out Directly to Subject Specialists for Advice

Accept that your education, training, and experience may not prepare you for managing neurodivergent employees. Summon the courage to ask others for assistance in your leadership role. Seek advice from subject specialists if you lack answers. Be open to deferring to their wisdom and incorporating their insights. Reach out to your business network to see what has worked for others.

Strategies

- **Consult experts:** Hire a neurodiversity consultant to provide tailored advice and training.
- **Network with peers**: Join forums or groups where leaders share best practices for managing neurodiverse teams.
- **Utilize online resources:** Explore online platforms and webinars that offer guidance on neurodiversity in the workplace.

Take Steps to Create a Supportive Environment

The key to managing neurodivergent people is building a supportive base where they can optimize their potential. Engage neurodivergent workers one-on-one. Be transparent as you explore their strengths and needs. Ask how you can support them.
The key to managing neurodivergent people is building a supportive base where they can optimize their potential.

Strategies

- **Regular check-ins:** Schedule one-on-one meetings to discuss their needs and progress.
- **Customize workspaces:** Employees can personalize their workspaces to suit their sensory preferences.
- **Offer flexible hours:** Provide flexible working hours to accommodate different working styles and needs.

Walk the Extra Mile by Providing Extra Mentoring

Achieving Career Growth for ND Employees

Continuous Support

Regular check-ins and flexible accommodations ensure sustained success.

Career Progression

Provide clear career paths, promotions, and leadership roles tailored to diverse thinking styles.

Peer Networking

Foster a sense of belonging through structured networking and recognition programs.

Skill Development

Offer tailored learning experiences based on ND employees' strengths and learning preferences.

Guidance & Onboarding

Pair ND employees with mentors to support their transition and early career growth.

Every new employee requires guidance when starting a career with your company. Neurodivergent people, however, may need extra support interpreting job requirements as well as a more supportive work environment. (Morris et al., 2015) To effectively manage neurodivergent employees, acknowledge that their desire for enrichment and success matches yours. Put yourself in their shoes to help them find the extra support they may need.

Strategies

- **Pair with a mentor:** Assign a mentor who understands neurodiversity to provide additional guidance.
- **Buddy up:** Assign a workplace buddy to guide newcomers through essential information, such as office navigation, sensory room etiquette, and kitchen protocols.
- **Create clear guidelines:** Develop step-by-step instructions for tasks to aid understanding.
- **Provide feedback:** Offer regular, constructive feedback to help employees improve and grow.

Empower Employees to Reach Their Full Potential

Neurodivergent people think differently. Tap into this potential by questioning those boundaries you thought were fences. Empower your neurodivergent employee to challenge your tried-and-tested ways of doing things. Have the courage to be open to fresh perspectives. Accept that the company normal is not the only way.

> ***Empower your neurodivergent employee to challenge your tried-and-tested ways of doing things.***

Strategies

- **Encourage innovation:** Create a culture where new ideas are welcomed and explored.
- **Assign challenging tasks:** Give neurodivergent employees tasks that challenge their thinking and creativity.
- **Acknowledge contributions:** Publicly recognize and celebrate the unique contributions of neurodivergent employees.

Place Your Neurodivergent Workers Where They Best Belong

A neurodivergent worker becomes a real asset when you place them in a role where their differences can shine. Identify their best skills, then find a role that complements them. Wait until you have a neuro-appropriate match for their skills.

Strategies

- **Skill assessment:** Conduct assessments to identify the strengths and skills of neurodivergent employees.
- **Job matching:** Align their skills with roles that allow them to excel and contribute meaningfully.
- **Flexible roles:** Be open to creating new roles or adjusting existing ones to fit their abilities better.

Reconsider Whether Coming into Work Is the Best Option

Some neurodivergent people, especially those with autism, prefer to work alone. They may have a home environment that inspires them more than a workplace setting. Bright lights, noise, and constant interaction with co-workers may be counterproductive. Ask them where they would prefer to work to be at their best.

Strategies

- **Remote work options:** Offer remote work opportunities to those who find it more productive.
- **Quiet spaces:** Provide quiet areas in the office where employees can work with minimal distractions.
- **Flexible locations:** Allow employees to work where they feel most comfortable and productive. This might be a common area, a cafeteria, or their home.

Chapter 8 provides information on how to set up a sensory room or space.

Reach Out and Learn What Others Are Doing

Be humble and accept that you may not have all the answers, especially if you are managing a neurodiverse workforce for the first time. Reach out to your peers and ask them about their experiences with placing neurodivergent employees in fun, creative, and rewarding roles. You may discover that a neurodiverse workforce gives you the competitive advantage that's been missing in your team.

Strategies

- **Peer learning:** Join industry groups or forums to learn from the experiences of others.
- **Case studies:** Research successful case studies of companies with neurodiverse workforces.
- **Collaborate:** Partner with other organizations to share best practices and resources.

Encourage Neurotypical Employees to Celebrate Diversity

Hiring people who think differently cannot be a one-way street. Neurotypical employees interacting with colleagues who think alternatively will also experience intellectual stimulation, growth, and a rejuvenated imagination. Create training and educational programs to help neurotypical workers understand and work with their divergent thinking counterparts.

Strategies

- **Diversity training:** Implement training programs focusing on understanding and celebrating neurodiversity.
- **Inclusive activities:** Organize team-building activities that encourage collaboration and mutual respect.
- **Open dialogue:** Foster an open environment where employees can discuss and learn about neurodiversity.

Keep Thinking and Growing Your Neurodivergent Perspective

Invest time to understand what makes neurodivergent people tick. Lower your shields as you enter their world. They may think and behave differently from you, but this does not mean they are wrong. Connect with the neurodivergent community, read their words, and seek out their voices. Learn to appreciate their experiences and perspectives.

Invest time to understand what makes neurodivergent people tick.

Strategies

- **Continuous learning:** Commit to ongoing education about neurodiversity through books, courses, and seminars.

- **Community engagement:** Engage with neurodivergent communities through events and social media.
- **Personal reflection:** Reflect on your own biases and assumptions about neurodiversity regularly.

Continue Being Accommodating

Neurotypical employees were born into a world where most things seem natural and work for them. For neurodivergent thinkers, the world, and particularly the workplace, can be chronically challenging and disheartening. As the need for accommodation arises, stay flexible and focus on creative solutions. Managing neurodivergent employees takes time and energy because it forces growth, and growth is hard. It is an enriching experience to see your employees' talents come together on their teams to achieve success for the individuals, the team, and the company.

Strategies

- **Flexible policies:** Develop flexible policies that can be adjusted to meet individual needs.
- **Problem solving:** Encourage a culture of creativity in finding solutions to accommodate diverse needs.
- **Ongoing support:** Provide continuous support and check-ins to ensure that accommodations are effective.

Allow Team Members to Adapt without Having to Ask

Provide all employees with noise-canceling headphones, balance balls to sit on, and other sensory objects or accommodations. Don't force social interactions. Create "chill spaces" that are available to employees throughout the day. Make accommodations freely available to everyone in the workplace to create a productive work environment. When bringing on new talent, proactively explain that these options are freely available. Ensure they understand they can take advantage of all these accommodations without any formal review process.

Provide all employees with noise-canceling headphones, balance balls to sit on, and other sensory objects or accommodations.

Strategies

- **Universal access:** Ensure that all accommodations are accessible to everyone without the need for special requests.
- **Proactive communication:** Inform new hires about available accommodations during onboarding.
- **IDWD:** Design the workplace environment to include these accommodations naturally.

Be Flexible during Group Sessions

In every team, members have different interpersonal skills. They each have their own strategies for influencing group thought. Allow space for everyone to make their unique contribution in a way that is comfortable for them. Allow the use of adaptive technologies such as voice-to-text tools for note taking or video recording as an alternative to note taking. Permit extra time; interaction is a process, and team meetings may take longer. Again, this flexibility benefits everyone on your team, whether ND or NT. Every new hire should have their options laid out so they understand they are free to work in the manner that best suits them.

Strategies

- **Adaptive tools:** Provide adaptive technologies like voice-to-text and video recording for all meetings.
- **Clear options:** Communicate the available options for participation to all team members.
- **Extended time:** Allow extra time for discussions to ensure everyone has the opportunity to contribute.

Managing neurodivergent employees involves accepting that they think and feel differently from you. But by working together, your organization can achieve more.

Optimizing Team Productivity: Strategies for Inclusive and Efficient Meetings

Team meetings can be exhausting for employees in the neurodiverse workplace. Employees with ADHD or dyslexia may feel that they're unprepared or that they've missed important information.

Have you ever led a meeting and seen one of your employees tune out? Do you struggle to get a team member to join impromptu stand-ups? Do some team members seem to understand the task you give them in a meeting, only to forget the assignment or not know how to do it?

Understand that neurodivergent employees don't tune you out on purpose. They may need some simple accommodations, which are also helpful for neurotypical employees and can make meetings much more valuable for everyone.

Is the Meeting Necessary?

Meetings are an effective way to share information with several people at once. They can help teams solve problems and find breakthroughs to meet their objectives. They build a sense of camaraderie and remind employees of the company's purpose and mission.

On the other hand, meetings can hinder progress when misused, especially in the neurodiverse workplace. Excessive and overly long meetings can have a significantly negative effect on neurodivergent employees. Structure is essential to maintaining a neurodivergent employee's sense of security and ability to perform job functions successfully. Unscheduled, disorganized meetings can torpedo their productivity and cause them to lose confidence in their abilities.

A frequent joke in today's office and work-from-home environment is, "This meeting could have been an email." And in some cases, that's true. If you can solve an issue with a brief email exchange, there's no need to assemble the entire team in person to discuss it.

Provide a Schedule Before Meetings

Providing a meeting agenda can be incredibly helpful for everyone, especially neurodivergent employees. Knowing that a specific number of topics will be discussed, what those topics will be, and even how long the team will discuss each item can help employees stay focused on the meeting.

Limit Meeting Length and Frequency When Possible

Team stand-ups are a popular way to help everyone prepare for the workday or workweek. But they're called stand-ups for a reason: They are quick meetings, initially just a group meeting at the edge of the cubicles, of five to fifteen minutes. Their purpose is not to solve problems immediately but to ensure everyone is on track and that nothing hinders their work.

A team meeting is most effective between thirty minutes and one hour. After that, most people's focus begins to break down. It's better to address one issue per meeting and then plan future meetings as part of the "next steps" part of the problem-solving process.

Take "Brain Breaks" during Long Sessions

Every company is different, and sometimes, longer meetings are unavoidable. This significantly affects government contractors because daylong and even multiday conferences are required regularly.

Strategies

Here are some recommendations based on current research and best practices in adult learning and cognitive science:

- **Frequency of breaks:** It's generally recommended to provide a break every sixty to ninety minutes.
- **Length of breaks:** Short breaks of five to fifteen minutes are typically sufficient for most learners. However, a longer break (thirty to sixty minutes) should be provided for lunch.
- **The "90/20 rule":** Some experts recommend ninety minutes of focused learning followed by a twenty-minute break.
- **Microbreaks:** Besides longer breaks, incorporating two- to five-minute microbreaks every twenty to thirty minutes can help maintain attention and reduce fatigue.
- **Flexibility:** It's essential to be flexible and responsive to the group's needs. If participants seem fatigued or disengaged, it might be beneficial to take an unscheduled break.

Incorporate Reinforcement Exercises

An excellent reinforcement and refocusing activity is "Think/Pair/Share." If the team is getting unfocused or chatting with one another, or if you are sharing information that you want everyone to retain and understand, build this exercise into the last fifteen to thirty minutes of the meeting.

Here's How to Do It

- Have everyone think individually for a couple of minutes about the information or problem on the agenda.
- Pair everyone up and have them discuss their take on the problem (or their understanding of the information) with their partner.

- Have each pair share their thoughts with the rest of the team and then discuss. (If there isn't time for a broader discussion, write the shared ideas on the agenda and table them for the next meeting.)

Enhancing Communication: High-Impact Presentation Techniques for Diverse Teams

So often, managers call a meeting, share information, and then end the session, expecting employees to understand, assimilate, and implement the new information into their work endeavors. When this does not happen, a manager may feel frustrated with employees who can't do what they've been told to do. Or a more self-reflective manager may wonder what is wrong with their presentation style. Add the fact that more managers are managing neurodivergent employees, and the challenge increases exponentially. It's crucial for managers to adapt their presentation style to accommodate neurodivergent employees, promoting inclusivity and ensuring better understanding and retention of information.

Learning new skills and adding to an existing skill set is essential for every employee in your organization. However, every individual learns slightly differently and at a different pace.

It is crucial to ensure that all employees, particularly those who are neurodivergent, can effectively retain and process new information to maximize their ability to recall and apply it.

It's crucial for managers to adapt their presentation style to accommodate neurodivergent employees, promoting inclusivity and ensuring better understanding and retention of information.

Why would I focus just on introducing new material? As a former teacher, I know that presenting new material effectively is critical to my students' success. Understanding that not everyone learns the same way and being comfortable with varying presentation techniques are keys to success regardless of the learner's age.

It's no different in the working world. In fact, learning new material can be more difficult for neurodivergent employees because their focus must shift from an output mindset (completing their assigned work) to a receptive learning mindset.

LMS does an excellent job of presenting information that needs to be retained and understood by every employee, such as compliance requirements, workplace expectations, and best practices for team success.

However, there are many times when a team or individual employee needs to learn information more specific to their responsibilities. This is important for career development and can impact performance. For example, a new VoIP phone system is rolled out companywide with many new features, including better integration with customer contact lists. But as with all new software, there's a learning curve. How can a manager train their team to use all the new features they need without overwhelming them?

- 45 percent of employees spend at least fifteen minutes searching for information previously discussed. (Leadem, 2017)
- 77 percent of trainers spend at least fifteen minutes explaining concepts over again.
- 65 percent of learners will completely forget new information if they don't apply it within a week! (Glaveski, 2019)

As these statistics indicate, absorbing new information is challenging for most employees, even when they want to retain what they've learned! Realistically, it may take more than one session for employees to learn new information well enough to implement it.

For more effective presentations and meetings, consider the following strategies when managing neurodiverse teams.

Effective Meeting Preparation for Neurodiverse Teams

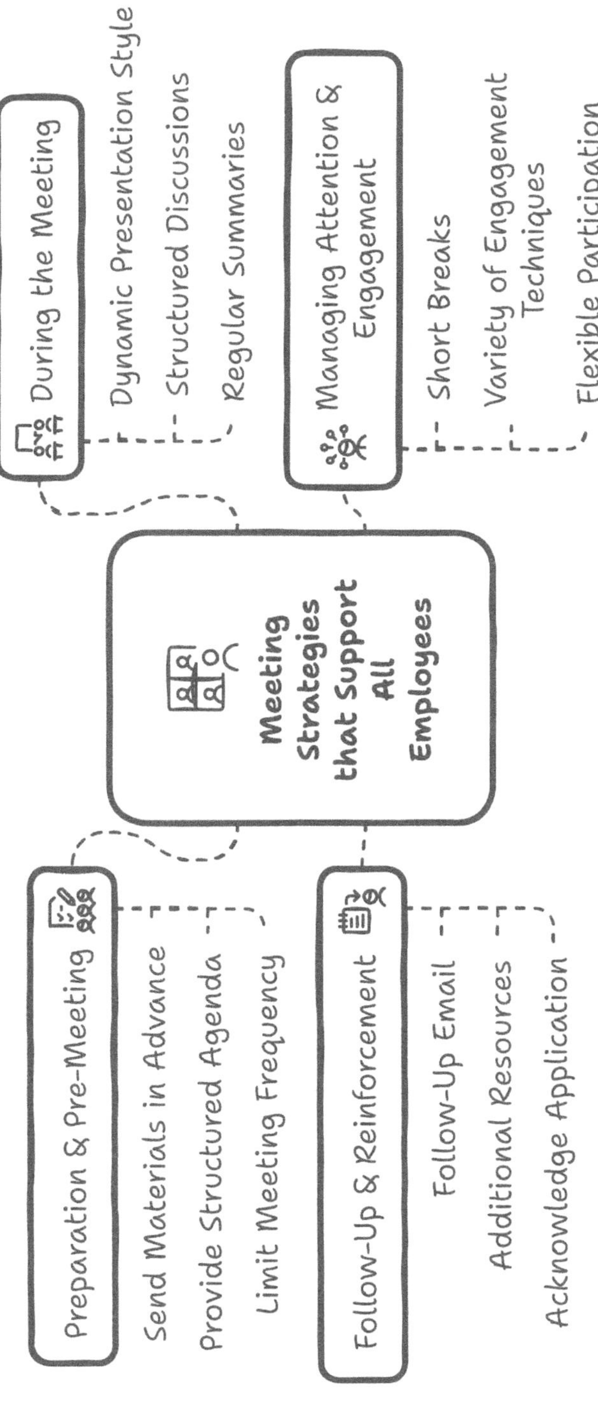

Preparation and Pre-Meeting:

- Where possible, send material out in advance so attendees can read and absorb it. This will give them an idea of what's coming up and allow them to formulate questions ahead of time.

Presentation Style:

- Avoid dispensing important information to your employees "lecture-style." A lecture voice puts people to sleep.
- Mix it up. Keep your style dynamic, not static. Make good eye contact. Establish a relationship with the audience and vary how you engage with meeting attendees.
- Show enthusiasm for the subject. If you don't seem to care about the material, your employees won't care, either. If the boss isn't invested in the message, why should they be?

If you don't seem to care about the material, your employees won't care, either. If the boss isn't invested in the message, why should they be?

Content and Organization:

- Include material that is not in the manual or handbook. Effective presentations offer material that can't be read from a book or slide deck. Use your resources as jumping-off points, not a script.
- Provide quality, not quantity. Don't overwhelm your team with new information. Studies show that the more introductory material is in a lecture, the less participants retain.
- Keep your meeting delivery organized, and don't veer off course. Start with a brief schedule of what you want to discuss, then use "signposts" to keep

your presentation on track (for example: "Now I want to talk about..."; "That's the end of our discussion of...").

- Use the Rule of Three. The brain tends to remember information presented in threes: beginning, middle, and end.
- Ideally, deliver new information in short, targeted sessions.

Engagement Techniques:

- Early in the meeting, generate curiosity about the material being shared. Introduce new ideas and push your team to develop their perspectives where appropriate.
- Use group discussion as a reinforcement technique during the meeting. Pause for a few minutes at the end of the session and ask participants to discuss among themselves what they've learned.
- Check in with participants at the end of the meeting and throughout the session. Summarize important concepts periodically. Encourage active discussion and avoid tangents that derail your message.
- Always integrate collaborative discussion when presenting new information. If possible, combine that delivery method with discussion, analogies, gamification, visuals, and hands-on components.
- Add a practice exercise. Whether it's a group discussion, a simulation, or a team project, applying new knowledge in an interactive environment will stimulate retention through active recall.

Visual Aids and Technology:

- Don't over-rely on technology. Use PowerPoint slides and online resources to support the discussion with visuals and main points. Ditch the multi-bulleted slides that tempt you to read from the screen!
- Use large imagery and bold colors in your slide deck. Choose large images and text that pop with color. Just don't put too many different colors on one page.

- Don't clutter slides with too much text. Less is more. One to three bullets is ideal.

Follow-Up and Reinforcement:

- Follow-up is the one most important practice that can make the difference between implementing the learning or not, and it is rarely done! Send a follow-up email after the presentation outlining the critical information covered.
- Notice when you see your employees implementing their learning. Say, "I see you are making effective use of your training. I appreciate your effort." Never underestimate the power of positive feedback.

Additional Considerations:

- A typical adult's concentration starts to wane after ten to twelve minutes, so chunking new information during longer meetings allows teams to process it more effectively.
- Assign readings, use online discussion boards, and direct employees to read articles online.
- Pique their curiosity: Short training sessions can keep employees curious and excited to learn more.

A typical adult's concentration starts to wane after ten to twelve minutes, so chunking new information during longer meetings allows teams to process it more effectively.

Aligning Individual Strengths with Organizational Objectives: A Strategic Approach to Goal-Setting

How can neurodivergent employees set job, task, and career goals and follow through on them?

> ***Empathy is an essential skill for managers, especially when one or more of their team members is neurodivergent.***

Managing a neurodivergent employee, someone with autism, dyslexia, ADHD, or another diagnosis, can be a perplexing challenge. Each neurodivergent employee is an individual with their own unique set of skills and challenges. Some have trouble retaining information, others have difficulty focusing, and so on. How do you, as a manager, help neurodivergent employees meet their goals successfully?

Empathy is an essential skill for managers, especially when one or more of their team members is neurodivergent.

Determine Whether You Must Adjust the Process to Accommodate the Employee

ND people often process information differently from NTs and, therefore, may approach a task from a different angle or at a different stage of the process. Find out as much as you can about how employees address specific tasks and what they understand about their assigned tasks. Then adjust the process where possible.

What would this adjustment look like?

Approach the employee with curiosity and a positive willingness to listen to their approach to a process, task, or situation. Genuinely show interest and empathy in the interaction. It's amazing what you can learn about employees when you take the time to listen to their take on their jobs and related tasks. These divergent thinkers who do things differently may astound you with how their process may be even better than the status quo way of getting the work done.

One of my clients had an engineer who was intelligent and capable but was not filling out the required reports on time. The problem was not willful noncompliance. We determined that the employee had trouble remembering sequential instructions and could not access and use the reporting system very well. Additional hands-on instruction and a written cheat sheet helped resolve the problem. The manager extended the reporting deadline so the employee could file reports correctly.

These divergent thinkers who do things differently may astound you with how their process may be even better than the status quo way of getting the work done.

How Does the Employee Best Retain Information?

For example, a person with ADHD or on the autistic spectrum may have trouble listening to and recalling verbal instructions, especially if they are complicated or have several sequential steps. A written recap with step-by-step instructions is extremely helpful. For some employees, a video recap from a Zoom meeting or screen capture video showing how to complete a task would be invaluable.

Some employees remember details better when they're shown the task or can perform the steps under instruction. Have a team member work directly with them to walk through the task a few times. Record the tutorial so the employee can access it later for review.

Is Anxiety Hampering Employee Performance?

One client I work with has a brilliant employee who has trouble delivering information to an audience of any size, whether in a team meeting, in a large conference room, or at an event. Another client has employees who get overwhelmed when presented with a large project or task outside their usual daily work.

Strategies

To minimize anxiety, help these employees prepare, whether it's for a presentation or for achieving a specific goal.

- Break down the project into smaller, easily achievable steps. Give each step a mutually agreed-upon deadline.
- Communicate by sending a recap each week (or each day, if necessary) of the goal, the steps they have already completed, and the next step on the list.

For presentations, hold a rehearsal, or two, or three! There's a reason why actors rehearse plays for months before a performance. Presenters need to rehearse, too.

- Have the employee present in front of one person. Then have them present in front of the team.
- Go over scenarios that may happen during a presentation and determine how to handle each. What if the microphone cuts out? What if the projector doesn't work that day? What if a moderator asks a curveball question? How do they field that?

Most important, listen to your employees. They can often see a different way to approach a problem or task and get the same result. If they know that they can explain this to you without judgment or being told they must do things exactly as initially laid out, they'll be much more confident in telling you when there's an issue. When you work with them to find a solution, they'll feel respected and seen and that their contribution to the team makes a difference. It's a win-win when you approach goal-setting with an open mind, open ears, and genuine empathy.

Most important, listen to your employees. They can often see a different way to approach a problem or task and get the same result.

Team Building for Innovation: Leveraging Neurodiversity for Creative Problem-Solving

Does your team seem unfocused, less productive, or stressed out? Changing the rhythm of the workday can help employees feel recharged and more focused. A team-building exercise or another type of group activity can help.

Team building is essential, especially for neurodivergent employees who may have difficulty building a social rapport with their colleagues. However, traditional team-building exercises can cause extra anxiety for neurodivergent teammates. Here are some group activities that can benefit everyone on the team.

Team building is essential, especially for neurodivergent employees who may have difficulty building a social rapport with their colleagues.

Think/Pair/Share

- Add this exercise to meetings that run longer than usual or where a lot of information is being imparted. Have employees think about the information you want them to process and understand for a few minutes. Then have them pair up (or even triple up) and share their thoughts about the information. This social activity enables neurodivergent and neurotypical employees to speak with their peers without fear of judgment.

Tell a Story, Then Discuss

- People remember stories; they are stored in long-term memory and can be recalled quickly. That's why speakers frequently open their talk with a story: It engages the audience while making a point about the topic. Because a story has a beginning, middle, and end, it creates a pattern the mind can follow. It also helps employees engage with the discussion once you've completed the story (or reached a point where discussion is helpful).

People remember stories; they are stored in long-term memory and can be recalled quickly.

Pattern Out Problems and Solutions

- Patterns are helpful for all employees, but especially for neurodivergent workers. It helps them associate concepts with visual images. Uncover all the whiteboards in the meeting room. Set out colored markers and pencils. (If your team is meeting online, have everyone pull up OneNote, Google Docs, or another group-enabled app.) Discuss the problem at hand and encourage colorful and artistic note taking. Designs might include colored graphic organizers, grouping and classification charts, and sequence charts, including timelines and workflows.

Note: As the meeting leader, you may need to start things by associating concepts with visual images. When presenting new information to your neurodiverse team, include diagrams, tables, outlines, and so on. After introducing new ideas, concepts, or challenges, ask the group to visualize how various statements relate to one another and draw a graph, chart, picture, or some other representation of the material.

Tongue Twisters

- This is a great starting exercise to get everyone relaxed and focused. Tongue twisters increase the activity of the cells in a part of the brain called the Broca's area, which controls speech articulation. Create tongue twisters, which can be random, fun, or designed to review material the team needs to remember. This exercise can be combined with the Think/Pair/Share exercise: Have a contest to see which team pair can develop the best tongue twister! Not only will your team be laughing, but they will also remember critical information.

Structured Virtual Happy Hour

- This is a variation on a popular "Zoom party" or happy hour. The difference is that it's structured so neurodivergent employees can participate and socialize without struggling to connect. Set a date and time for the happy hour and designate where it will take place (online via Teams or Zoom, or in person at the office). Include a structured schedule in the invite, including the time it starts and ends, as well as key activities.
- One key activity in a structured happy hour is "getting to know you." Before the event, send an email explaining that each person will get to answer one or two pre-set questions about themselves during this activity. As the activity proceeds, assign one person to ask each participant questions. This structure gives neurodivergent employees time to prepare and think about their answers before the activity begins.
- Consider other supportive activities, like combining Trivial Pursuit with a Think/Pair/Share. Employees can support one another to come up with answers.

Meaningful involvement is important to every employee, both neurodivergent and neurotypical. Supportive group exercises that encourage workers to help one another learn and understand new information and build camaraderie can make the workplace a positive environment. They can help stimulate creativity and improve productivity, and they can help employees build lasting connections.

Meaningful involvement is important to every employee, both neurodivergent and neurotypical.

Chapter Six Reflection Questions

1. How can managers effectively balance the need for structure with flexibility when leading neurodivergent teams? Provide specific examples based on the strategies outlined in the chapter.
2. Discuss the potential benefits and challenges of implementing a mentoring program for neurodivergent employees. How might this approach impact both the mentors and mentees?
3. How can organizations create an environment that empowers neurodivergent employees to reach their full potential? What specific strategies from the chapter could be most impactful?
4. Analyze the importance of adapting communication styles and meeting structures for neurodivergent teams. How might these changes benefit all employees, not just those who are neurodivergent?
5. Reflect on the concept of brain breaks during long meetings or training sessions. How might this practice impact productivity and information retention for diverse teams?
6. How can managers effectively set goals and track progress with neurodivergent employees? What considerations should be taken into account when developing performance metrics?
7. Evaluate the effectiveness of the team-building activities suggested in the chapter. How do these activities address the specific needs of neurodivergent employees while fostering overall team cohesion?
8. How can organizations strike a balance between providing necessary accommodations for neurodivergent employees and maintaining a sense of fairness and equality among all team members?
9. Reflect on the importance of continuous learning and growth in understanding neurodiversity. How can managers and organizations cultivate a culture of ongoing education and adaptation to support neurodivergent employees effectively?

Accelerating Talent Development: Optimizing Learning Strategies for a Competitive Edge

Maximizing ROI on Learning Management Systems: Avoiding Pitfalls and Driving Engagement

Ben was working in sales for a very well-known company. He always knew he was a slow reader but didn't know why. When his daughter was diagnosed with dyslexia, he realized that he also had dyslexia. He saw that she experienced the same struggles he had dealt with when he was in school. It had never occurred to him that he might be neurodivergent.

He successfully concealed his dyslexia for decades until his company shifted toward a Learning Management System (LMS) to deliver information about new products more quickly. The new LMS required employees to take computerized tests to earn the certification needed to sell the latest products.

As Ben took these tests, the numbers and letters flipped and turned backward. When he brought the issue to senior management, begging for alternative learning options, he was turned away.

As a result, after being one of the top-performing sales reps for years, he received a less-than-stellar performance review.

These tests cast a glaring light on his dyslexia.

Eventually, he felt he had no choice but to find another job with a company that was more flexible and willing to work with him despite his dyslexia. His now former company, which ironically spearheaded an initiative to hire neurodivergent employees, let one of their top-performing neurodivergent sales reps go out the door. What a senseless loss to the company and to the employee.

It had never occurred to him that he might be neurodivergent.

A Missed Opportunity

Learning challenges are more common than you might think. They follow individuals from school to work. This matters because when companies fail to recognize that the path to learning is different for everyone, they risk losing valuable employees, even their top performers. More important, they risk losing seasoned employees and decades' worth of acquired institutional knowledge because of a system change that requires upskilling.

> ***Companies that don't recognize that there are many ways to teach their employees will continue to lose great talent.***

It's not just a matter of losing talent. It's expensive for a company to find and replace talent. Companies that don't recognize that there are many ways to teach their employees will continue to lose great talent and incur significant financial costs in the process.

Pay Attention to People, Not Numbers

Sadly, companies often embrace initiatives like LMS to save money. They bring in LMS systems that use algorithms and AI to determine whether an employee is hitting the mark. When salespeople pitch these systems, they glorify numbers that present a picture of substantial savings.

However, what is often missing from that colorful pie chart is the cost of replacing hardworking, loyal employees lost due to the lack of personalization, human understanding, and people-centered problem solving in their LMS metrics.

The idiom "one hand doesn't know what the other hand is doing" might be appropriate here. Companies often make decisions in silos. Ben's manager recognized his value and knew he was one of their top-performing sales reps. However, she found herself constrained due to rigid policies regarding certification for selling new products. She was well aware that he could sell the product better than anybody else in the department, yet he couldn't demonstrate his understanding on a standardized test.

Looking at the test scores alone, the number crunchers didn't see Ben as a human being who brought profit to the company. They only saw him as a number on a spreadsheet.

Finding the Person in the Middle

So what's the solution? That answer, unfortunately, is not simple. And the larger the corporation, the more complicated it gets. Possibly, it starts with a company culture that is more people-centered and less numbers-centered. Yes, profit is important; however, "It doesn't take long before the employee is seen and treated as a cog in the machine. They feel like second-class citizens, not unique, creative beings capable of great things." writes Jeb Banner in "Four Ingredients for a People-Centered Workplace." (Banner, 2016)

For Ben, the only solution was to leave a company that he loved and that had profited from his hard work for years. That is not the scenario any company hopes for when it implements an LMS or some other performance measurement initiative. What a loss for the company, financially (it's expensive to hire, onboard, and train new employees) and in intellectual property (IP). Companies face a 37 percent chance of losing IP when employees quit. (VB Staff, 2022)

Has your company experienced this issue? Are you wrestling with the problem of good employees leaving because of a policy change or new performance initiative?

Taking steps to improve training benefits all employees. State-of-the-art instructional models are available that make the workplace more inclusive of all learners.

Beyond Training: Strategies for Measurable Skill Acquisition and Performance Improvement

There is only one constant in how different employees apply their brain power to learn and retain information: We all learn differently.

As employers, we must recognize this reality. Every employee processes the information that we provide in training or meetings in their own unique way. Ultimately, their goal is to upskill efficiently and perform tasks successfully. How they do that depends on their learning preferences, strengths, and mindset.

The Trainer Called Me Out in Public!

I was attending a sales training session when the trainer suddenly called me out, believing I wasn't paying attention. What she didn't realize was that I have auditory processing disorder (APD). She paused her presentation to point out how rude it was that I was using my iPad while she was speaking. She failed to understand that I was actively connecting her training content to real-world information necessary for completing the paperwork she was referencing.

You see, I'm not a strong auditory learner. My auditory processing speed is slower than the average human's, and my auditory memory is poor when not associated with visual cues or immediate interaction. In this session, the trainer's PowerPoint consisted of filler images without text. Crucial information was being delivered solely through her verbal presentation.

As she mentioned websites and specific keywords to help us with the sales paperwork, I entered them into my iPad's browser search box. I thought, "I need to connect this information to a real application.

I have to make connections to what she's saying." I began finding the websites she referred to and exploring them. I could hear her words, and now I could also see what she was trying to communicate. I was linking her message to the actual sales information I needed.

Being called out on the spot like that left me feeling embarrassed and frustrated. I wasn't idly playing on my iPad; I was on task, locating the websites she discussed and visually confirming that the information she provided was exactly what I needed to complete those sales documents. I was working in the way my brain learns best.

The presentation itself wasn't problematic for me; I know how to manage my learning needs. The issue stemmed from her erroneous conclusion about my behavior.

For those unfamiliar with APD, it affects how the brain processes spoken language. This can make it challenging for individuals to understand speech when delivered in noisy environments, to follow verbal instructions, or to differentiate between similar sounds. Adults with APD often find themselves repeatedly asking for repetition, mishearing information, or experiencing fatigue from the effort of listening. They frequently struggle with auditory memory.

Adults with APD may need assistance remembering spoken instructions, comprehending conversations in noisy settings, and recalling details of what they've read or heard.

Customized Learning Pathways: Tailoring Professional Development for Maximum Impact

As more businesses implement programs to attract and retain neurodivergent workers, focusing on supporting their professional development is crucial. Traditional training programs often fall short for neurodivergent individuals, including those with autism, dyslexia, ADHD, or other unique neurological profiles. According to recent esti-

Learning Strategies for the Modern Workforce

Spaced Learning

Breaking training into shorter sessions for better retention.

Blended Learning

Combining in-person and online learning for diverse styles.

Microlearning

Offering content in small, manageable modules for easy understanding.

Interactive Content

Engaging learners through quizzes and hands-on activities.

Real-World Application

Ensuring training is relevant to the workplace for better engagement.

Teaching Others

Promoting peer teaching to enhance comprehension and retention.

Learning in Flow

Integrating learning materials into daily work tasks for accessibility.

Regular Testing

Implementing quizzes with immediate feedback to monitor progress.

Multimedia Use

Incorporating videos and interactive modules for engagement.

Storytelling

Using narratives to enhance memory retention.

Training Formats

Offering diverse training methods for various preferences.

Presentation Styles

Engaging learners with multiple instructors or speakers.

Follow-Up

Implementing activities to reinforce learning.

Self-Directed Learning

Allowing learners to choose their learning paths.

Experience Connection

Relating new knowledge to past experiences.

Problem-Solving

Encouraging critical thinking through real-world challenges.

mates, neurodivergent individuals may make up as much as 15 to 20 percent of the global population. (Doyle, 2020) This suggests that a significant portion of your current workforce—potentially one in five employees—may benefit from more inclusive training approaches.

Large, classroom-based programs (in-person or virtual) that require quick, on-the-spot thinking, presenting responses in front of the group, or attending long lectures can be counterproductive for over 50 percent of your employees. Webinar-style training often encourages employees to click through while multitasking. Heck! No one can see what they are doing. Admit it; you've done it, too! Okay, I'm also guilty of multitasking during a boring webinar.

Despite the training challenges, employees must have the opportunity to learn and grow in their place of work. So how can professional development training programs be designed differently, with the other 40 percent in mind?

You can safely assume that 40 percent of your staff does not learn through traditional methods. I've spent my entire career in education. Forty percent of students need differentiated instruction. Their brain wiring doesn't change just because they become adults. Most adults just figure out how to hide their learning challenges as they move into the workplace.

Designing programs with the knowledge that employees have different learning preferences and brain wiring is key to helping them get the most out of their training. When they engage and learn because the training meets their learning needs, they can give the most back to their place of work. While no two employees will have the exact learning needs, some best practices make professional development training more accessible to all employees, including your neurodivergent talent.

Designing professional development training programs with the neurodivergent employee in mind creates programs that benefit all employees. The gold standard is well-designed training programs that support different learning preferences by offering multiple training formats, clearly articulated instructions, and clear expectations provided in advance. To maximize training efficacy, add follow-up support and flexible methods for employees to demonstrate understanding.

> ***Designing professional development training programs with the neurodivergent employee in mind creates programs that benefit all employees.***

When Planning Training Events

One of the things we need to think about when planning training events is how the people working for us can maximize their brain power to grasp what we're saying. How can they focus on the sales projections, complete new budget requirements, or understand new regulations in a way that will allow them to carry forward what you need them to do?

In Inclusive Dynamic Workplace Design™, it's fundamental that each employee is allowed to learn in the way they learn best.

Universal Design for Learning

Often, managers overlook neurodivergent employees for professional development training opportunities, or the training is delivered in a way that isn't optimal. "A full 67% of workplace learning programs are instructor-led, and 53% of those are in face-to-face formats, including virtual learning." (Gronseth & Hutchins, 2020)

Conduct Training by Design

Some companies use Universal Design for Learning (UDL) practices to develop professional development training programs. UDL acknowledges that people learn differently and builds in multiple approaches from the start.

Options for professional development should be tailored to reflect employees' diverse needs so that they can fully take advantage of available resources. So often, companies provide a one-size-fits-all training format. Unfortunately, this disadvantages many capable, talented, divergent learners.

Worse is the trend toward computerized assessments determining whether an employee has mastered a topic. Some employees have a depth of knowledge about a topic and can utilize their knowledge successfully on the factory floor, in sales, and in conversations with key stakeholders. However, if they put a standardized, computerized test in front of them, they will fail. It is the wrong way to assess these individuals' understanding and knowledge of any topic.

The convenience of digital testing to determine whether an employee knows their stuff ignores current research about how brains learn and demonstrate knowledge.

The convenience of digital testing to determine whether an employee knows their stuff ignores current research about how brains learn and demonstrate knowledge.

Enhancing Knowledge Retention: Evidence-Based Approaches to Accelerate Skill Mastery

Inclusive workplace training for adults requires options that cater to their unique learning needs and preferences. Here are some proven strategies that trainers can use to enhance information retention among adult learners.

Include Neurodivergent Employees in the Development of Training Programs

When designing professional development courses or materials, the goal is for the training to be effective for all employees. How about including neurodivergent employees in the creation process? Their input allows for programs to be developed that do not unnecessarily exclude a portion of the workforce.

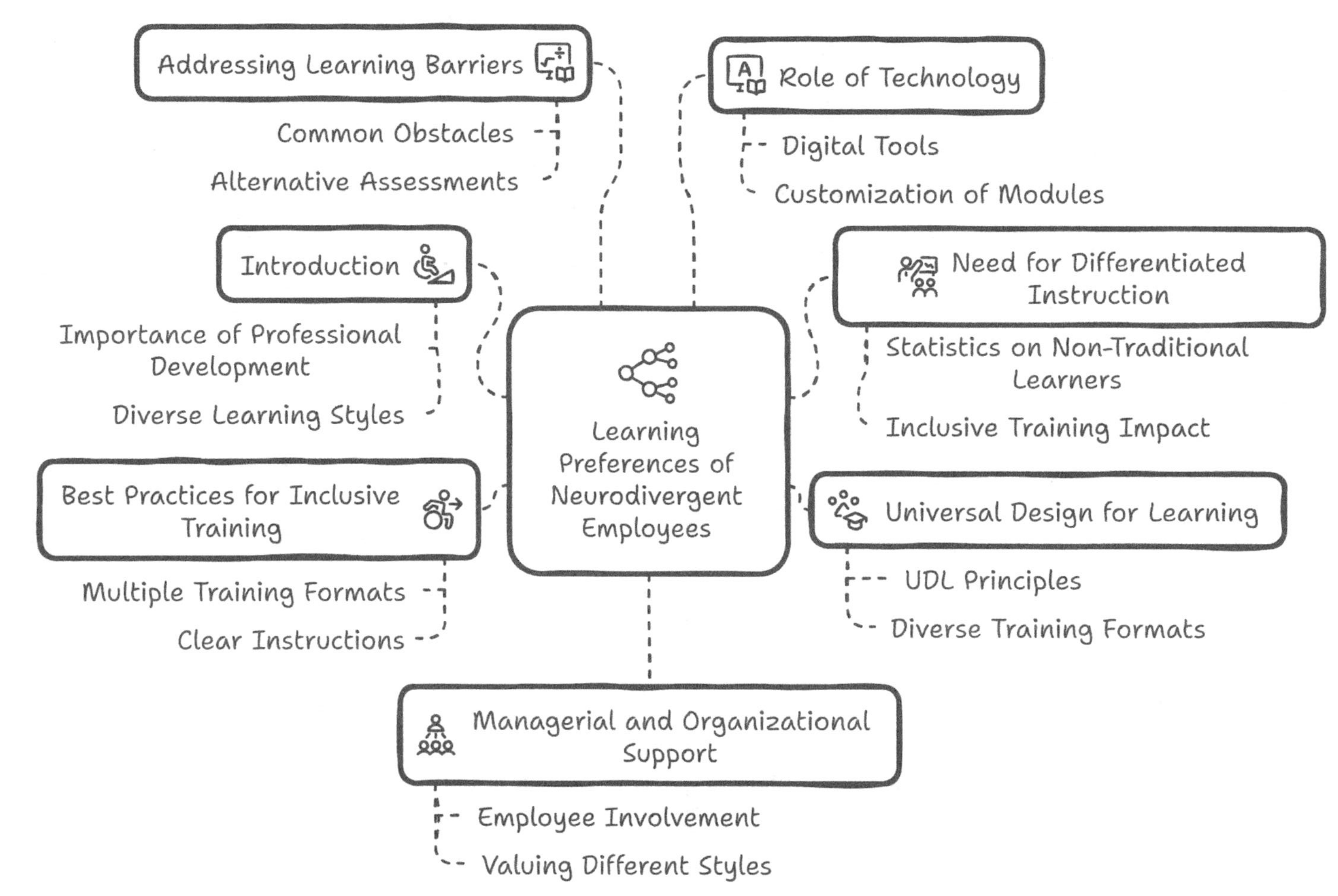
Inclusive Workplace Training
Addressing Learning Barriers
Common Obstacles
Alternative Assessments
Role of Technology
Digital Tools
Customization of Modules
Introduction
Importance of Professional Development
Diverse Learning Styles
Learning Preferences of Neurodivergent Employees
Need for Differentiated Instruction
Statistics on Non-Traditional Learners
Inclusive Training Impact
Best Practices for Inclusive Training
Multiple Training Formats
Clear Instructions
Universal Design for Learning
UDL Principles
Diverse Training Formats
Managerial and Organizational Support
Employee Involvement
Valuing Different Styles

When designing professional development courses or materials, the goal is for the training to be effective for all employees.

Most professional development is planned according to the status quo, which is how teaching has been done forever! If you compare a picture of a college classroom taken a hundred years ago with a photo of a college classroom today, you'd likely see little difference: Rows of students facing a teacher who lectures from the front while students take notes. We still overwhelmingly teach to verbal-linguistic learners who read well and have excellent auditory memories. That instructional format does not consider the needs of employees with dyslexia or ADHD, those who need extra time to process and reflect on the concepts being taught, or hands-on learners. I could go on, but you get the idea.

Provide as Much Information in Advance as Possible

Providing information about learning expectations in advance can ease anxiety and allow employees to undertake the training program feeling more in control of the experience. Wille and Sajous-Brady suggest that employers "clearly describe key expectations and instructions in writing," along with providing task checklists and flowcharts in advance (2018). Front-loading doesn't benefit neurodivergent employees alone. The introverts on your staff also appreciate having the information ahead of time.

Follow-Up Support Is Key

A support network for neurodivergent employees can significantly improve job performance and support their mobility within a company. Providing mentors or coaches can help employees follow through on completing professional development training tasks. An accountability partner can be a game changer when training is in self-paced modules. (Volpone et al., 2022)

Innovative Learning Modalities: Optimizing Knowledge Transfer for the Modern Workforce

Spaced Learning

Breaking down extended training programs into shorter sessions with spaced intervals helps learners recall and retain information over the long term. This method leverages the spacing effect, known to improve memory retention.

Blended Learning

Combining traditional face-to-face learning with e-learning engages different types of learners and ensures better retention. This approach allows for flexibility and caters to various learning preferences.

Microlearning

Dividing learning content into small, bite-sized modules makes it easier for learners to absorb and retain information. This method is particularly effective for complex topics that can be overwhelming if presented all at once.

Interactive and Engaging Content

Creating interactive content such as quizzes, role-playing, and hands-on activities fosters active participation and enhances retention. Engaging learners through interactive methods helps break the monotony of traditional lectures.

Real-World Application

Designing learning units directly applicable to the learners' work lives improves retention by making the content relevant and practical. Real-world problem-solving exercises help learners see the immediate value of the training.

Teaching Others

Encouraging learners to teach the material to others is one of the most effective ways to help them master a subject and retain knowledge. This method reinforces learning through repetition and explanation.

Learning in the Flow of Work

Providing access to learning materials and answers to queries in real time helps learners apply new knowledge immediately, reinforcing retention. This approach integrates learning with daily tasks.

Regular Testing and Feedback

Incorporating quizzes, tests, and assessments into training courses helps learners retrieve knowledge and monitor their progress. Immediate feedback on performance can motivate learners and highlight areas for improvement.

Use of Multimedia and Technology

Incorporating multimedia elements like videos, infographics, and interactive e-learning modules makes learning more dynamic and appealing. Technology can cater to different learning styles and enhance engagement.

Storytelling and Emotional Engagement

Using anecdotes, real-life examples, and narratives to illustrate concepts can captivate learners' attention and help them connect with content on a personal level. Emotional engagement deepens the impact and retention of information.

Provide Training in Multiple Formats

Recent research from Volpone et al. (2022) shows that providing professional development training in the form of self-paced tutorials or, when appropriate, on-the-job training was preferred by neurodivergent employees over in-class or online courses. Additionally, providing information in multiple ways, such as verbally, through short video clips, microteaching, gamification, hands-on learning, or mentoring, accounts for differences in learning preferences and yields better results.

Variety in Presentation Styles

Varying presentation styles by using different instructors or guest speakers can prevent boredom and maintain interest. Each presenter brings a unique perspective and teaching style, which can enhance the learning experience.

Strategies That Support Recall and Comprehension

Follow-Up and Reinforcement

Implementing follow-up activities, quizzes, or refresher courses ensures that key concepts are reinforced and retained over time. Continuous reinforcement helps solidify learning.

Self-Directed Learning and Autonomy

Offering choices in how and when learning occurs respects adults' preferences and constraints, fostering a sense of control and motivation. Self-directed learning options can empower learners and enhance engagement.

Connecting to Previous Experiences

Encouraging learners to draw on their previous experiences and relate new information to what they already know can enhance understanding and retention. This method leverages relational learning.

Problem-Solving Exercises

Including exercises that allow for problem-solving and unveil new perspectives can create aha moments for learners. These exercises make learning more interactive and relevant.

Take Notes by Hand

Encourage employees to take notes by hand as a speaker talks. Some people listen better and process information better by writing it down. This only works for some. Some people listen better by typing the notes. Some can only listen and observe. For these learners, any other activity pulls their attention from the speaker to the mechanics of writing or typing.

Close Your Eyes while Listening

Have employees close their eyes or look away from the speaker during information-intensive parts of the presentation. Japanese businesspeople are well known for doing this as it lets them focus more completely on the speaker's voice. (Kopp, 2011)

Put Your Body Where You Are Most Comfortable

Make sure employees can stand up and stretch or walk around occasionally. Encourage this by setting up a table opposite the speaker with water and coffee so they can walk to and from without passing the speaker.

Devices Can Be a Critical Learning Aid (When Not a Distraction)

Allow employees to take notes or look up information on their laptops or tablets. Many professional speakers encourage this during parts of their presentations to actively engage participants.

Use Compelling Visuals to Assist Learning

Research over several decades has shown that three days after a training session, employees retain only 10 percent of the content presented through listening. However, they retain an astounding 65 percent of content when the training is visual.

You can use this knowledge to your advantage in training and employee engagement. An informative, eye-catching slide can enhance an employee's learning better than hours of lectures or reading through written information. "The brain processes visual information 60,000 times better than text," the Visual Teaching Alliance reports. This visual approach is critical if you have employees with dyslexia or who are on the autistic spectrum. These neurodivergent thinkers need visual input to process verbal and/or textual information.

The brain processes visual information 60,000 times better than text.

Mind Mapping Is an Active Learning Activity

Instead of getting frustrated, managers can encourage their employees to use "mind mapping" during a meeting. This inclusive approach allows everyone to contribute in their own way, whether it's doodling, creating improvised flowcharts, taking notes, or any other method that helps them visualize the topic being discussed. It fosters a sense of connection and understanding among team members. Encourage them to doodle, create improvised flowcharts, take notes, or do whatever they need to do to visualize the topic being discussed.

I'll give you a real-life example. I was working with a vice president at a company that does a lot of electronic media publishing. When I talked about the mind-mapping concept, she snapped her fingers. "That just happened in a meeting!" she told me.

"I was on a Zoom call with my team, and one of my people had her head down almost the entire time. She wasn't talking or contributing except to nod her head a little bit. She's a lead developer, so her input was important, but during this meeting, when we were problem-solving a critical issue, she wasn't contributing. I didn't want to call her out and embarrass her," the vice president told me. "So near the end of the meeting, I asked if she had anything to add to the discussion. She looked up and said, 'Yes. I've been mapping out the conversation. I think I have a solution.' And she held up a hand-drawn flowchart that she'd put together while we were discussing the problem. She had identified the break in the process by mapping out the conversation!"

That's the kind of visual learning that managers need to encourage. That employee listened the entire time but also processed the information being communicated and put it into a visual map. Seeing the problem visually allowed her to problem-solve, figure out the break in the system, and develop an innovative solution.

Measuring Learning Outcomes: Authentic Assessment

Providing flexible options for presenting work and showing understanding is essential. Videos, written responses, presentations, and one-on-one discussions are good ways to demonstrate an understanding of training program materials.

My Employee Is Both a High Performer and an Underperformer—How Can That Happen?

So you have somebody on your team that other employees are complaining about. That person is not getting key assignments in on time and is holding up a project. You've got an underperformer, right? Not. He's also an engineer whom most would say is a high performer when doing what he does best: engineering. What do you do?

One of my clients, Anita, came to me with this problem. She supervised an engineer who excelled at execution, problem-solving, and collaboration. Yet he needed to catch up on documentation and metrics reporting, which was another part of his job. Without those pieces, projects couldn't move forward and were often delayed.

"He's one of our top-performing engineers," the manager explained. "He's analytical; he can look at a problem, sift through all the ambiguity, and solve the problem." She continued, "He's great to work with, and his team members love him. And he's fast! His team

> *would outperform all expectations if he'd get the documentation in on time. Unfortunately, writing his reports takes him so long that he loses efficiency."*
>
> *I suggested that he use speech-to-text to write the first draft to get his thoughts out.*
>
> *Anita explained that she'd considered offering that option to him, but she did not think it would help. She continued, "When he presents his findings to the team, he is so random that he goes off on tangents. So even when presenting verbally, he struggles to be clear and concise in his explanations." Consequently, using speech-to-text would not be a viable solution.*
>
> *Anita cared about her people. She wanted a solution that would work and be fair to the rest of the team. This talented engineer provided tremendous value. However, his difficulty meeting his job's writing requirements became a serious problem.*
>
> *Understand that this employee was not avoiding a task because he didn't like doing it. He didn't have the skill set to complete the task in a timely way. This is not an uncommon problem in engineering departments. Engineers are not known for their excellent writing skills!*

Here's the key: This company hired him for his engineering skills. They did not hire a writer. If they wanted a technical writer, they would have hired a writer. Thirty years ago, he would have had a secretary, and this would have been a non-issue.

Getting to the Root of the Problem

Many people excel in math or English, but few excel at both. Some who excel at math are not the best communicators, especially if they are neurodivergent and on the autism spectrum. Having worked with divergent thinkers my entire career, I suspected that this employee may have an expressive language disability.

So the question became, "How does a company keep a top-performing engineer (a difficult position to replace) when the task the engineer is struggling with is not where he delivers his greatest ROI to the company?"
The standard HR solution was to put the employee on an improvement plan. My client considered this. However, she understood that his ability to write would not improve. Instead, it would probably push him out the door, and she'd lose a brilliant, well-liked team member. It was unlikely that an improvement plan would help him if his problem was due to his different brain wiring.

Perceptive managers value employees who think differently. They understand the value of divergent thinking and realize that innovation, problem-solving, and efficiency improve when they are part of a team. These employees may have ADHD, be on the spectrum, or have difficulty speaking or explaining things verbally.

Perceptive managers value employees who think differently... These employees may have ADHD, be on the spectrum, or have difficulty speaking or explaining things verbally.

Those cognitive differences are the very reason they boost the success of their teams. However, they need accommodations to support their success. These accommodations rarely cost the company money. Instead, they push the limits of outdated corporate policies and adherence to "the way we've always done things" in exchange for the benefits of divergent thinking in the workplace.

Managers may feel frustrated because they can't figure out how to help an employee comply with workplace norms and policies. They may not have the flexibility or structure to provide the necessary accommodations.

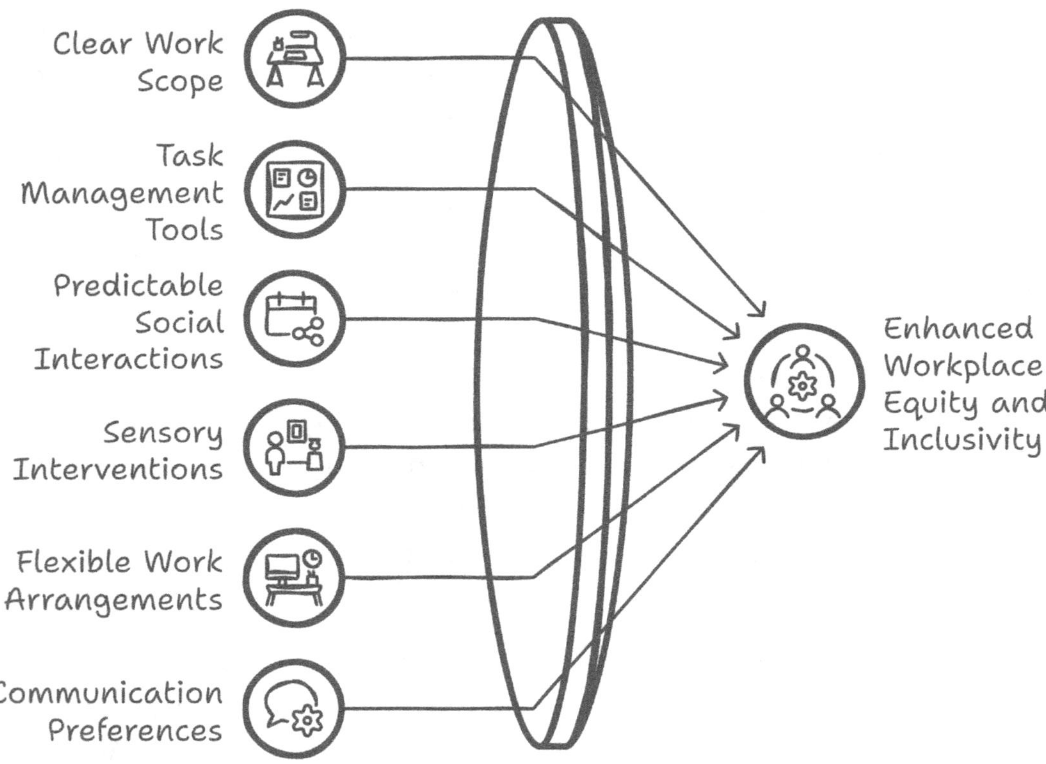

The Solution: Flexibility and Creative Problem Solving

Back to my client Anita and her dilemma: I suggested she try a buddy system. What if they matched the engineer with someone on his team who wrote well? He could be paired up with a teammate who excelled at written communication and the required process documentation. His teammate would interview him to help him verbalize his process and write the information down. Then the engineer could review it, make any edits he needed to make, and submit that documentation. The ideal scenario would be one where the writer benefits by learning from the engineer. He mentors his teammate, and his teammate helps him with the documentation. It's a win-win.

We both realized that such a solution would require selling the idea to upper management and the team. It was outside the parameters of how things were always done. Even so, this wise manager realized that the win for the company and the team was worth trying to find a solution that benefited everyone.

H3: Tailor Solutions to the Individual

Managers must focus on the bigger picture to get the best out of our divergent thinkers and our teams. Sometimes that means going against the status quo. Research shows that companies that amplify the talent that a person was hired for by providing accommodations for their challenges will not only be more innovative but also increase employee retention.

Research shows that companies that amplify the talent that a person was hired for by providing accommodations for their challenges will not only be more innovative but also increase employee retention.

Cognitive Capital: Investing in Employee Potential for Exponential Returns

How can we help our employees focus and process information better and have meaningful interactions with management and peers?

A healthy brain is as important as a healthy body when it comes to employee learning and productivity. Wise company leaders support both facets. Healthy employees are more productive, and that helps improve the bottom line. That's what is behind the rise in employer-supported programs that address nutrition, exercise, and wellness.

A healthy brain is as important as a healthy body when it comes to employee learning and productivity.

Implementing supports that maximize your employees' brain power delivers a significant ROI.

Embrace and Support Diverse Ways of Working and Learning

I've worked with neurodivergent people for many years. Yet even among those we consider neurotypical, we all have our own way of processing information and completing tasks. From assembly-line workers who perform prescribed movements to truck drivers or landscapers, employees learn in slightly different ways from the person next to them.

This learning difference is even more pronounced in office environments, especially when the work is goal-oriented and employees can take different paths to reach their goals.

Here's what I mean. I've known for my entire adult life that I cannot sit for a long time and focus my attention on a speaker in front of me. I tune out, and I don't retain as much information. I'm not alone. But if I can look down and take notes as I listen or even doodle little cartoons on paper, I retain much more of what is said. I can write down questions about what's being said. If I have a tablet in front of me, I can look up more information.

When I present training, I often supply mandala coloring pages and markers for my audience to color while listening. Over the years, countless participants approached me after my workshop

> *and thanked me for allowing them to color a mandala. They'd say, "I was worried I'd struggle to pay attention, but coloring the mandala not only helped me to listen, it made the time fly by."*

"An estimated 80% of students and 25% of adults admit to being chronic procrastinators, and with the internet and smartphones offering an endless number of distractions from what we should be doing, it may be getting worse." (Williams, 2014) Why? Too many distractions interfere with our ability to focus and get things done.

To a manager leading a meeting, what I'm doing might look like I'm goofing off. I know it can be frustrating to see that. In a big room or on a remote video call, you probably can't see what an employee is doing and can't tell if they're playing mobile Scrabble or taking notes.

Given that people learn and process information differently, it's possible that your employees aren't goofing off. They're consciously or unconsciously using a stronger learning path: visual learning.

Improve Learning Agility

Some employees could be better at rolling with change. Leaders who create workplace environments that support and encourage learning agility help employees adapt to changes.

Leaders who create workplace environments that support and encourage learning agility help employees adapt to changes.

"The hard truth is that not everyone is born an agile learner," said Elenie Zoe in an eFront blog post. (Zoe, 2019) But that competency can be taught.

We saw a real test of agility all through 2020. The most successful companies were able to help employees adapt to dramatic changes in work hours, work locations, and, well, everything! Projects were changed or canceled. Industry events evaporated. At this level of adaptation, there is an emotional and mental toll. A healthy company recognizes this. However, the ability to adapt to new processes or routines can be taught and supported with the right approach.

Consider bringing aboard a learning manager who can guide your company and employees on dealing with uncertainty and improve learning agility across the organization.

Support Brain Breaks

Most white-collar workers are engaged in deep work for several hours during their workday. However, as those hours increase, an employee's effectiveness decreases. It's important to build in what teachers call brain breaks and literally rest the brain. These breaks can and should take many forms. It can be a walk around the office, an hour at the gym, a simple five-minute stretch routine, a twenty-minute nap, or playing casual games on the phone for five minutes. A brain break works best when the person completely disengages from the deep work they're doing and does something undemanding for a few minutes.

It's important to build in what teachers call brain breaks and literally rest the brain.

Think of this type of break as a short but fast recharge for the brain.

Help Employees Build Connections

When someone refers to building connections, most of us think of mixer events like the social hours at conferences where people network. Those are valid connections, but not all employees do well at mixers, and employers shouldn't rely solely on these events.

Instead, they should look at the many pathways available to help employees build connections with their peers within the company and the industry. These are crucial career development steps, but they're also personal development steps. We need peer interaction. It's healthy for us, keeps our brains pliable, and teaches new skills that make an employee an even better performer.

Building connections internally is equally important, and there are plenty of ways to do it. A company can set up an internal social page where employees can share pictures, stories, and anecdotes. Another possibility is setting up a peer-to-peer celebration program so employees can cheer one another on and recognize one another's efforts.

Implementing any one of these ideas will help our employees focus and process information better. Those that encourage soft skills and connections create the opportunity for meaningful interactions with management and peers. Remember, a healthy brain is as important as a healthy body when it comes to employee learning and productivity. Wise company leaders support both facets.

Uncovering Learning Preferences: A Key to Unlocking Workforce Productivity

Millions of adults in the United States have some form of learning challenge. You likely work with a neurodivergent co-worker, manager, or employee. One of the hardest things for many of these adults to do is to reveal that they have a challenge.

As an employer, it's important to know that this is a big issue for some of your employees.

Meet Ella

A colleague of mine, Ella, is a career coach. She's phenomenal at her job and works beautifully with people. Part of her unique skill set is an innate sense of exactly what her clients need. She helps them create plans to tailor their careers and target jobs that fit best. Her company loves her in this role; she's perfect.

Recently, while creating a special program for her clients, she needed to create a computerized form. The app available to create the form was new to Ella, so she had to learn how to use it. Nobody at her job knew Ella couldn't do trial and error on the computer as most people could. Most of us pick around and figure out how to use a computer program to get our jobs done, but Ella doesn't learn that way.

Typically, she calls the IT person and has him come over to show her how to use programs with which she's unfamiliar. But on this day, he was unwilling to help. He may have been too busy or stressed when she emailed him for help. Instead of coming over, he replied, "I don't have time to go over there. Here are the instructions for how to use the app to create the form."

Ella read that email, and her heart sank. "Oh my gosh! He doesn't know that I can't read these instructions and figure it out," she told me later. She wrote back and said, "Look, this is great, but could you please come over and show me? Or I'll come to you. Just show me." Instead of agreeing to help, he wrote, "Look, here's the steps. This is what you've got to do; just do it. What's wrong with you?"

She was crushed.

"I was so upset that I didn't know what to do because I didn't want people to know about my disability. I have a nonverbal learning disorder (NVLD), and I can't learn that way. I realized that I had to tell him. I had to say. 'I have a disability, and I need you to come and show me.'"

I listened as she explained, "I had to out myself. I was so humiliated." She continued, "I went home that night, and I wanted to cry. It's hard for people like me to get through those days at work. When we must out ourselves, we fear possible backlash."

Ella is not alone. There are many people in your workplace, working on-site or remotely, with similar issues. They are hardworking, productive employees who are nontraditional learners. Quietly, they work around their learning challenges to get the job done. They've learned through experience how to compensate for their challenges and maximize their talents.

They are hardworking, productive employees who are nontraditional learners.

Support Employees without Embarrassment

Here are some ways to accommodate employees who have learning challenges. There is no reason a person needs to out themselves as neurodivergent. These strategies increase their success on the job without embarrassment. An organization implementing Inclusive Dynamic Workplace Design is on the path to supporting employees with the following strategies.

Allow Employees to Work to Their Strengths

For example, consider an employee with dyslexia. They may struggle with written instructions yet have an exceptional memory. Instead of providing written instructions, provide verbal or recorded instructions until they are memorized.

To take this a step further, consider providing all instructions to your employees in multiple formats: written, audio, or video, and through visual diagramming. Allow your staff free access to choose the format that best complements their learning strengths.

Record Digital Whiteboard Meeting Notes

It's common for meeting attendees to photograph a whiteboard or take good old-fashioned notes. Yet for some people, that's not enough. Remembering meeting discussions requires strong auditory memory and processing skills. A solution is to record meeting notes on a digital whiteboard. Store the video recording in the cloud for download or streaming after the meeting.

Of course, these are just a few ways to accommodate your employee's secret learning challenges. What's the biggest learning challenge you or your employees are struggling with? What strategies do you employ in your office? So often, we think of neurodivergence as being a serious condition that requires extreme accommodations.

But the truth is, most people who fall on the neurodivergent spectrum are people who have what has been referred to for years as learning disabilities. Most HR staff, managers, and company leaders don't think about accommodating these learning challenges because they don't make it onto our radar as needing accommodation.

Like Ella, millions of workers are masking or hiding their difficulties with learning. They've learned how to work around their issues, avoid calling attention to themselves, and blend into the surroundings of a neurotypical-centered workforce. By incorporating just these three simple strategies, you are taking those first giant leaps toward supporting a neurodiverse workforce.

When Being Neuro-Different Holds You Back

Do you see yourself in this person?

Twelve-year-old Joe frustrated his teachers. He had difficulty focusing on his work and preferred socializing with the students sitting next to him rather than getting his work done. He paid attention to the teacher for about ten minutes and then gazed into space. He struggled to remember what he'd been taught, and, more important, he couldn't seem to implement what he had learned to complete his work or pass tests.

"Joe is intelligent and wants to do a good job, but he just does not apply himself, especially when he's required to learn information that he thinks is boring," one of his teachers wrote.

Fast-forward to thirty-five-year-old Joe, who is a source of frustration for his boss. Joe has difficulty focusing on his work. He prefers to socialize with his colleagues rather than get his work done. His job requires continuous learning to keep up with current regulations and industry specs. He's observed staring off into space when attending training required to update his skill set.

He can use the company's Learning Management System (LMS) as an alternative option, yet he procrastinates and does not complete the modules promptly. Even when he does get through them, he struggles to remember what he's been taught, and, more important, he can't seem to implement what he's learned to complete his work.

"Joe is intelligent and generally motivated to do a good job. He just doesn't apply himself when required to upskill," his boss writes.

Do you see a pattern here?

Adult Joe has many of the same problems he had as a boy. He is aware that he's struggling at work. His career has just about stalled. He's struggling with anxiety and depression. And he doesn't know what to do about it.

Before we go further, let me mention that Joe is a real person (I'm just not using his real name) whom I coached. He was referred to me by his boss, who, like Joe's teachers in school, saw a bright, hardworking person who balked at completing certain tasks required for career progression.

After talking to Joe and getting a sense of his personal history, his career goals, and what he perceived as his failures, I had a suspicion. "Joe, were you ever evaluated for a learning disability when you were in school?" I asked him.

After getting assurances from me that his boss would not be told about anything we talked about in the coaching session, Joe admitted that he was diagnosed with ADHD and dyslexia when he was a boy.

As an adult, he thought he had outgrown his impulsiveness, disorganization, and trouble focusing. "I figured, once I finished school, I would never have to deal with it again. I honestly thought I grew out of it. I mean, I went to college and graduated with a four-year degree. And now I have my dream job. But I don't want to do any more learning," he told me.

The Hidden Neurodivergence

Like many adults, Joe's neurodivergence is hidden. He learned to manage it somewhat during his school years and kept it unknown to his peers and bosses—except when faced with challenges like learning new information in a text-heavy LMS curriculum. A 2006 study (Kessler et al., 2006) found that 4.4 percent of US adults, about fourteen million people, have been formally diagnosed with ADHD. Only 10.9 percent of those diagnosed are receiving treatment. And considering how many children are diagnosed with ADHD—9.4 percent—the number of adults with ADHD may be far underreported. (CDC Staff, 2024)

Other learning challenges like dyslexia, dyspraxia, APD, dyscalculia, dysgraphia, language processing disorder, nonverbal learning difficulties, and visual perceptual visual motor deficit are lifelong challenges.

Many adults with learning challenges do their best to hide them. They may choose jobs and careers that are less challenging. Or they muddle through a job they thought would be fun and filled with opportunity, hoping no one realizes they are having trouble with some aspects of it.

The Bright Side

Like many neurodivergent adults, Joe has many positive qualities that outshine the challenges he faces. He's empathetic to his co-workers, a great team player, and a creative problem-solver—all characteristics that earn him high scores on his performance review each year.

While adults with learning challenges have fewer resources available to them than school-aged children, there are still ways for Joe to manage his ADHD and dyslexia better. (Cicerchia & Freeman, n.d.; Smith, 2024) The recognition of undiagnosed ADHD and other learning challenges in adults is improving as more attention is paid to the issue.

Joe's neurodivergence was stopping him from pursuing key career development opportunities. But it wasn't too late to ease his anxiety about learning. Adults of any age can benefit from working with a professional to manage their disability.

Further, Joe's disability had some protection under American Disabilities Act (ADA) requirements. He could inform key people in the company, including HR and his boss, about his challenges and the need for accommodation. I knew that he was nervous about doing so: Not every company handles this well, and many people with disabilities find themselves in the uncomfortable position of having to advocate for themselves while worrying about the possible repercussions of revealing their disability. (Staff Writer, n.d.)

For Joe, the outcome of our coaching was positive. He had a close relationship with his boss and colleagues, and when he finally approached his boss and revealed his neurodivergence, the reaction was positive and supportive. HR immediately offered him LMS courses that better accommodated his dyslexia. His boss began looking for resources to help him manage Joe's career development better. Because the company knew that Joe had experience and valuable interpersonal assets, they were more than willing to help get him past the learning hurdles that had unintentionally been placed in his way.

If only every work situation could be this way for adults with learning disabilities. We have a long way to go, particularly in building awareness in the workplace, but we can hope.

Hindsight and Office Environments Before and After a Pandemic

Another often overlooked way employers can make their workspaces truly inclusive of neurodiversity is in the actual physical design of the workspace.

Companies can make their office layout truly welcoming for all employees, both neurodivergent and neurotypical, through IDWD. As America gears up for a return to the office, now is the perfect opportunity to create an office that works for everyone. It's interesting that before the pandemic, many companies were remodeling their offices to reduce the quiet spaces in their environment. Out went the frequently maligned cubicles; in came "group spaces" with minimal privacy. Workers got lockers for personal items, just like high school! The reintroduction of open-concept design forced people into communal areas to work without regard to a person's need for privacy, personal effects, or relief from sensory stimulation.

The new "open" design responded to what company leaders felt millennials wanted in their work environment. However, they did not consider the needs of introverts, people in the spectrum, or people overwhelmed by too much sensory input.

Common Workspaces Are Exhausting

I'm married to an introvert who, starting a couple of years before the pandemic, came home exhausted after work every day. His company had eliminated all personal workspaces and cubicles in favor of common workspaces, lockers, and group desks. He hated the updated office environment. To get deep work done, he needed his own work cave.

While open space is appealing in the pages of a design magazine, jumping into a completely open layout is a mistake; being visible to others all the time can induce anxiety in many people. "Doubts flourish under fluorescent lights that expose every slight, every interpersonal hurdle," a *New York Times* article on office design for neurodivergent employees noted. (Dominus, n.d.)

Office design must respect the needs of introverts and neurodivergent workers to have their own low-sensory-stimulating space to work. For introverts and many employees in the autistic spectrum, that work environment is akin to torture.

Rather than increase productivity, it reduces productivity. Instead of supporting collaboration, it creates tension and stress for those whose working and learning preferences are for quiet, low-stimulation office environments.

Provide quiet spaces. Autistic employees enjoy having a designated space to focus and work on projects without interruption.

That said, all employees benefit from access to quiet spaces. A good example of this concept is many recently remodeled airport lounges. Many have a quiet room where people cannot talk on their cell phones or converse with other members.

Not only will autistic employees appreciate the space, but your introverts or other employees who need quiet to focus will, too. It's a win-win for everyone.

Lockdown Changed Everything about Office Work

When the pandemic hit, people who relish that personal space and reduced stimulation could work from home. My husband couldn't be happier working alone in his work cave, interacting with colleagues via Microsoft Teams (with the video off), phone, or chat. He hopes to never have to go into the office again.

What does this mean for workers who were called back to those open-design office spaces after the pandemic ran its course? As companies strive to create workplaces where all employees can thrive, they need to consider ergonomics that go beyond how we sit or stand at our workstations.

The science of ergonomics encompasses more than the distance between your eyes and the computer screen. "It involves designing workspaces in such a way that they truly fit the needs of those who work in them," an Arc Alliance post explained. (Polec, 2018) "Thus, it considers various disciplines, including anthropometry, biomechanics, and applied and social psychology. It also focuses on environmental factors that can promote comfort in a workspace. These factors include noise, light, heat, cold, hearing, vision, and sensations, which can determine comfort and work performance for those with autism."

Sound/Noise as a Problem

During my interviews with both neurotypical and neurodivergent employees to understand their challenges in a neurodiverse workplace, one interviewee shared this experience:

"Aaliyah had this big fan under her desk that she ran all day. When she first turned it on in the morning, I thought I could stand the soft whirring noise it made. But at 4:30 p.m. when she turned it off, it was utter relief to my ears. White noise hell!

"I assumed the fan was a menopause thing, but when I asked her about it, she said that she needed the white noise to block out distractions. After some discussion, we came to an agreement: She'd turn the fan off when she left her desk, and I was allowed to turn it off if she forgot.

"This small compromise made a big difference in our ability to work together comfortably."

This story illustrates the importance of open communication and finding mutually beneficial solutions in a neurodiverse workplace. What one person needs to focus might be distracting to another, but with understanding and flexibility, co-workers can create an environment that works for everyone.

For many workers, large open spaces without walls create a cacophony of noise and distraction, especially for neurodivergent employees with ADHD, autism, or sensory sensitivity. To get the best out of these workers, we need to consider office design that respects their need for a quiet, less stimulating space.

Have you ever been to a restaurant in a renovated mill yard where the ceilings are high, the floors are concrete, and the walls are wood or brick? Many people seem to love this type of environment. However, for people with sensory sensitivities, APD, autism, or ADHD, these environments are incredibly uncomfortable.

If you've been in an office environment like this and felt that it was just too loud, imagine the employees who feel that way when they're trying to work in these large, open corporate spaces.

It's a death sentence for productivity.

Harsh Lighting Affects Overall Health

The fluorescent lighting used in most workspaces can lead to a host of difficulties for employees, including migraines, not to mention the distractions of flickering or buzzing lights. Instead, diffusing these harsh lights and introducing more natural lighting into the workspace jives with the body's natural circadian rhythms, indicating to the brain that it's time to be awake and alert.

The fluorescent lighting used in most workspaces can lead to a host of difficulties for employees.

Studies have also theorized that natural lighting improves visibility, health, mood, and focus. Even if you can't increase the natural light in your office, you can approximate natural daylight by using full-spectrum lighting as well as increasing blue lighting (natural daylight includes a lot of blue light). One option is to cover fluorescent lights with blue fluorescent tube sleeves.(S. Me. C. Fitzell, 2021)

Office Design Can Accommodate Personal Needs

"It is important for companies to be aware of possible needs as well as to have open communication with their employees," according to The Arc Alliance. (Polec, 2018) "Some people with autism need space to rock or swing since it relaxes them; others are soothed by touching their back to a wall, and some others do need open space. Design that can accommodate the individual needs of employees can make all the difference in terms of comfort within the office."

Open design can affect the eye and ear. But what is often not considered is smell and touch. Even the scent in the air and the feeling of a chair or desk surface can impact our work comfort level.

Consider that there are hotels that develop and trademark a specific scent to permeate their reception area. When people enter the lobby, that scent provides an experience that is remembered as part of that hotel brand.

"The Sheraton Carlsbad Resort & Spa uses a bergamot, jasmine and freesia scent, designed to evoke warm memories, relax the body and calm the mind," a Premium Scenting post reports.

Have you ever been to a hotel where the scent conjures up feelings of nausea? Or causes a migraine? I have, and I won't go back to those hotels. Sometimes, scent is used in the guest rooms because it is believed that spraying perfume on the rug is better than the scent of the previous occupant. For me, when I go into a hotel room that has a strong scent, my first reaction is to want to check out. I usually call down to the front desk and ask them to remind housekeeping not to use any sprays in my room during my stay.

Now apply this to consider the office environment. How might the scent of the workspace impact employees?

Communication Is Key!

When my husband's workspace was scheduled to be reconfigured, he came home from work on a Friday and said he would be home the following week. When I asked him why, he said, "Well, they're remodeling our workspace, so they want us to just work at home for a week so that they can get that done." I asked him if he knew what they were doing. Of course, he did not.

Whoever was on the design committee didn't consider talking to the employees who would be using that space. This lack of communication is one of the places where those brilliant people in charge of designing office space disconnect from the employees who must work in that space.

Communication is critical when making changes to an office environment, whether small or drastic.

Now that employees are returning to the office, whether on a hybrid schedule or full-time, companies need to consider their neurodivergent employees' needs when deciding the environment where they're going to work. Some workers feel trapped in quiet cubicles; they need the open space and movement of an open plan, and that's great for them. For others, an open design is akin to the House of Horrors.

Get feedback from employees on the kind of workspace they'd like to have. Do they prefer a more private cubicle? Would they like a more open, collaborative space? Or a mix of options? Work with the HR department to communicate with and create a means for employees to give honest feedback, whether through a survey or suggestion process.

Get feedback from employees on the kind of workspace they'd like to have.

I guarantee the results will be illuminating and could lead to a new way of thinking about how dedicated workspaces, designed for individual needs and preferences, can boost employee productivity.

Chapter Seven Reflection Questions

1. How can organizations balance the need for standardized training with the diverse learning needs of neurodivergent employees? What are some potential challenges and solutions?
2. Discuss the potential impact of poorly designed Learning Management Systems (LMS) on neurodivergent employees. How can companies ensure their LMS is inclusive and effective for all learners?
3. How might traditional performance metrics and assessment methods disadvantage neurodivergent employees? What alternative approaches could be more equitable and effective?
4. Analyze the concept of brain breaks in the workplace. How might implementing them benefit both neurodivergent and neurotypical employees?
5. Reflect on the importance of physical workspace design in supporting neurodivergent employees. How can companies create inclusive environments that cater to diverse sensory needs?
6. How can managers effectively support employees with hidden neurodivergences without compromising privacy or creating stigma?
7. Discuss the potential benefits and challenges of implementing Universal Design for Learning (UDL) principles in corporate training programs.
8. What strategies can organizations use to foster a culture of continuous learning that is inclusive of diverse learning styles and preferences?
9. Reflect on the role of communication in creating an inclusive learning environment. How can managers and HR professionals improve their communication strategies to better support neurodivergent employees?

Accommodations

Are Workplace Accommodations for Neurodivergent Employees Favoritism?

Consider these statements overheard by my client at a typical tech company:

- "Yeah, she gets a cubicle on the quiet side of the floor, but the rest of us have to work in the open-plan area. Must be nice to be the boss's favorite (forced laughter)!"
- "Yeah, he's weird and super intense. He comes into the office when he wants and leaves when he wants."
- "He wears those heavy-metal T-shirts and sweatpants, but management likes him because he's brilliant and gets things done."

Comments such as these reflect unconscious biases that often exist in a workplace dominated by neurotypical values.

So let's talk about the Heavy-Metal T-Shirt and Sweatpants Guy. He was an unmasked neurodivergent (ND) person. Yet the quality of his work made up for the liberties he took with the dress code and work hours. That brilliance is what "won" him the right to create a work situation that was best for him.

Those co-workers might not have realized that Sweatpants Guy had to negotiate these accommodations. He demonstrated a work ethic that earned him the respect of his supervisors, and they knew they had to be flexible with him because they saw that he was an invaluable asset to the company.

Yet these same accommodations may be considered favoritism if anyone else asks for them.

Let's look at the bigger picture.

The Difference Between Reasonable Accommodations and Outright Favoritism

Let's start with an example:

Women in the workplace know all about the guilt (and even shame) that comes with taking time off to tend to sick kids. Women know that they risk the perception that they are less reliable because of this. As a result, many women work twice as hard to make up for it.

Workplace accommodations for women have come a long way in recent decades. That said, unconscious bias and resulting microaggressions still exist. (Olkin et al., 2019)

Now imagine a woman who also has a neurodivergent condition. She's in a spot, isn't she?

We are familiar with and often accommodate a parent's need to leave work early to pick up a sick child from school. How might we react to:

- An autistic programmer who might need to use noise-canceling headphones in an open-plan office?
- An autist who may decline invitations for after-work drinks? (Dubiks, 2018)
- A neurodivergent employee who skips a team-building session because of sensory overload?

The Balance Careers article "Is Displaying Favoritism in the Workplace Illegal?" states, "Favoritism in the workplace is when a person (usually a manager) demonstrates preferential treatment to one person over all the other employees for reasons unrelated to performance." (Lucas, 2020). This definition leaves the matter open for interpretation regarding the needs of neurodivergents in the workplace.

How the Law Supports a Neurodiverse Workplace

Research has proven that a neurodiverse workforce increases productivity and gives businesses a creative cutting edge by harnessing the entire spectrum of human thought processing.

However, one important factor that many people in the neurodiversity movement tend to skip over: the law.

So, what legal requirements exist to encourage neurodiverse workplaces?

For Readers in the United States: What Does the Law Say?

I'm not too fond of complicated legalese. But some things are worth knowing.

Section 503 of the Rehabilitation Act of 1973 states, "The party contracting with the United States shall take affirmative action to employ and advance in employment qualified individuals with disabilities." (US DOL Staff, 2024) This federal law applies to federal contractors and subcontractors. The affirmative action requirement goes beyond mere nondiscrimination, compelling contractors to actively seek and promote the employment of individuals with disabilities.

This law aims to help close the gap between employed and unemployed disabled workers. Businesses subject to Section 503 should have a stated goal of 7 percent of their workforce falling into the "disabled" category and a verified affirmative action system in place to help meet this goal. Compliance with this law is necessary if a company wants to get a contract with the federal government.

The Americans with Disabilities Act (ADA), which is broader and protects all disabled Americans, is not quite so easy to quote. To keep it brief, it basically states that Americans with disabilities have a right to "reasonable accommodations" not only to do their jobs but also to the interview process to get that job and to "enjoy equal benefits and privileges of employment."

But wait a minute...I feel like there is something here that needs to be clarified before we proceed.

Neurodivergent people are not necessarily disabled, right? Neurodivergence isn't a disability. I have said it time and again.

But—and this is a very big *but*—

It cannot be denied that neurodivergent conditions create specific difficulties for those trying to make their way as independent adults in a neurotypical world. This is especially true when trying to hold down fulfilling employment. This is why the protection of the ADA is so vital to the neurodivergent community.

For legal reasons, the ADA defines a disabled person as someone who:

- "Has a physical or mental impairment that substantially limits one or more major life activities;
- "Has a record of such an impairment; or
- "Is regarded as having such an impairment."

Under the law, neurodivergence may be considered a disability because it falls under the category of "mental impairment." Depending on their circumstances, neurodivergent employees are protected by the ADA and have the right to "reasonable accommodations."

Universal Accommodations: Be Compliant with the Law through "Accommodations" for Everyone

I have spoken to many business leaders who balk at implementing a neurodiversity inclusion plan. They immediately see red tape, paperwork, and reworking of their entire HR system. There is an unfortunate misconception that welcoming and accommodating neurodivergent employees is complicated.

I am happy to tell you that this is not true.

There is one easy and unilateral way to ensure your company complies with all the laws protecting neurodivergent workers: Create a company culture (and the policies to support it) where accommodations once reserved for certain individuals are universal. My solution to this dilemma is IDWD™.

The primary goal of neurodiversity at work initiatives is to create a work environment where every employee feels safe, accepted, and supported.

For instance, if you provide noise-canceling headphones for one worker, why not make them available for everyone? This is the essence of universal accommodations. If you will create workspaces that limit sensory stimulation for sensitive individuals, ask yourself if it is possible to extend that option to any employee who may benefit from that kind of workspace.

This being said, if a neurodivergent worker does need to request a specific accommodation, they have a right to do so under the ADA. This requires them to disclose their condition. The employer must authorize the requested accommodation unless it would create unreasonable hardship for the company. In that case, it is recommended that an alternative arrangement be made that both meets the employee's needs and is within the reasonable capabilities of the company.

Most neurodivergent workers choose not to reveal their neurodivergence. This is especially true in the workplace, where stigma, misunderstandings, and prejudice against divergent thinkers are common and have dire consequences. It may only be when problems arise and an employee feels backed into a corner that they decide to reveal their diagnosis and ask for accommodations.

At this point, there may be a conflict between the worker and management. This could lead to allegations of discrimination and potential legal actions.

Complicated situations can be avoided by intentionally creating a company culture that values neurodiversity in both words and actions. Universal "accommodations" are an easy way to avoid red tape, legal complications, and unnecessary paperwork by ensuring your workforce feels supported and empowered.

Creating a company culture where accommodations once reserved for certain individuals are universal is the essence of inclusive design.

Self-Disclosure: Why It's Important for Compliance with the ADA and Section 503

One of the fundamental pillars of the ADA and Section 530 is confidentiality. All workers who disclose their neurodivergent condition to request accommodations or participate in affirmative action hiring programs must trust that their medical information will be held in strict confidence.

There are countless reasons why divergent thinkers may opt never to self-disclose their neurodivergent condition. One is the fear of being called out publicly for their "differences" and held up as an "example" of the company's neurodiversity at work initiatives. For those who have carried the weight of a stigma-laden label around for their entire school lives, the workplace can be an opportunity to leave that baggage behind. Many divergent thinkers prefer to stay in the shadows, mask, and pass as neurotypical to the best of their ability.

When workers refuse to self-disclose their condition, it can create some potential problems. Companies may struggle to meet that 7 percent goal as laid out by Section 503. Without self-disclosure, there is no way to measure the success of neurodiversity at work initiatives. This makes it difficult to monitor and track progress in an organization's diversity, equity, inclusion and accessibility (DEIA) programs.

How can a company promote self-disclosure by neurodivergent workers?

- Have clearly defined policies that respect absolute confidentiality.
- Promote a company culture free of bullying, stigma, or shame surrounding accommodations and neurodivergence.
- Offer accommodations to all through IDWD without the requirement of self-disclosure.
- When onboarding new employees, encourage them to voice their needs early on and educate them about the procedures and policies surrounding voluntary self-disclosure and accommodation requests.
- Appoint a dedicated accommodations officer, allowing employees to voice their needs to someone other than their immediate supervisor or manager.

Why not create a work environment where neurodivergent employees feel safe, supported, and inspired to reveal a very private part of their identity so that they feel safe being their full authentic self? Again, this can be accomplished with IDWD.

Best Practices to Protect the Rights of Neurodivergent Workers

In addition to all the steps I outlined above, some complementary actions can be taken to guarantee compliance with the law while going above and beyond to create a neurodivergent-friendly workplace.

- Conduct an annual internal audit to determine the success of your neurodiversity at work initiatives. Is your business in compliance with its own policies?
- Reach out to state and local advocacy organizations. How can they help you create a more neurodiverse workforce?

- Review for pay gaps. Are your neurodivergent workers earning less than their neurotypical counterparts?
- Create an employee resource group (ERG) for neurodivergent workers and allies to promote workplace inclusion, equality, and advocacy.
- Take advantage of public resources such as Job Accommodation Network (JAN) and Employer Assistance and Resource Network on Disability Inclusion (EARN) when you need assistance or advice on accommodations or legal matters. (AskEARN Editor, 2024; JAN Staff Editors, 2024)

Protecting the Rights of All Workers

Slowly but surely, as our understanding of the human mind evolves, society is learning to leave harmful stereotypes in the past. Understanding is beginning to replace stigma. Empathy is overtaking judgment. However, it is still an imperfect world, and the protections provided by the ADA and Section 503 continue to be necessary to protect the rights of workers, especially those with seemingly invisible disabilities.

Where IDWD and universal accommodations are a reality, the law becomes an afterthought. Legal compliance is a natural consequence of a work environment and company culture organized to respect every employee's unique needs.

> ***Universal 'accommodations' are an easy way to avoid red tape, legal complications, and unnecessary paperwork by ensuring your workforce feels supported and empowered.***

Why Are Accommodations Needed?

There are many ways to be human. Yet without an understanding of neurodevelopmental conditions (McGregor, n.d.), accommodations can be misinterpreted as favoritism. For example, on the surface, wearing comfortable attire and being flexible with work hours can look like preferential treatment.

A thought experiment:

You are about to take a flight for a solo business trip. It's midsummer, and you board your plane after the usual awkward encounter with airport security. You've found your seat, shoved your bag into the overhead, and are sitting in a middle seat, the only one available on check-in. Since people are still boarding, you take out your laptop and get a head start on some work. People are streaming in, loud, hot, annoyed, and confused. The row behind you is occupied by a six-year-old, his baby sister, and their mom.

The six-year-old noisily opens a bag of Cheetos and puts his feet up on the back of your seat. The baby sister wants Cheetos, too, so they fight. The baby cries and is inconsolable. The smell of Cheetos overtakes you as you try to focus on your work. The seats on either side of you have filled up now, and the elbow space is cramped for working.

You hear a flight attendant announce that the flight will be delayed, but they can't say for how long. As the plane sits delayed on the runway, you worry about being late for your meeting. But you can't do anything, so the anxiety builds. Someone starts coughing. You panic quietly but carry on. The plane eventually gets off the runway. You can hear a weird clicking sound and can't figure out where it's coming from. Also, the seat in front of you smells like spilled soda. You have to ignore this, you say to yourself. The baby behind you bursts into tears now and then. You feel sorry for the mom, but at the same time, it hurts your ears.

Would this flight exhaust you?

This airplane analogy is a caricature of the sensory hell that's daily life for an autistic. Possibly, you're thinking, "If I were in this situation, I'd use headphones. I'd ask for a different seat if that were a remote possibility." Your request is reasonable. You need to concentrate, and the environment isn't conducive to it.

For some, abiding by corporate dress codes is a sensory nightmare. Belts, heels, ties, and makeup hurt and irritate. What might be insignificant to neurotypicals can be intense and overwhelming to an autistic, especially if repeated day in and day out.

The scents from co-workers' lunches, the constant office chatter, and the pressure to contribute in meetings are common workplace experiences. However, these can be particularly challenging for neurodivergent individuals. For those on the autism spectrum, there's an acute awareness of how word choice, facial expressions, tone of voice, and difficulty in reading social cues can affect their success. As one of my autistic colleagues shared, "So, I mentally rehearse what I want to say. But then, I'm spoken over, misinterpreted, or worse, ignored."

For neurodivergent people, dealing with these microaggressions while knowing that their ability to make a living depends on how they navigate these situations erodes energy reserves and motivation.

So what can be done? "I would use headphones and ask for a different seat."

It's as simple as that. It's not favoritism. It's a change of scenery so that you can work at your best. In an airplane, you have the autonomy to put on your headphones. You have some freedom to create the kind of space you need. This freedom may not exist in the office.

What autistics need to work at their best is incompatible with the standard office dynamic. Thus, flexibility is vital to harness neurodivergent talent and let it shine. Consider making headphones and seating flexibility a norm for all employees.

Accommodations That Work for Neurodivergents

Repeatedly, autistics in work situations mention the same kinds of accommodations. According to an anonymous autistic blogger for Spectroomz, an online resource for autistics looking for employment, the following accommodations are what helped them (Blanchard, 2022; Marmorstein, n.d.):

- A clearly defined scope of work.
- Solid task management—for example, a ticketing management hub. (Spacey, 2017) However, even email would work in a pinch. This prevents misunderstandings that might occur when only verbal instructions are given.
- Predictable social interactions that an autistic employee can mentally prepare for.
- Limited need to mask. (Oswald, 2020)
- Clearly defined performance metrics.
- Openness to sensory interventions such as noise-canceling headphones or a quiet room to work in.
- Flexible work hours.
- Flexible work location such as partial work-from-home arrangements. Even a private space will work.
- Consideration for individual communication preferences. For example, communicate in writing or detailed instructions.

Asking for these accommodations should be as risk-free as asking to change seats on a plane.

How to Reduce the Perception of Favoritism

In the workplace, employees from underrepresented backgrounds frequently encounter situations where they feel their presence is viewed as disruptive or inconvenient. This discomfort often prevents them from requesting necessary accommodations, fearing it will reinforce negative perceptions. To create a more inclusive environment and eliminate perceived favoritism, employers can implement the following strategies:

Create awareness of the value of cognitive diversity in the organization. Most people's understanding of neurodiversity comes from how autistic characters are portrayed in the media.

Corporate values must foster an environment where all employees can thrive. Forward-thinking organizations with a positive attitude toward cognitive diversity and mental health are key to successful initiatives. The C-suite mindset trickles down to employees. A results-only or profit-only attitude shapes organizational culture. A culture driven by the numbers without regard to employee wellness will fail the inclusivity test.

Emphasize the value of team success (as opposed to individual achievements). Think of a team as the ragtag assembly of superheroes who, individually, can't get much done but all bring something to the party to save the world. Every superhero team has a singular focus on one goal, not on self-gain. Even the weirdest hero brings something valuable to the table. This is a change from the workplace idea of teamwork, where each person tries to work with others for a vague common goal, but self-gain is still top of mind. Self-serving behavior in a team creates an Us versus Them dynamic. This makes conditions ripe for the accusation of favoritism.

Foster respect for neurodivergents by celebrating strengths and supporting areas that need improvement. Encourage curiosity over judgment and dismissal of unconventional ideas.

Hold true to IDWD philosophy and create clear, easily accessible policies for workplace accommodations for neurodivergent employees. Ad hoc accommodations are generally not well received.

To Sum Up, Is it Favoritism?

No, it isn't. If we say, "Everybody is unique" and "Just be yourself," we can't then say, "No, not like that!" With uniqueness comes different strengths. Accommodations for unique needs are appropriate and necessary to allow those strengths to shine. Those accommodations are not one-size-fits-all. The beauty of an inclusive philosophy is that employers, neurotypical employees, and neurodivergent employees all benefit.

With uniqueness comes different strengths. Accommodations for unique needs are appropriate and necessary to allow those strengths to shine.

Free from the "Culture of Normal"

For divergent thinkers, the pandemic provided an unexpected and unprecedented opportunity to thrive. In response to the nationwide shutdown in 2020, radical changes were implemented on campuses and in the workplace across all sectors of the economy. With a sigh of relief, neurodivergent (ND) students and employees experienced the benefits of finally having their needs accommodated.

They no longer had to try to fit a mold that often caused them anxiety and stress and reduced their productivity. This mold was the Culture of Normal.

The Culture of Normal in many workplaces often conflicts with how neurodivergent brains function. This mismatch can lead to reduced productivity and increased stress for neurodivergent employees. Common workplace features that can be challenging include:

- Open office environments with high levels of sensory input.
- Noisy communal areas and cafeterias.
- Poor acoustics in classrooms or conference rooms.

These environments can cause sensory overload, which is often particularly exhausting and stressful for neurodivergent individuals. By recognizing and addressing these challenges, companies can create more inclusive workspaces that allow neurodivergent employees to thrive and contribute their unique strengths.

It's no secret that the pandemic has had devastating consequences. Scrolling the internet for only a few seconds can reveal all the dooming statistics of the coronavirus outbreak and the global shutdown of life as we knew it.

Yet the pandemic showed us that humans have an incredible ability to adapt to extreme circumstances. From moving to a virtual workspace to adapting various safety strategies, society has proven its ability to make accommodations when necessary. Many of these accommodations are ones that neurodivergent folks have been asking for throughout the years. Teachers or employers rarely felt these accommodations were fair or appropriate, let alone possible.

However, the pandemic showed us the opposite: Accommodations *are* fair, and *everyone* benefits from the flexibility these necessary changes allow. Quarantine accommodations were fundamental because we had no other options. Contrary to what the decision-makers believed, they were possible.

Things we were told were impossible were imperative to continue doing business. One of the primary pandemic-induced accommodations, working from home, was overwhelmingly helpful for neurodivergent thinkers.

Going Virtual: Sensory Relief for Neurodivergent Students and Workers

For ND individuals, the most significant impact of the pandemic was how they attended school or work. Moving to a virtual environment was an accommodation that was emotionally difficult for a lot of people, but many ND students and workers thrived.

Going virtual through remote learning or workspaces allows the neurodivergent person to do their work in a comfortable environment. While change and adaptability can be extremely difficult for ND people, certain aspects of the move proved helpful.

Sensory Overload

Sensory environments can more easily be controlled at home. At school or work, background noise, bright lights, and chatter are next to inevitable. What can be even more frustrating is that these stimuli cannot be controlled.

However, in a home environment, it is easier for ND individuals to create a space that suits their personal needs. For example, they can have dimmer lights or a quiet study space.

Social Interaction

There is a certain subsection of ND thinkers who find social interaction challenging. In a virtual space, neurodivergent folks are much more in control when they take breaks, are called to speak, and choose to interact with their peers. Of course, it's not wise to become completely isolated, but regaining a sense of independence and personal power in social situations can make a world of difference for divergent learners.

Turning one's camera on or off as desired allows those who struggle with eye contact and body language to do what's most comfortable. For those needing to monitor their facial expressions and body language constantly, it can be onerous to do so while concentrating in a school hall lecture or a workplace meeting. Virtual spaces allow ND thinkers to take breaks from social self-monitoring.

What Is "Social Self-Monitoring," and Why Is It Necessary?

Stimming is a common form of self-expression attributed to the autistic community. But did you know that we all stim, neurotypical and neurodiverse alike? We all use repetitive behaviors to calm ourselves. For some of us, it's shaking our leg. For others, it's biting our fingernails or twirling our hair.

Stigma still exists around stimming, unfortunately, and ND people often feel judged if they show these behaviors in public. Most of us can pick up social cues to let us know when our behavior is disruptive or annoying, but for people with autism, picking up social cues and being able to stop is a challenge, if not impossible.

Going remote creates a private space and removes physical barriers to stimming. (There's more about stimming later in this chapter.)

Physical Comfort

Other behaviors may not be socially appropriate in the school or work environment but are natural and soothing for an ND thinker. These relate to the person's physical comfort and ability to focus.

A university student, for example, may choose to pace around while listening to a lecture. This self-stimulating behavior is found calming by many on the autistic spectrum. Pacing around while listening to a lecture would be quite impossible, or at the very least difficult, in a classroom.

Working remotely also allows divergent thinkers to choose how and where they sit or stand to work. Standard desks can feel like a cage to an ND person. Having the freedom to decide how to work allows a neurodivergent student or worker a better range of motion and the freedom to meet their physical needs.

Focus and Attention

Finally, those with attention difficulties can take short brain breaks in a virtual workspace or classroom without fearing judgment or unpleasant consequences. For those with ADHD, these breaks can include leaving their workspace altogether if needed. Ultimately, this space to rest the brain and refocus helps some ND folks be more productive.

On the flip side, autistic people, or those with ADHD, often hyperfocus on projects. When this happens, they keep going for hours, sometimes without even stopping to sleep. Breaking this focus is disruptive to their flow and productivity. Yet in most university settings or corporate spaces, it's impossible to hyperfocus for twenty consecutive hours.

Remote learning and virtual workspaces are the perfect accommodations for ND students and workers who face challenges with the Culture of Normal regarding their individual ways of focusing.

A Silver Lining for Neurodivergent Thinkers

The pandemic forced everyone to shift focus and reassess their priorities. We have seen the development of greater empathy for humankind and human differences. As the world changed, our perspective changed.

As we all wrestled with reorganizing our lives, even the most neurotypical person needed certain accommodations.

Many of us needed extended deadlines or flexibility in school or work attendance. Considering the circumstances, university professors and workplace supervisors were more willing than ever to allow accommodations that supported people's success.

The unprecedented challenges of the pandemic led business and academic leaders to understand that those accommodations once thought unfair, inappropriate, or impossible *are indeed feasible.* Many of those quarantine-induced accommodations that benefit neurodivergent thinkers have become normalized.

Post-pandemic, it may be more socially acceptable to ask for the help that we need. There's less stigma associated with being different. With the new "normal" of creative accommodations, we are all more successful in reaching our goals, whether at the university level or in the corporate space.

When everyone realizes that accommodations bring out the best in us, it reduces the stigma and labeling that often result when they are requested exclusively by "outed" neurodivergent individuals.

A New Post-Pandemic Reality for the Neurodivergent Community

The pandemic forced us to overcome the barrier of "It's always been done this way" when it came to accommodations.

In the post-pandemic hybrid approach that many universities and corporations have implemented, neurodivergent thinkers will benefit from the option of learning or working from home or in person. Such flexibility allows the neurodivergent community to regain control and agency in their coursework and careers.

Overall, the pandemic has offered an opportunity for all of us to learn. It's shown us that we can create a world where all types of neurodivergence are welcome and accommodated. The world has proven its incredible ability to adapt. The time is now to create a future that is inclusive to all.

> ***The world has proven its incredible ability to adapt.***
> ***The time is now to create a future that is inclusive to all.***

How Mind Mapping Can Help You Connect with Neurodivergent Employees

Managing a neurodiverse workforce has its challenges, but it's also an opportunity to use some of the most important skills a manager can develop: listening, empathizing, and driving positive change for employees.

For managers who have a neurodivergent worker reporting to them, learning and implementing mind-mapping techniques with that employee could help put them on the path to better productivity.

Suzanne, a neurodivergent worker on the autism spectrum, shared how mapping out critical issues with one of her managers helped her immensely, both personally and professionally. (Clark, 2020)

"As I began struggling to cope with aspects of the job (mostly due to sensory issues), the two managers tried implementing strategies which (although well intentioned!) did nothing to empower me and only made me feel even more of a problem and a failure," she explained. "The assistant manager intervened and one day suggested going to the conference room with a sheet of flip chart paper and some colored pens. We spent an afternoon creating a mind map of what I found difficult and shared ideas around solutions. As a visual person, this was perfect for me."

By working with Suzanne and mapping out problems and solutions, the assistant manager and her other managers became aware of things that were creating stumbling blocks for her. They then worked with her to adapt her schedule and work environment so that she could be much more effective at her job.

Suzanne noted that the assistant manager "treated me like the highly skilled, intelligent, professional person I am. He trusted me to get on with my job without micromanaging me by being positive, creative, and pragmatic. This was a perfect example of good management."

Mind mapping can help neurodivergent employees express themselves clearly to managers. For example, a person on the autism spectrum may have trouble verbalizing how they feel yet have no problem expressing themselves in writing. A collaborative mapping session where the employee can express their thoughts on a whiteboard can create a communication bridge. The ROI is a greater understanding of their needs so that adjustments allow them to perform at their best.

Mind mapping can be particularly beneficial for neurodivergent employees who may struggle with overwhelm when faced with complex problems. By visually breaking down issues into smaller, interconnected components, mind mapping helps to:

- **Identify specific stumbling blocks:** The process of creating a mind map allows employees to isolate individual challenges that may be contributing to a larger problem.
- **Reduce overwhelm:** By separating a seemingly insurmountable issue into smaller, manageable parts, employees can focus on addressing one aspect at a time.
- **Prioritize concerns:** The visual nature of mind maps makes it easier to recognize which issues are most pressing or have the greatest impact.
- **Brainstorm solutions:** Once specific challenges are identified, employees and managers can use the mind map to brainstorm potential accommodations or solutions for each issue.
- **Plan implementation:** The mind map can serve as a road map for implementing accommodations, allowing the employee and manager to track progress and adjust strategies as needed.

By using mind mapping in this way, managers can help neurodivergent employees move from a state of general overwhelm to a focused, actionable plan for addressing workplace challenges and implementing effective accommodations.

For employees with dyslexia, a whiteboard mind-mapping session that utilizes distinct colors and shapes can help managers communicate concepts and spur creative solutions. (DiversityQ Writer, 2019)

Managers can also use mind mapping to help employees—both neurodivergent and neurotypical—set goals and outline the achievable steps to reach those goals. Mind mapping enables leaders "to align a team around key objectives, to delegate tasks and to define timelines," according to a *Training Industry* article. "Since mind mapping mimics how the brain works in organizing and understanding information, it is effective in cultivating individual accountability and collective understanding." (Grosskopf, 2019)

For a how-to primer on mind mapping, see chapter 9.

Sensory Rooms—Facilitating Neurodivergent-Friendly Workplaces

Before we get into the details of sensory rooms, it helps to understand why they were invented in the first place. Children on the autistic spectrum have often been described as engaging in repetitive actions, such as hand flapping, hair twirling, and skin picking, often referred to as "stims." The reasons for this behavior were unclear, and it was frowned upon for a long time. As a result, caregivers and clinicians sought to prevent it. Now, though, the benefits of stimming are known and more accepted among professionals.

To facilitate the beneficial side of stimming, schools and care centers have begun to create sensory rooms to help kids of all neurotypes express their sensory needs safely, without judgment and/or harming themselves.

What Is Stimming?

What is stimming? According to *Medical News Today,* stimming is a "self-stimulatory behavior that normally involves repetitive body movements or repetitive movement of objects."

Researchers associate stimming with conditions such as autism, ADHD, and sensory processing disorder. Still, the fact is that people outside of these groups stim as well. How so? Nail biting, knee bouncing, clicking your pen, twirling your hair, or chewing your pencil are all commonplace and examples of stimming.

If stimming is so common and spans all neurotypes, why are we discussing it? In the case of neurodivergent individuals, stims can be particularly noticeable and distracting to themselves or observers. In some cases, these behaviors can also physically harm the individual and thus present a danger.

Much discussion has taken place around why these habits develop. A nail biter will tell you that they think they do so because it does something to calm them or alleviate some other discomfort in a situation. Could this be a clue to understanding the more "unusual" stims in neurodivergent people?

Why do neurodivergent people stim? While stimming in neurotypical people is often anxiety-related, in neurodivergent people, it can have a few other sources as well. Stimming helps regulate stress, anxiety, boredom, fear, sensory overload, happiness, and joy!

Stims can either provide stimulation for sensory-seeking individuals or dampen stimulation for the sensory-overloaded. (Delacato, 1974)"Common stims for people with autism include hand flapping, rocking, flicking or snapping fingers, bouncing or jumping, pacing, head banging, spinning objects, and repeating words."

Researchers have identified various stims that fall into several broad sensory-system-related categories illustrated in the chart below.

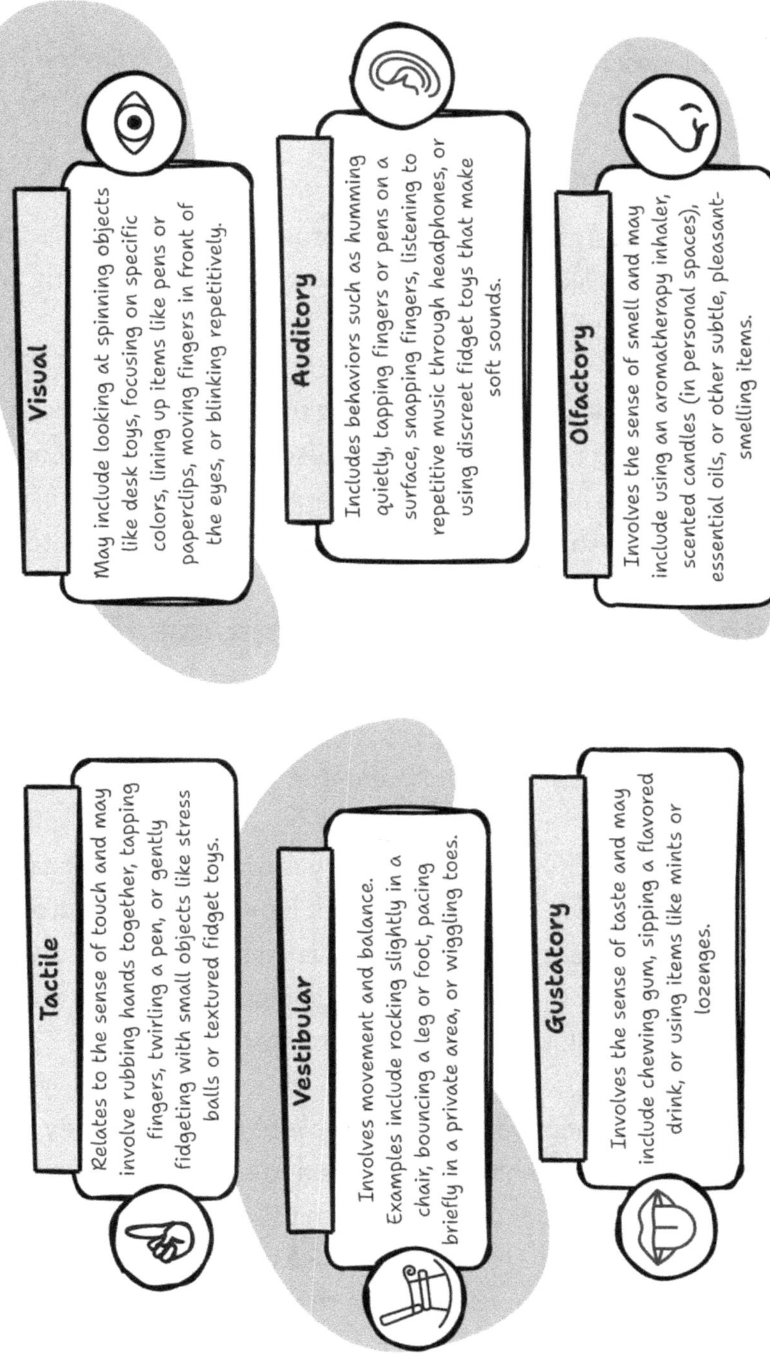
SENSORY STIMMING
Visual
May include looking at spinning objects like desk toys, focusing on specific colors, lining up items like pens or paperclips, moving fingers in front of the eyes, or blinking repetitively.
Auditory
Includes behaviors such as humming quietly, tapping fingers or pens on a surface, snapping fingers, listening to repetitive music through headphones, or using discreet fidget toys that make soft sounds.
Olfactory
Involves the sense of smell and may include using an aromatherapy inhaler, scented candles (in personal spaces), essential oils, or other subtle, pleasant-smelling items.
Tactile
Relates to the sense of touch and may involve rubbing hands together, tapping fingers, twirling a pen, or gently fidgeting with small objects like stress balls or textured fidget toys.
Vestibular
Involves movement and balance. Examples include rocking slightly in a chair, bouncing a leg or foot, pacing briefly in a private area, or wiggling toes.
Gustatory
Involves the sense of taste and may include chewing gum, sipping a flavored drink, or using items like mints or lozenges.
*This list of examples is not all inclusive

Suppressing Stimming?

Most nail biters will describe how they've been discouraged from the habit, often by force or other painful measures, with little regard for addressing the cause of the behavior.

Sadly, for many neurodivergents, the same approach has been applied to their stimming. So while things like nail biting, skin picking, and hair pulling are damaging, banning the behavior is not beneficial.

These behaviors help alleviate some issues that the person is experiencing in their environment. Suppressing harmless stims because they appear odd or unusual to neurotypical colleagues is harmful to neurodivergent people. Suppressing stimming, a basic need of many autistic individuals, can lead to detrimental outcomes.

Sensory Rooms Accommodate Stimming in a Healthy Way

As we've seen, stimming is a response to a sensory need. Hundreds of stim toys and objects exist for children, including fidget toys, chewable jewelry, and more. Weighted blankets also provide a sensory stimulus, and they are increasing in popularity.

The dedicated sensory spaces known as sensory rooms play a crucial role in addressing the sensory needs of neurodivergent individuals. They provide a safe and comfortable environment where children can escape when they feel the need to stim, thereby preventing the use of harmful coping mechanisms such as head banging, skin picking, or lashing out physically to name a few.

Sensory rooms for children can range from simple to elaborate. They might be quiet rooms with creature comforts known to soothe and help regulate the senses. They are also designed to accommodate a wide range of sensory needs in one space. The facilities in these rooms are related to the sensory types mentioned above and contain items and amenities that can address these.

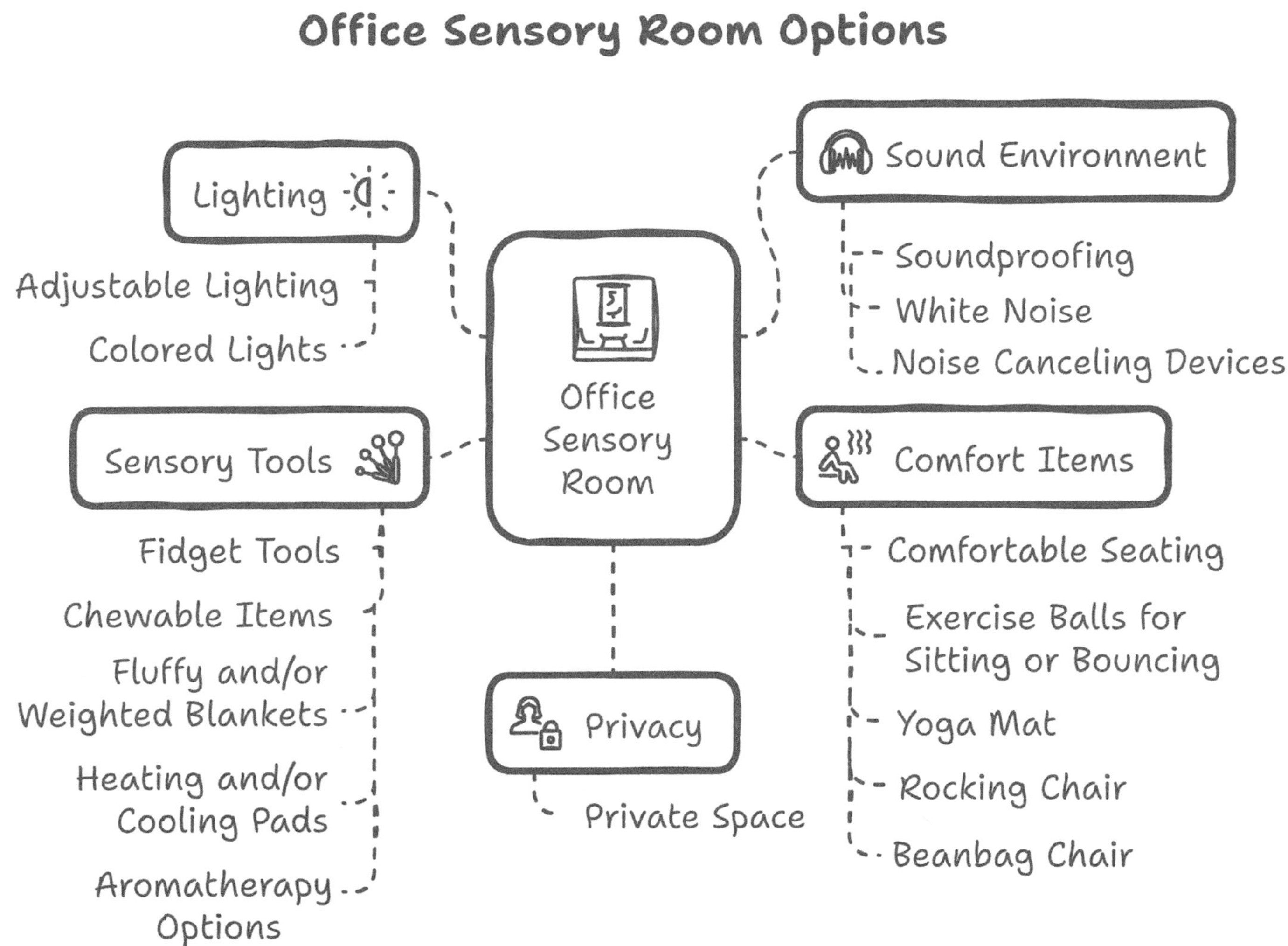
Office Sensory Room Options
Lighting
Adjustable Lighting
Colored Lights
Sensory Tools
Fidget Tools
Chewable Items
Fluffy and/or Weighted Blankets
Heating and/or Cooling Pads
Aromatherapy Options
Office Sensory Room
Privacy
Private Space
Sound Environment
Soundproofing
White Noise
Noise Canceling Devices
Comfort Items
Comfortable Seating
Exercise Balls for Sitting or Bouncing
Yoga Mat
Rocking Chair
Beanbag Chair

Children who stim grow up to be adults who need to stim (and become stressed when putting their energy into masking it).

Sensory needs do not go away for a neurodivergent adult. In fact, sensory stress may accumulate for those who are employed and actively trying to fit in to society unnoticed! This is part of the reason so many neurodivergent are unemployed, are underemployed, or can't seem to stick with a job. Sensory rooms are, thus, not just for kids. Adults can benefit, too. This situation is entirely addressable by making an effort to meet a very human need.

How to Set Up a Sensory Room

An autistic woman in the workplace describes her plan for a sensory room for adults.

"I worked remotely and only had to go into the office once a week. I will say that the lighting was so bright that I felt uncomfortable and exhausted by the end of the day. Normally, I can cope with a little bit of bright light, if only for eight hours a week. One day, when I had a particularly emotional issue on my mind, the lights and open-plan setting just seemed worse. I couldn't think or breathe properly or concentrate on my work, and my heart rate was elevated. I remembered that this office had private work rooms, which one could book for private teleconferences or to focus on work. I asked my team lead if I could use one of them. He agreed. I locked the door and sat in that darkened room, alone, on the velvety couch, got into a child's pose, and focused on my breathing. I calmed down after about ten minutes and could get back to work. The brightness of the office lights seemed less bothersome after that."

This experience reveals a few things. First, she was sensitive to lighting and noise. Most of the time, she could cope with these inputs. Still, one additional stressor, a personal problem, caused her to lose her ability to manage the sensory inputs. The solution was to be alone in a dark room where she did what was needed to self-regulate. She is hypersensitive to light and sound; thus, a sensory room would be a space where she can control the lighting and the audio or noise levels. She also talks about lying in a child's pose to calm her down. This suggested vestibular sensory needs.

A good sensory room would allow a person to control the environment concerning the different sensory functions.

Practically, a sensory room in a workplace can include the following features:

- A private room or set of spaces with some level of privacy enabled.
- Ability to control the lighting using dimmers, lampshades, or colored lights.
- Soundproofing and the ability to play white noise or other sounds that soothe. A place where the person can use their own noise-canceling devices.
- A set of mild fragrances to sniff if needed. Aromatherapy.
- Gummy candies or other kinds of safe, chewable items.
- A place to sit or lie down. A couch with a neutral-textured surface.
- Fluffy blankets.
- Weighted blankets/cushions.
- A yoga mat on the floor for those who prefer to sit or lie on the ground.
- As a bonus, rocking seating or a swing chair or hammock chair fastened to the ceiling for vestibular sensory seekers.
- Exercise balls to sit on or bounce on.
- A selection of fidget toys and other interesting textural items to choose from.
- Electric hot pads or cooling pads.
- Beanbag chairs.

As you can see, a workspace sensory room need not be an expensive or complicated project. Whether you are neurotypical or neurodivergent, the appeal of having such a space available is apparent. Fair usage policies should be set up to manage access and maintenance and to prevent abuse. Managing those factors will be much easier if the workplace culture accepts neurodiversity-inclusivity.

Humans have unique needs. Meeting those needs instead of ignoring them has many benefits. With the increased focus on employee mental wellness, such a space would enhance the employee experience. This simple idea, a dedicated, safe, comfortable escape room, can be just what's needed to bring out the best in employees.

Help Employees Manage Their Cognitive Differences

Create an environment where everyone is given the benefit of the doubt.

One of my clients told me he had an engineer who always wore headphones to team meetings. My client would notice, and one day, he called him out in front of everyone, asking why he was listening to music in the meeting. The engineer explained that he wasn't listening to music; the headphones helped block out the background noise so he could hear my client better.

I tell this story often when I speak on podcasts or when I write articles because it is a perfect example of the struggles neurodivergent people face in the workplace. This engineer's needs differed from those of other people. When people go against what is considered the norm, it is often seen as rudeness or antisocial behavior.

In response to this story, Rabbi Yonason Goldson remarked that an ethical leader wouldn't call someone out in front of people. Even if it was someone being rude, the conversation should've happened in private. I agree; all it would've taken in this situation was for my client to talk to the engineer privately and ask why they were wearing headphones.

Giving people the benefit of the doubt and asking polite questions goes a long way toward creating an understanding work environment.

Work environments bring together people of all different backgrounds and needs. Giving people the benefit of the doubt and asking polite questions goes a long way toward creating an understanding work environment.

Encourage Self-Advocacy

People with neurocognitive differences may feel intimidated about speaking up about things that affect them. Provide a safe way for all employees to voice concerns and address issues effectively, ensuring your organization runs smoothly.

Now, more than ever, businesses are embracing innovation and flexibility to meet the needs of their workforce. If the COVID pandemic taught us anything, it's that with a bit of creativity, solutions can be found for even the most insurmountable obstacles. Since early 2020, nearly every business has had to make accommodations for their workforce of one kind or another to keep their "doors open" and ride out the instability and uncertainty that defined that year and a half.

We are now at a historic moment when business as usual is being reexamined. Recruitment and hiring practices, onboarding, and even worker evaluations are under the microscope. There is a sudden collective questioning of how we can do things better across the entire business community.

We are now at a historic moment when business as usual is being reexamined.

When it comes to the neurodivergent community in the workforce, there has never been a more opportune moment to advocate for meaningful accommodations. Managers and executives are more receptive than ever to implementing the changes necessary to meet their workers' needs and increase productivity.

When it comes to helping workers manage their cognitive differences in the workplace, it boils down to the ability to listen to each individual, provide reasonable accommodations, and empower neurodivergent workers to help themselves.

I had a conversation with Ken Blackwell on his *Insight at Work* podcast. We touched on this subject a lot, but Ken said something that stuck with me that day. He said that we need to give managers and leaders permission not to have all the answers and not expect them to know everything when giving direction. This is one of the most accurate statements I have ever heard, especially regarding creating workplace accommodations for workers with cognitive differences.

So what can the leaders in the workplace do to support the neurodivergent thinkers on their teams?

Promote Communication and Active Listening in the Neurodiverse Workplace

The single most important factor in helping neurodivergent workers help themselves is having a workplace culture that values open communication with leaders who are skilled in active listening. This way, when you see a worker who is tripped up by OCD, dyslexia, or some other cognitive difference, you can have productive conversations that lead to collaborative solutions.

> ***The single most important factor in helping neurodivergent workers help themselves is having a workplace culture that values open communication with leaders who are skilled in active listening.***

Ask the right questions. What obstacles does the worker perceive in the workplace? Are they overwhelmed by the physical environment and sensory stimulation? Do they struggle with irregular schedules or strict deadlines? What possible solutions do they suggest? The best person to provide suggestions for viable solutions is the struggling employee!

Several years ago, I consulted at a middle school to support teachers working with neurodivergent learners. Most of these "different learners," also called "students with learning disabilities," struggled to succeed with traditional teaching practices. At the time, in addition to training and coaching, I offered my clients the option of having me work one-on-one with a student to do a full assessment and then make recommendations. That full assessment included going through their school records from kindergarten through the present day and interviewing all their teachers and the student himself. The student I evaluated was struggling in all his classes. In his frustration, he acted out, disrupting the learning process for everyone in the room.

In the one-on-one interview with this kid, I asked him to tell me what he would do differently if he were the teacher. What he said left me gobsmacked. He said, "I would draw pictures on the board."

I responded, "What kind of pictures?"

He went on to explain, "I love science. In class yesterday, Mrs. Smith was teaching about water systems. She was talking about the hydrosphere and salt water and oceans and all that. But she was talking and writing notes on the board to take down in our notebooks. If I were teaching it, I would draw pictures. When I see pictures about what the teacher is teaching, I remember it better."

Jimmy's response was so simple.

Nowadays, every teacher has learned the importance of using visuals when teaching lessons in the classroom. But sadly, most publishing companies don't include enough visuals in eighth-grade curriculums and teacher lesson plans. Even if they do, some teachers teach according to their own learning preferences. If they learn best with linear notes and verbal lectures, they might not even consider that students need diagrams, flowcharts, or visuals.

I shared what Jimmy told me with his team. It was an aha moment for everyone in the room. Again, this student's behaviors were so disruptive that the team was at a loss for what to do to engage him in learning.

One month later, I returned to sit with the team. When I asked how Jimmy was doing, every teacher shared that his behavior had improved 100 percent. They said it was like he wasn't even the same kid. I asked what they thought had changed. Every one of them explained that they started including diagrams and visuals with their lectures, and that's all that was needed.

Now, the pictures helped Jimmy. But another piece of this solution might be that someone finally asked him what he needed, listened to what he said, and then took action to ensure his needs were respected and met.

This concept is no different in the workplace: If an employee is struggling, ask them their perception of the issue and what can be done to support them. I've learned throughout my career that there's very little difference between what a kindergartner needs, what a tenth grader needs, and what an adult needs to be a successful learner.

When it comes to accommodating cognitive differences, there is no one-size-fits-all template. This is true even when it comes to accommodating workers who have specific diagnoses such as ADHD or dyslexia. Most neurodivergent adults have learned, through life experience, what they need to accomplish their goals and get their jobs done.

Managers and leaders will benefit from training that promotes active listening skills and positive communication techniques. This allows true collaboration between management and workers to design individualized solutions.

Dedicate the Time Necessary to Design Effective Accommodations for Divergent Thinkers

Even though solutions should be tailored to the individual, a lot of time and productivity can be lost if you improvise accommodations for each neurodivergent employee. If you want to allow your workers to manage their own cognitive differences, your organization should incorporate IDWD to create structural accommodations that support neurodiversity in the workplace in general. The beauty of this is that those same accommodations benefit all employees. Having these in place will save managers a lot of time and energy.

If you have one worker overstimulated by excessive noise, you could allow that person to use noise-canceling headphones judgment-free! That is undoubtedly a great start. If it is within the realm of possibility, you could also designate an area of the workspace that is "noise-free." If finances allow, make noise-canceling headphones freely available for any worker needing them. You may be surprised at how many employees take advantage of simple accommodations made available to all. The ROI is increased productivity, innovation, and problem solving.

Forward-thinking organizations must invest the time necessary to design meaningful accommodations for divergent thinkers in their workplace. Research on companies making this investment verifies the payoff.

Forward-thinking organizations must invest the time necessary to design meaningful accommodations for divergent thinkers in their workplace.

Remember to ask: "How can we support everybody on the team?"

This approach will save you a lot of extra work in the long run while benefiting every member of a neurodiverse workforce.

Trust in the neurodivergent workers' capabilities.

Your neurodivergent employees got their jobs for a reason. I'm willing to bet they are good at what they were hired to do. The reality is that they often get into trouble for things they were not hired to do or are not good at!

When it becomes evident that a worker's cognitive difference is interfering with their ability to do their job, the team leader might proactively engage the employee using positive communication and active listening strategies. Approach the conversation with a gifts-mindset as opposed to a deficit mindset. A hard-line, critical, authoritarian approach will likely provoke a negative response. Criticism, put-downs, and perceived failure are the story of a neurodivergent's life. It's a lose-lose approach.

When the appropriate accommodations have been identified and implemented, it's time to step back and leave that person alone. Let them do their job.

When divergent thinkers in a neurodiverse workplace can count on empathetic management and supportive accommodations, they will impress you with a dramatically improved performance. The idea is to give support and then back away. Eventually, your employees will adapt to the different processes designed for their benefit, allowing them independence and autonomy to get their job done.

What it boils down to is management's need to be human.

Be flexible. Take the time to build relationships, ask the right questions, and set your assumptions aside. As a manager, you don't have to have all the answers. As Ken said in that podcast interview, "It is as simple as listening to your employees and finding solutions from a place of co-creation."

When workers feel seen and heard, they do their job better.

Chapter Eight Reflection Questions

1. How might the perception of workplace accommodations as favoritism impact the overall company culture? What strategies can be implemented to address this misconception?
2. Analyze the concept of universal accommodations as presented in the chapter. How might implementing this approach benefit both neurodivergent and neurotypical employees?
3. How can organizations balance the need for standardized processes with the diverse needs of neurodivergent employees? What potential challenges might arise, and how can they be addressed?
4. Discuss the role of self-disclosure in accommodating neurodivergent employees. What strategies can companies use to create an environment where employees feel comfortable disclosing their needs?
5. How might the use of mind-mapping techniques benefit both managers and neurodivergent employees in communication and problem-solving? Provide specific examples based on the chapter's content.
6. Reflect on the concept of sensory rooms in the workplace. How might implementing such spaces impact employee well-being and productivity for both neurodivergent and neurotypical individuals?
7. Analyze the importance of active listening and open communication in managing a neurodiverse workforce. How can managers develop these skills to better support their teams?
8. How can organizations strike a balance between providing necessary accommodations for neurodivergent employees and maintaining a sense of fairness and equality among all team members?
9. Discuss the potential long-term benefits of investing time and resources into designing effective accommodations for neurodivergent employees. How might this approach impact company culture, innovation, and overall success?

Finding Your Voice: A Guide to Self-Advocacy for Neurodivergent Professionals

This chapter is for employees. The target audience is neurodivergent employees; however, what is in this space supports all employees. Every time I deliver a keynote or training on neurodiversity in the workplace, I find myself in a conversation about self-advocacy afterward. Inevitably, someone asks me how to advocate for themselves.

It's a topic that's not widely discussed, but it's crucial for employees to understand how they can advocate for themselves without fear of getting fired. This article aims to empower individuals to take control of their work environment, feel confident, and succeed.

More companies are recognizing the unique strengths of neurodivergent employees like you. These employers know that the talent you bring to the table is invaluable. Effective leaders invite you to help them understand what you need. Awareness is growing, and with it comes the normalization of workplace accommodations that let you perform at your best. When you thrive, the company benefits, too.

"Effective leaders invite you to help them understand what you need."

These accommodations are usually simple to set up. This guide focuses on the challenges you might face and how you can address them. Remember, everyone is unique, so there's no one-size-fits-all list. However, some common themes have emerged from studies and personal stories from neurodivergent people.

Empowering Self-Advocacy: Building Confidence and Overcoming Imposter Syndrome

After publishing an article on self-advocacy for neurodivergent professionals, I received a thought-provoking comment that resonated deeply with me. A reader shared:

"I like that this article has practical suggestions. But speaking for myself, self-advocacy is an emotionally and mentally difficult thing to do. Many autists, especially those who are trying to mask in order to work, suffer from a high degree of imposter syndrome, making self-advocacy emotionally fraught. If you have some suggestions about overcoming this self-doubt—about how to work up the strength and boldness to speak up for ourselves—that would be really useful to the community."

This candid feedback struck a chord. It highlighted a crucial aspect of self-advocacy that I hadn't fully explored: the emotional hurdles many neurodivergent individuals face when attempting to speak up for themselves in the workplace.

Reframing old negative patterns of thinking was the most effective way to help myself.

Recognizing the importance of this issue, I delved deeper into research and consulted with neurodivergent professionals across various industries. From my decades-long work of overcoming these same obstacles, I have learned that reframing old negative patterns of thinking was the most effective way to help myself. So focusing on verbal scripts that address the underlying emotional challenges, particularly imposter syndrome, makes sense to me.

In this section, we'll look at ways to reframe negative thoughts, build confidence gradually, and develop the mental resilience needed for effective self-advocacy. Whether you're new to self-advocacy or looking to enhance your existing skills, you'll find practical approaches to help you overcome self-doubt and speak up confidently.

Remember, self-advocacy is not just about what you say—it's about believing in your inherent worth and the value you bring to your workplace. Let's begin this journey of empowerment together.

Self-advocacy is not just about what you say—it's about believing in your inherent worth and the value you bring to your workplace.

Reframing Negative Thoughts

- **Recognize your unique strengths:** Instead of thinking, "I don't belong here," try, "My unique perspective adds value to this workplace."
- **Challenge self-doubt:** Replace "I'm not good enough to ask for accommodations" with "I deserve support to perform at my best, just like everyone else."
- **Embrace your neurodiversity:** Rather than thinking, "I'm different, and that's bad," think, "My neurodivergent traits offer valuable insights and abilities."

Building Confidence for Self-Advocacy

- **Start small:** Begin by advocating for minor needs before tackling larger issues. This can help build confidence gradually.
- **Practice with trusted allies:** Role-play self-advocacy scenarios with friends or family to gain comfort and confidence. Role-playing what to say and how to say it with a trusted friend was incredibly effective for me.
- **Document your achievements**: Keep a journal of your successes and positive feedback. Refer to this when self-doubt creeps in. I kept a "feel-good file," and every time I received a thank-you, positive feedback, or a validation of my worth, I added it to the folder. Reading through it could make me smile on my most challenging days.
- **Educate yourself:** Learn about your rights and the specific accommodations that could benefit you. Knowledge can be empowering.
- **Join support groups:** Connect with other neurodivergent individuals to share experiences and strategies for self-advocacy. If your company has an employee resource group (ERG), consider joining it.

Verbal Scripts

When requesting accommodations, you might say something like, "I've identified some strategies that could help me perform even better in my role. Could we discuss implementing these?"

When you're facing self-doubt, change your self-talk to this: "I remind myself that my unique perspective is valuable, and advocating for my needs benefits both me and the organization."

Repeat this affirmation when preparing for a self-advocacy conversation: "I have important insights to share. My voice deserves to be heard, and this conversation is an opportunity for positive change."

Remember, self-advocacy is a skill that can be developed over time. It's okay to start small and gradually build up to more challenging situations. The key is to recognize your worth and the value you bring to your workplace.

Document your achievements: Keep a journal of your successes and positive feedback.

Common Challenges and Practical Solutions

Problem: Executive Dysfunction

"Executive dysfunction is a term used to describe the range of cognitive, behavioral, and emotional difficulties that often occur as a result of another disorder or a traumatic brain injury. Individuals with executive dysfunction struggle with planning, problem solving, organization, and time management." (Rodden, 2021)

Executive functioning disorder can present itself in various ways in the workplace, affecting an individual's ability to plan, organize, and complete tasks effectively. Here are some common manifestations.

Time Management and Planning

- **Difficulty meeting deadlines:** You may struggle to estimate how long tasks will take and often underestimate the time needed.

- **Procrastination:** You might postpone starting tasks, especially those that seem complex or overwhelming.
- **Poor prioritization:** There may be challenges in determining which tasks are most important or urgent.

Organization and Task Completion

- **Disorganized workspace:** Your desk or digital files may be cluttered and disorganized.
- **Incomplete projects:** You might have difficulty following through on tasks to completion.
- **Forgetfulness:** Important meetings, deadlines, or tasks may be forgotten.

Attention and Focus

- **Easy distraction:** You may have trouble maintaining focus, especially in open office environments.
- **Difficulty multitasking:** Switching between tasks or handling multiple responsibilities can be challenging.

Emotional Regulation

- **Impulsivity:** You might act or speak without considering consequences.
- **Emotional outbursts:** Difficulty managing stress or frustration can lead to inappropriate emotional responses.

Adaptability and Problem-Solving

- **Resistance to change:** You may struggle with changes in routines or processes.
- **Difficulty with complex problem-solving:** Breaking down large projects into manageable steps can be challenging.

Communication and Social Interaction

- **Misinterpreting social cues:** You might have trouble reading nonverbal communication or understanding office politics.
- **Difficulty following conversations:** You may lose track in meetings or struggle to remember important points.

It's important to note that executive functioning challenges can vary widely among individuals and may be associated with conditions like ADHD or exist independently. Recognizing these signs can help in developing appropriate accommodations and support strategies in the workplace.

Solutions

- **Use task management tools:** Tech tools can help you stay organized and keep track of what needs to be done. Many great tools can track productivity. There are also apps for focus, time management, and memory. Use these apps to help you stay focused, manage your time, and remember important tasks. Some examples are:
  - Digital calendars and reminders.
  - Time-tracking apps.
  - To-do list apps.
  - Project management software.
  - A timer and the Pomodoro technique.
  - Visual aids such as mind-mapping software or whiteboard apps.
  - Mood-tracking apps that can help identify patterns in mood and productivity.
- **Clarify work priorities and urgency with your manager:** Make sure deadlines are clear and on your calendar.
- **Highlight key directions and important words:** Use color to highlight essential information in work instructions.

- **Flexible workdays/hours:** Work with your manager to arrange your schedule to match your most productive times.
- **Communicate clearly about breaks and lunchtimes:** Make sure you understand when to take breaks and lunch. If you need flexibility, work with your manager to find options that work for you, your team, and your manager. Proactive communication can help avoid misunderstandings.
- **Organize your workspace:**
    - **Digital file organization:** Use cloud storage solutions like Google Drive or Dropbox to keep files organized and easily accessible.
    - **Physical organization tools:** Implement systems like color coding or labeled storage to keep your physical workspace tidy.

Problem: Concentration and Distractibility

Being easily distracted is common for many neurodivergent individuals and isn't a sign of laziness or unwillingness to work hard. If you're on the autism spectrum or have ADHD, your way of focusing is different. Once you find what works, your creativity and output can be remarkable.

> ***Being easily distracted isn't a sign of laziness or unwillingness to work hard.***

Solutions

- **Time blocking:** Try "uninterruptible time" or time blocking. This means setting aside periods when you can't be disturbed. It helps you stay focused and get back to work after interruptions. Plus, it helps you tackle routine and "boring" tasks more easily without getting sidetracked.
- **Designated private working areas:** Find or request a private area where you can work without constant interruptions.

- **Noise-canceling headphones**: Use these to block out background noise and help you concentrate better.
- **Mobile partitions between desks:** These can create more private space and reduce visual and auditory distractions.
- **Minimize visual distractions:** Keep your workspace tidy and free from unnecessary visual clutter.
- **Flexible work hours:** If possible, arrange your work hours to match your most productive times.

Problem: Auditory Processing Disorder (APD)

You're not alone if you find it challenging to understand your colleagues in noisy environments. For individuals with auditory processing challenges, even subtle background sounds—like a fan humming nearby—can interfere with comprehension. This difficulty may not be apparent to peers who don't share these sensitivities. Auditory processing disorder can be particularly problematic in open-plan offices or when receiving verbal instructions. The challenge lies in separating relevant speech from background noise. Here are some strategies to manage APD in the workplace.

Solutions

- **Use voice transcription tools:** These can help you keep track of verbal instructions.
- **Ask for written instructions:** Having things in writing can make it easier to follow tasks.
- **Use noise-canceling tech:** This can help eliminate background sounds and let you focus on the relevant audio.
- **Find a quiet place for phone calls:** This can help you concentrate better.
- **Explore alternative communication methods:** Consider using sign language, writing, or typing if verbal communication is challenging.

Problem: Language/Speaking

Some neurodivergent employees may have problems with verbal communication due to neurological differences, such as autism spectrum (which can present varying degrees of impairment). In addition, there may be some deficits in information processing and the ability to focus. But again, simple workarounds can help you mitigate these challenges.

Solutions

- **Communicate in alternative ways:** Use writing or typing if speaking is difficult.
- **Divide tasks by skill set:** For example, if you're a neurodivergent software engineer, you can write the code while another team member presents the functionality and design to the team.

By taking these steps, you can create a work environment that supports your needs. Advocate for yourself and take action to ensure you can work comfortably and effectively.

Problem: Dyslexia and Other Reading Difficulties

One of my clients, a software engineer, frequently needed clarification on his team's software requirements specification (SRS) document. The issue arose because the functional requirements and technical specifications were often drafted by product managers or business analysts who weren't always versed in precise technical communication. Sometimes, the acceptance criteria would include domain-specific jargon or references to unfamiliar design patterns or architectural concepts. For instance, terms like *microservices architecture, RESTful API endpoints,* or *asynchronous event-driven processing* might be used without sufficient context. If you have dyslexia or another reading difficulty, parsing these dense technical documents can be especially challenging. Here are some strategies to help with understanding and processing written information in a software development context.

Solutions

- **Review official company documents for confusing language:** Ensure that you understand project descriptions, company rules, and training manuals. If you're not sure you know what a document says, be proactive and find help. This may come from a trusted colleague or from an app that can read it to you or reframe it for clarification.
- **Seek out examples to clarify concepts:** Examples can make complex topics easier to understand.
- **Ask for verbal responses:** If written instructions are challenging, ask colleagues or employers to provide verbal ones.

Problem: Writing/Spelling/Grammar

If you have dyslexia or another disability that makes writing, spelling, or grammar challenging, it can be tough to perform text-based tasks. Here are some tools and strategies that can help.

- **Use speech-to-text (STT) apps:** You can easily write an email or send a text using our voice, simply by hitting a microphone icon on your smartphone or tablet. Why not compose your best work using a voice recognition app?
- **Use Grammarly:** This app can run in the background and provide suggestions on spelling, sentence structure, and the like. The free version is helpful, but the paid version offers powerful features like a plagiarism checker. If security is a concern, there is an enterprise-grade version designed specifically for corporations that includes enhanced security.
- **Add color and graphics to text-heavy documents:** Adding visual aids can help you understand and retain information better. The bonus is that the process of adding meaningful visuals helps in itself. Some people find that after adding the visuals to their notes, they don't need to look at them again because drawing them solidifies the information in their memory. Your brain needs to understand information before it can illustrate it.

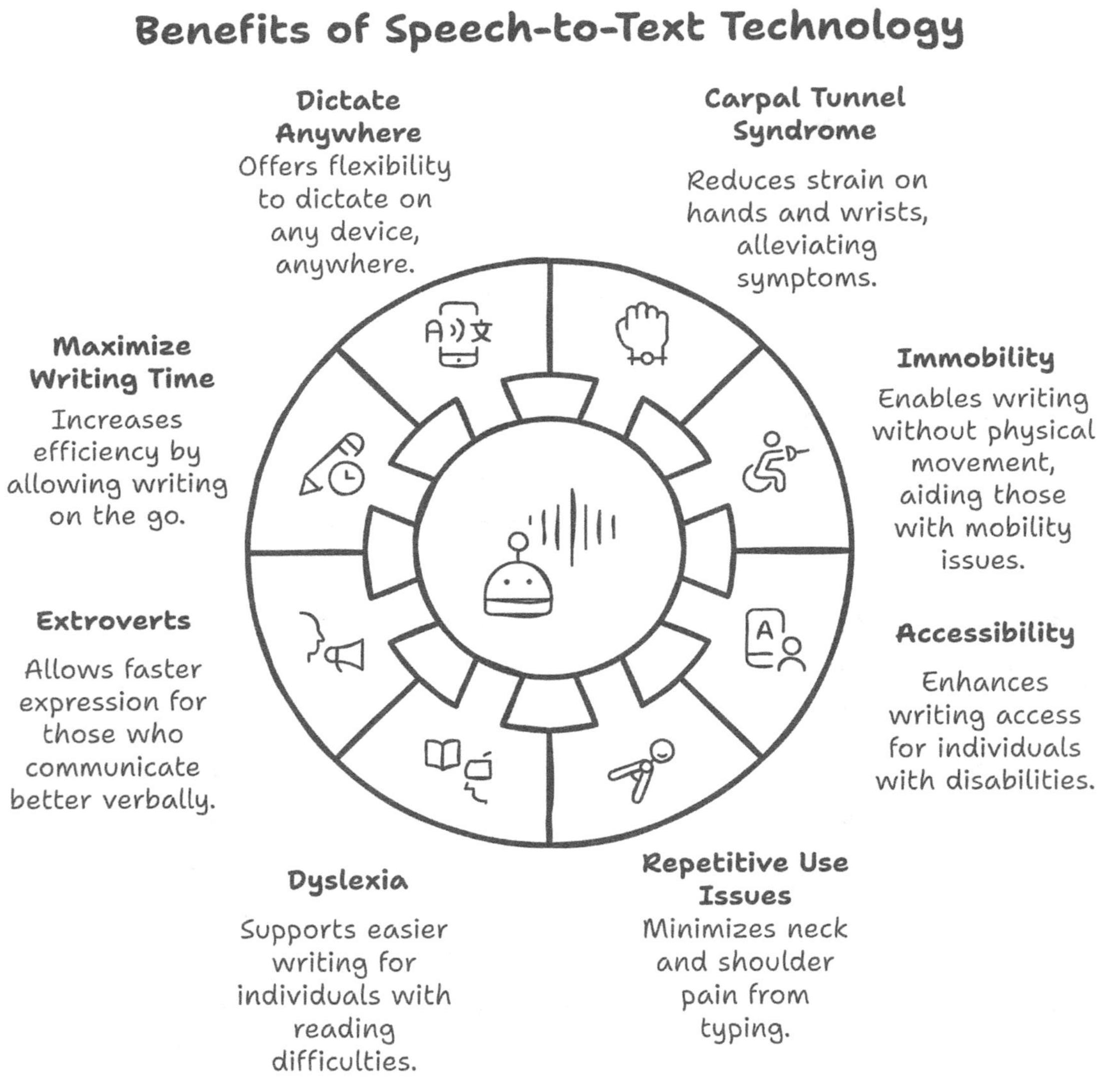

Benefits of Speech-to-Text Technology

Dictate Anywhere
Offers flexibility to dictate on any device, anywhere.

Carpal Tunnel Syndrome
Reduces strain on hands and wrists, alleviating symptoms.

Maximize Writing Time
Increases efficiency by allowing writing on the go.

Immobility
Enables writing without physical movement, aiding those with mobility issues.

Extroverts
Allows faster expression for those who communicate better verbally.

Accessibility
Enhances writing access for individuals with disabilities.

Dyslexia
Supports easier writing for individuals with reading difficulties.

Repetitive Use Issues
Minimizes neck and shoulder pain from typing.

- **Use bullet points:** Break down instructions into bullet points and short, clear sentences. This makes information more accessible.
- **Use text-to-speech (TTS) apps:** Listening to emails, memos, and documents can be easier than reading them. Ask IT to add a TTS app to your device or show you how to use the built-in TTS function.
- **Use Microsoft Office built-in tools:** Many companies already use Microsoft Office, which includes features like the Editor tool in Word and Outlook, offering grammar and spelling suggestions similar to Grammarly.
- **Install OpenDyslexic font:** This is a free, open-source font designed to increase readability for readers with dyslexia. It can be installed on most corporate computers without security concerns.
- **Re-read emails before sending them:** Make sure your emails are straightforward. If possible, read them to a colleague for feedback before sending them. You can also use AI to improve your email without changing your voice or adding information. For example, you might ask AI to edit the email for punctuation, grammar, and flow without rewriting it. You can also tell AI to adjust your tone to be positive and professional.
- **Consider peer review for important communications:** Implement a buddy system for reviewing important emails or documents before sending them out. This practice can be particularly helpful in stressful situations where emotions might affect communication. Having a colleague review your work helps ensure:
    - Professional language is maintained.
    - Emotional content is appropriately moderated.
    - Spelling and grammar errors are caught.
    - The message is clear and effectively conveys the intended information

This strategy not only assists with potential dyslexia-related challenges but also promotes a culture of collaboration and mutual support within the team.

Problem: Dyscalculia—Mathematics

If you struggle with math due to dyscalculia, some tools can help.

Solutions

- **Use specialized calculators:** Different industries have calculators tailored to their needs.
- **Try talking calculation devices:** These can call out numbers and data, making it easier to follow.

Strategies for Dealing with Sensory Overload

Navigating a world designed for neurotypical people can be exhausting. While proactive self-advocacy and self-care are crucial, here are some further strategies to help manage sensory overload.

Strategies for Dealing with Visual Overload or Photosensitivity

You're not alone if bright, pulsing, or aggressive lighting makes you uncomfortable or triggers seizures. This kind of lighting is common in many places, but there are ways to manage it.

Solutions

- **Fix flickering lightbulbs:** Report them to maintenance and ask for repairs.
- **Use blue lighting covers or natural lightbulbs:** These can reduce harsh lighting effects. You may need approval from your boss to enlist facilities maintenance or the building lighting technician to install blue lighting covers.
- **Wear sunglasses or glasses with colored lenses indoors:** This can help reduce visual discomfort.

- **Dim the lights or reduce screen brightness:** This can make your environment more comfortable. However, it may not be possible in an open-plan environment.
- **Take visual breaks:** Look away from screens or bright lights regularly to reduce eye strain.
- **Try alternative lighting solutions:** If possible, use LED lightbulbs in your workspace—they are often gentler on the eyes.
- **Wear UV-protective clothing if you work outdoors:** This can help reduce the impact of sunlight.
- **Get window tinting in your vehicle:** Tinting windows can provide relief from harsh sunlight while driving.
- **Choose natural lighting where possible:** If natural light isn't an option, discuss other solutions that might help. You often know best what works for you.

Strategies for Dealing with Temperature Sensitivity

If you struggle with the ambient temperature at work, it can be uncomfortable. This sensitivity can have various causes, from neurological to physiological. Here are some ways to manage it.

Solutions

- **Direct the airflow:** Consider using air conditioner vent deflectors or vent covers to direct airflow away from or toward you as needed. Be aware that modifying airflow can impact the overall heating/air-conditioning system in your building. Before making any changes, consult with your facilities maintenance team. Explain your temperature sensitivity issues and ask about approved methods for adjusting airflow at your workstation. The facilities team can advise on solutions that won't disrupt the building's climate control system and may offer additional options to manage your workspace temperature effectively.

- **Use fans:** Either request a fan or bring your own. Having a personal fan can help you stay cool.
- **Try heating or cooling gloves:** These can help regulate your body temperature.

Strategies for Dealing with Tactile Sensitivity

If certain textures or materials cause you discomfort or even pain, it can make required workplace attire unbearable. Here's what you can do.

Solutions

- Ask for flexibility around clothing choices. Wearing comfortable materials can significantly improve your happiness and productivity. Wear soft, seamless, and tag-free clothing to minimize irritation. Opt for loose-fitting clothes that don't cling or rub against the skin. Use compression clothing or accessories if deep pressure is soothing.
- Layer clothing under uniforms. This can create a barrier between your skin and uncomfortable materials.
- Carry an object with a pleasant texture. Handle it when you encounter uncomfortable textures.
- Place soft covers or padding on chairs and armrests.
- Politely decline or adjust activities involving uncomfortable tactile experiences, like participating in certain team-building exercises.
- Use weighted lap blankets for calming pressure.
- Incorporate textured gloves or grip-enhancing tools to improve comfort while handling objects.
- Wear comfortable clothing and remove tags. Choose materials that feel good on your skin.
- Use touch-friendly office supplies. Select items with textures that you find pleasant.

- Use deep pressure techniques. Weighted lap pads or compression clothing can help regulate touch sensitivity.

Strategies for Dealing with Auditory Overload

If loud or sudden noises overwhelm you, here's what you can do.

Solutions

- Use noise-canceling headphones or earplugs. These can reduce background noise and help you focus.
- Communicate your needs. Ask co-workers, students, teachers, or employers to help reduce triggering sounds. When requesting accommodations for auditory sensitivities, it's important to be clear, professional, and solution-oriented. Noise level accommodations are more sensitive than many others because they often require others to change their behavior. Here are some examples of how to approach the conversation:
- **To a manager:** "I've noticed that I'm having difficulty concentrating due to the noise level in our open office. Could we discuss some potential accommodations that might help me be more productive?"
- **To HR:** "I have auditory processing challenges that sometimes impact my work. I'd like to explore options for reducing noise distractions. Can we schedule a meeting to discuss possible accommodations?"
- **To colleagues:** "I hope you don't mind, but I sometimes use noise-canceling headphones to help me focus. If you need my attention, please feel free to send me a quick message or tap my shoulder."
- **Requesting a quiet space:** "I've found that I'm most productive when I have access to a quieter work area. Is it possible to relocate my desk to a less busy part of the office or for me to use a quiet room for focused work when needed?"

Remember to be specific about your needs and open to collaborative solutions. It's often helpful to suggest potential accommodations while also being receptive to alternatives your employer might offer.

Strategies for Dealing with Odor Sensitivity

If you have a highly acute sense of smell, it can be tough to deal with odors from the office kitchen or restrooms. This sensitivity can cause nausea, make it hard to concentrate, and lower your productivity. Here's how you can address it:

Solutions

- **Choose a scent-free work location:** Ask to work in a part of the office where strong odors are less likely.
- **Use a mask if you have to work in smelly places:** For example, if you're a cleaner, wearing a mask can help manage the odors.

Other Options for Sensory Overload

Even with strategies in place, you might still feel overwhelmed by sensory input. Here are some additional tips to help you manage these situations.

Solutions

- **Give yourself permission to step away:** If you're feeling overwhelmed, it's okay to remove yourself from the situation to regain control.
- **Use self-regulating behaviors:** Pacing, rocking, vocalizing, or other stims can help you manage sensory overload. You might need to inform your co-workers about these behaviors so they understand and respect your needs.

Strategies for Dealing with Stress Intolerance

Stress affects everyone, but it might worsen your symptoms if you are neurodivergent. Here's how you can manage stress at work.

Solutions

- **Mindfulness apps:** These can help you manage stress and improve focus.
- **Play calming ambient music:** Music at sixty beats per minute or less can create a calm and focused environment. Lower the volume as the workday starts and turn it off if it becomes distracting.
- **Use anxiety management apps:** These apps can help you manage stress and anxiety.
- **Seek counseling or therapy:** Professional help can provide strategies for dealing with stress.
- **Consider a support animal**: If possible, having a support animal can provide comfort.
- **Find a support person:** Having someone you trust at work can help you manage stressful situations.

Strategies for Dealing with Anxiety/Panic Attacks

Kelly, a project manager at a mid-market insurance brokerage, shared this story:

"Last month, I had to give a department-wide presentation about my new project. As the day approached, my anxiety spiraled. The morning of the presentation, I arrived feeling dizzy and nauseous. As people filed into the conference room, I felt a panic attack coming on. I abruptly excused myself and rushed to the restroom, where I had a full-blown panic attack. It took fifteen minutes to calm down enough to leave. By then, my manager had postponed the meeting. I felt humiliated and guilty for disrupting everyone's schedules. This incident has made me even more anxious about future presentations, and I'm worried about how it might affect my career and relationships with colleagues."

Kelly's concerns are valid. If you deal with generalized anxiety disorder or panic disorder, you know how challenging it can be. These conditions can be part of a neurotype or may stand alone, and many people face their effects daily. Here are some small interventions that can help.

Solutions

- **Maximize natural lighting:** Try to work in areas with plenty of windows or lights that mimic natural light. This can help calm you and boost productivity.
- **Try mandala coloring books:** Coloring mandalas can help focus your attention and boost creativity. Keep a book of mandalas and some markers, colored pencils, or crayons handy for when you need a break.
- **Institute flexible workdays/hours:** Work with your manager to arrange your work schedule to match your peak performance times.
- **Have backup plans:** This can help reduce the stress of unexpected changes.
- **Prepare in advance for schedule changes:** Knowing about office retreats or training days ahead of time can help you manage your anxiety.
- **Use doodling/fidget tools:** These can help you stay calm and focused.

Strategies for Dealing with Social Interactions in the Workplace

Alex, a neurodivergent software developer, often felt overwhelmed and isolated during team lunches and after-work gatherings. The loud conversations and unstructured social time left them feeling anxious and unsure how to engage.

Socializing with colleagues can be tough for some neurotypes, but it's important for building camaraderie, which can improve how you work together. If you find it challenging to fit in, here's what you can do.

Solutions

- **Find a work buddy or mentor:** They can help you navigate social interactions and feel more comfortable.
- **Ask for event details ahead of time:** Before meetings, ask for an agenda, outline, and notes. This way, you'll know what will be discussed and when, making it easier to follow along and participate.

After Alex tried these strategies, social interactions were much more manageable. They connected with a mentor who helped them prepare for social events and introduced them to colleagues in smaller, less overwhelming settings. By requesting agendas before meetings, Alex felt more confident contributing to discussions. Over time, they built stronger relationships with their team, improving collaboration and job satisfaction.

Strategies for Dealing with Self-Worth in a Neurotypical Workplace

Navigating a neurotypical workplace as a neurodivergent individual can sometimes be challenging. You may encounter situations that push you beyond your comfort zone or trigger sensory overload. These experiences, which can occasionally lead to meltdowns, might leave you feeling guilty or ashamed. Remember that these reactions are natural and not a reflection of your worth or abilities.

It's important to address the guilt or shame you might feel after a sensory-overload-induced meltdown. Here's how to cope.

Solutions

- **Allow yourself time and space:** Give yourself the time and space needed to process without judgment.
- **Work with a specialist:** Therapy can help you unlearn ableist ideals and develop strategies to manage sensory overload.

Remember, you wouldn't get mad at a fish for not being able to walk, so don't get mad at yourself for not functioning in neurotypical ways. It's important to recognize that both neurotypical and neurodivergent individuals can grow and learn from each other. Everyone has unique quirks, sensitivities, and strengths. All members can thrive by working together to create a team culture of acceptance and support.

Brain Hacks to Learn Faster

Much of my work is helping professionals see that they're not "bad at learning"; they're trying to learn in a way that doesn't work for their brains. While my work naturally helps many neurodivergent people, it also applies to neurotypical people with different learning preferences.

One of the things I wish I could put on billboards everywhere is that people need to stop fighting the way their brain works and instead lean into it. If you learn in a way that works best for your brain, you can process much more information faster. Here are some of my favorite brain hacks.

Problem-Solution Mapping: A How-To Guide for Self-Advocacy and Workplace Success

Problem-solution mapping, an application of the mind mapping strategy, is a powerful tool for organizing information, brainstorming, and problem-solving. It's especially valuable for neurodivergent individuals in the workplace, as it can be used for self-advocacy and communicating needs effectively. By visually mapping out your thoughts, strengths, and challenges, you can better articulate your unique perspective and requirements to colleagues and supervisors.

I love mind mapping. It is easily one of my favorite methods for organizing information, brainstorming for projects, and problem-solving. It can be used for teaching just as effectively as it can be used for learning. In the workplace, it is an incredible tool for negotiating, finding solutions, and reaching compromises—all crucial skills for self-advocacy and professional growth.

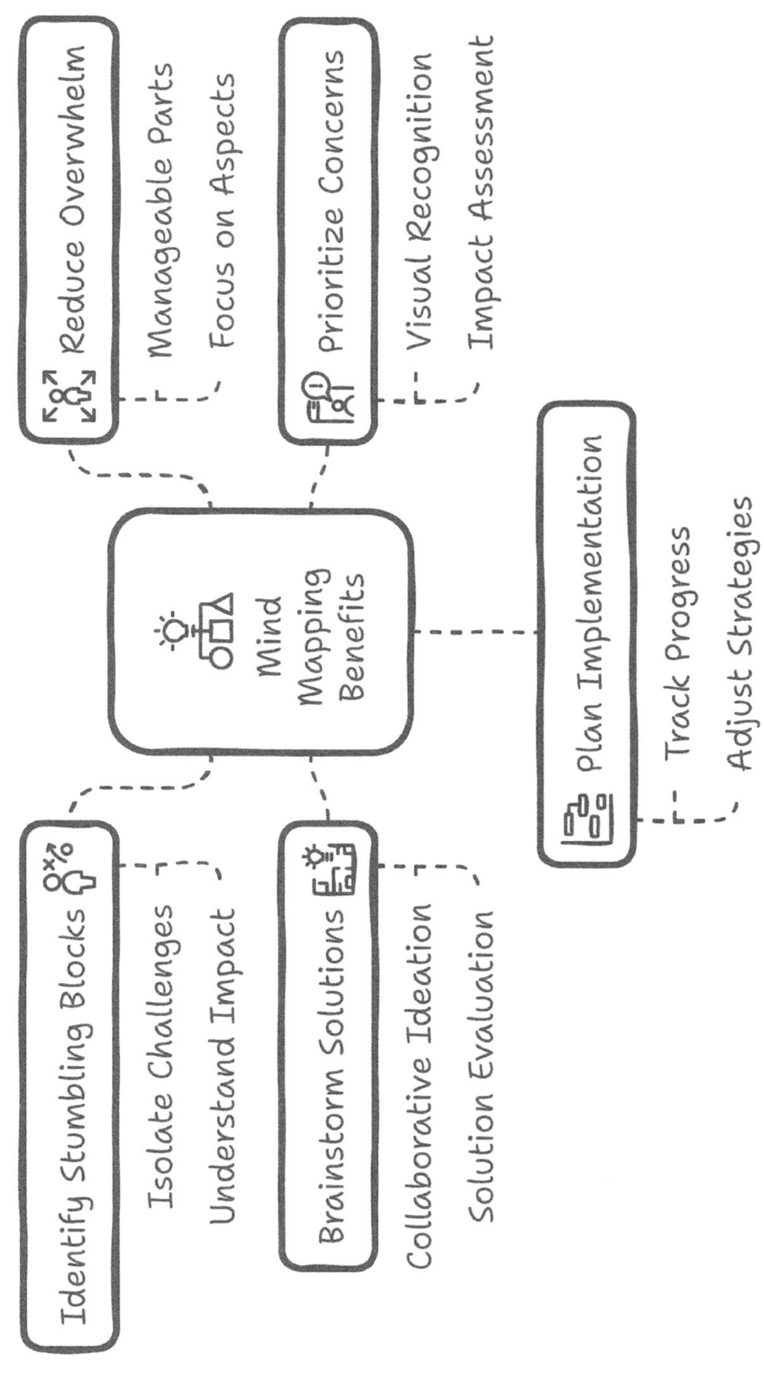
Benefits of Mind Mapping for Problem Solving
Mind Mapping Benefits
Reduce Overwhelm
Manageable Parts
Focus on Aspects
Prioritize Concerns
Visual Recognition
Impact Assessment
Plan Implementation
Track Progress
Adjust Strategies
Identify Stumbling Blocks
Isolate Challenges
Understand Impact
Brainstorm Solutions
Collaborative Ideation
Solution Evaluation

Problem-solution mapping is a technique that can be applied to every aspect of life: work, school, home organization, and even social and emotional issues.

So how do you do it?

Contrary to what many people imagine, mind mapping is not just spewing a bunch of random ideas onto a page. While it is an exercise anyone can do, mind mapping draws upon your instinct for connecting information and is best done with a bit of strategy. Let's use Suzanne's example from chapter 8 to illustrate how Problem-solution mapping can be useful when problem-solving with neurodivergent workers.

> ***Mind mapping is not just spewing a bunch of random ideas onto a page... it's an exercise that draws upon your instinct for connecting information.***

Problem-Solution Mapping Explained in Three Easy Steps

Suzanne required multiple mind maps to resolve multiple issues. Each mind map should deal with one central theme. To keep this example simple, let's focus on just one theme.

Step 1. Identify the main concept or central theme of your mind map.

Identify your central theme by asking yourself, "What is the main idea that needs to be dealt with?" If you are problem-solving, like Suzanne, your central theme will be the specific issue you are trying to solve.

Write this down. This will be the center of your mind map. If it helps, draw a circle around it, or some other shape. Maybe highlight it with an attention-catching color. You might even want to go so far as to give it its very own sticky note. Tap into your creativity to help visually connect to the main concept you want to address.

The best thing about Problem-solution mapping is that you can use whatever materials you have on hand or whatever inspires you. You can create your mind map using an app, a whiteboard, a giant notepad, or just a plain sheet of paper. Do whatever works best for you to get that main concept down, front and center.

Step 2. Identify themes that are directly related to the main concept. These will be your primary branches.

Continuing with Suzanne's example, which has a specific goal of problem-solving, the next step is to look at the "whys" or the circumstances that trigger the problem. In Suzanne's case, she might list an afternoon energy crash, frustration with her co-workers' communication methods, and irritation about being interrupted as the main reasons for her lack of patience when interacting with them.

Each issue will be a branch off the main concept. For problem-solution mapping, these branches typically explain the "why" at the root of the issue.

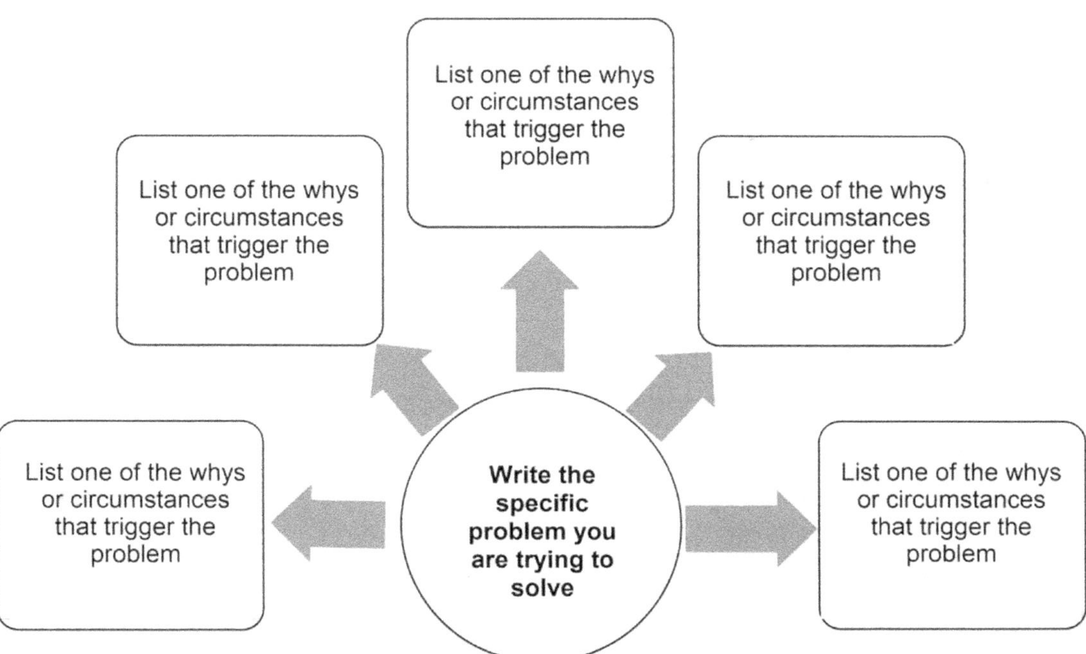

If you are creating a mind map for teaching or learning, these branches will provide the main supporting themes that back up or link to the central concept.

Step 3. Explore each supporting theme in depth by discovering associated concepts.

This is your opportunity to dig deep. If we examine Suzanne's afternoon energy crash issue with a magnifying glass, we might discover that she needs to incorporate some kind of physical movement into her daily routine. Maybe she would benefit from eating an earlier or later lunch. In the end, only Suzanne knows; this is her opportunity to lay out ideas for possible solutions to counteract that afternoon energy crash.

This third layer is essentially where the problem-solving happens. Suzanne can use this same discovery process to figure out ways to help her co-workers communicate more effectively with her and maybe minimize interruptions.

These associated concepts are basically the meat of any lesson when it comes to teaching or learning. They are the details that all build up to the main conclusion or central theme.

Why Problem-Solution Mapping Works

When I teach Problem-solution mapping, I like to think of it as building a pyramid from the top down. Start with the big idea and then fill in all the supporting information.

This way of looking at things is helpful because connections between seemingly unrelated subjects suddenly become clear. It is a visual method for learners to conceptualize how different ideas are tied together. For problem-solving, solutions that may not have been immediately apparent suddenly become glaringly obvious.

Mind Mapping for a Neurodiverse Workplace

When it comes to supporting a neurodiverse workforce, mind mapping should be considered an indispensable tool. Mind mapping helps support meaningful learning and strengthen your overall depth of understanding (Liu et al., 2014). This is particularly true when it comes to learning complex information or resolving complicated situations. It is an activity that helps create structure within understanding.

For divergent thinkers, it creates an effective alternative to the neurotypical systems of learning, teaching, and problem-solving that frequently cause unending frustration. Mind mapping allows for creative expression in the shape, style, and aesthetic details unique to the tastes of the person creating the map. It helps pair words with an image, increasing understanding for visual learners. Additionally, non-linear thinkers will find it easier to express their ideas and communicate in a way that is universally understandable.

With a bit of practice, mind mapping will quickly become your fallback tool for processing information and problem-solving. Learn how to do it. Recognize when it can be helpful, and use it frequently.

Overcome Writer's Block with this Clustering Strategy

A few years ago, I looked up from my computer and saw my husband standing at my office door with a look of intense frustration and angst on his face. He appeared as if he was about to rant about something, but he held it together.

Not knowing what could possibly have upset my steady and controlled husband, I asked what was wrong. Exasperated, he barked, "They want me to write an essay telling them how my past work experience would benefit the company. I've got over twenty years' experience in this industry. How am I supposed to answer that question in five hundred words!"

He was transitioning into a new phase of his career and needed to write this essay as part of the job application process. My husband is an engineer, and while he's a wizard at math and coding, it takes him an hour to write a paragraph in an email. He agonizes over the process of writing.

I knew I could help him, but the strategy that was perfect for him was a brainstorming and organizing technique that I'd been using for over a decade with students with learning disabilities as well as gifted students. I'd never introduced the strategy to an adult. Broaching the subject carefully, I suggested that he try this writing activity to organize his thoughts. I sat with him and walked him through the steps. Once he got going, there was no stopping him. It worked!

Don't Know How to Start That Job Application Essay or School Assignment?

Starting the writing process is the most difficult part for most people. We learned how to organize our writing in school, but working that linear outline and starting with the introductory sentence is torturously slow for many of us.

Why? Because some of us are not linear thinkers; the words just don't flow for us in sentence format all at once. Different people, learners, and writers work differently. Sometimes our working memory is so full of what we might write, we can't seem to get started with the process of writing. That's what we call writer's block! Thankfully, there is a better way.

By using a simple clustering activity, and starting with what we know, we can write more effectively, more quickly, and with much less anxiety and frustration. Here's how the clustering writing strategy works.

The images included with these instructions are intended to be generic so that a reader in any profession can relate to the example. Most of us have gone on a vacation at some point.

Materials

1. Unlined paper sized at 8.5 x 11 inches or larger.*
2. Lined paper cut into thirds (8.5 inches wide x 3.5-ish inches tall)
3. Highlighters
4. Writing utensil

*Some people prefer to do this exercise on a tablet or laptop and use colored fonts instead of strips of paper. Each strip of paper would be replaced by text in a different-colored font.

Step 1. Brainstorm your ideas.

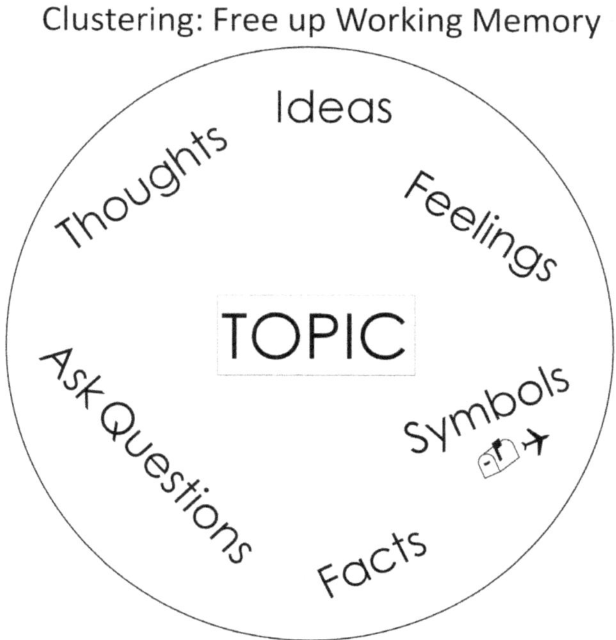

A. Draw a big circle on your piece of unlined paper.

B. Put the topic you are writing about in the middle of the circle.

C. Do a "brain-dump" and jot down all the keywords, facts, ideas, symbols, and questions that you have about the main topic. It's okay to draw pictures or symbols of your thoughts in the circle. Anything that comes to mind to help you write a paper is viable. Do not censor your ideas at this phase of the process.

D. Don't worry about spelling, grammar, or other conventions at this stage of the process. The purpose is to get your ideas out. Do the editing later.

For this example, let's pretend that we are writing about something we can all relate to—a vacation. Once you understand the process for a vacation, you can use the technique for anything you need to write.

Step 2. Prioritize, favorite, and eliminate.

A. Highlight the words, phrases, and images you might want to include in your writing.

B. Favorite your best ideas with a star—the ones you definitely want to include in your writing.

C. Cross out the words, phrases, images that you brainstormed but, on review, you decide don't fit.

Step 3. Start writing in small steps.

(See figure on following page).

A. Choose a word, phrase, or image from the starred words inside the circle.

B. Write a sentence about that word or phrase on a strip of paper. This will be your topic sentence for that idea. Do not write more unless it flows effortlessly.

C. Move on to the next favorite word and another strip of paper. Write a sentence about that idea on the strip of paper. Repeat the process for every idea you've starred.

D. Look at words that are highlighted but not starred. Decide whether you want to write about those ideas. If so, repeat the process above with those words.

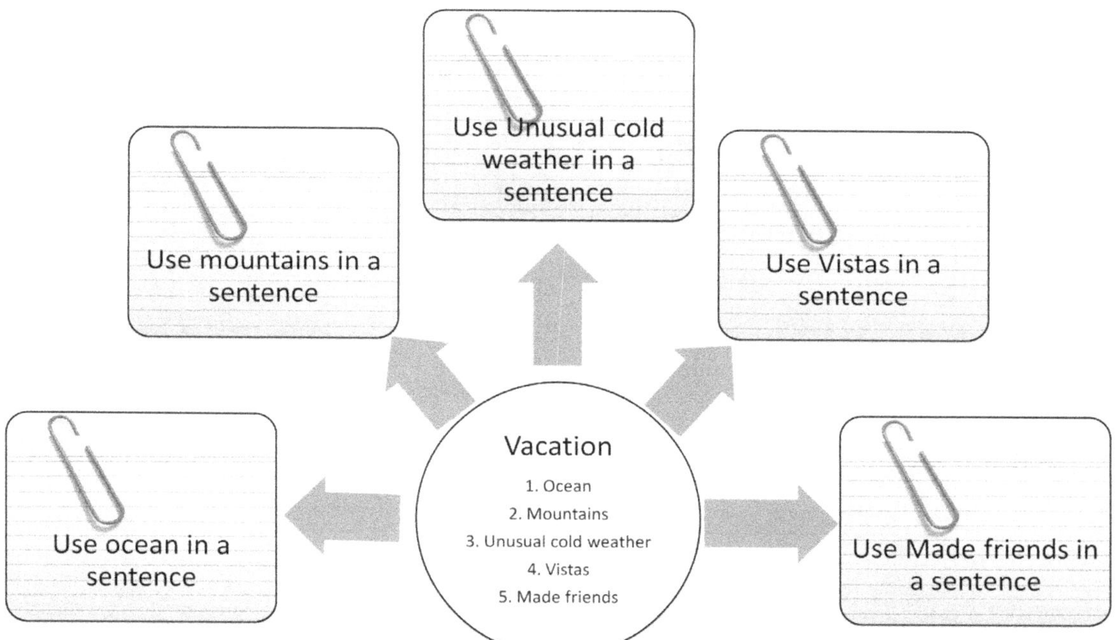

Step 4. Embellish your sentences.

(See figure on following page).

A. Choose any strip of paper with a topic sentence that you feel you can elaborate upon. Order is not important. What's important is that your ideas flow naturally and you are following your creative thought process rather than trying to constrain it into somebody else's rules for writing.

B. When you have elaborated as much as you can on that topic sentence, choose another strip of paper with another topic sentence and repeat the process.

C. Repeat until you have at least three to five sentences on each strip of paper.

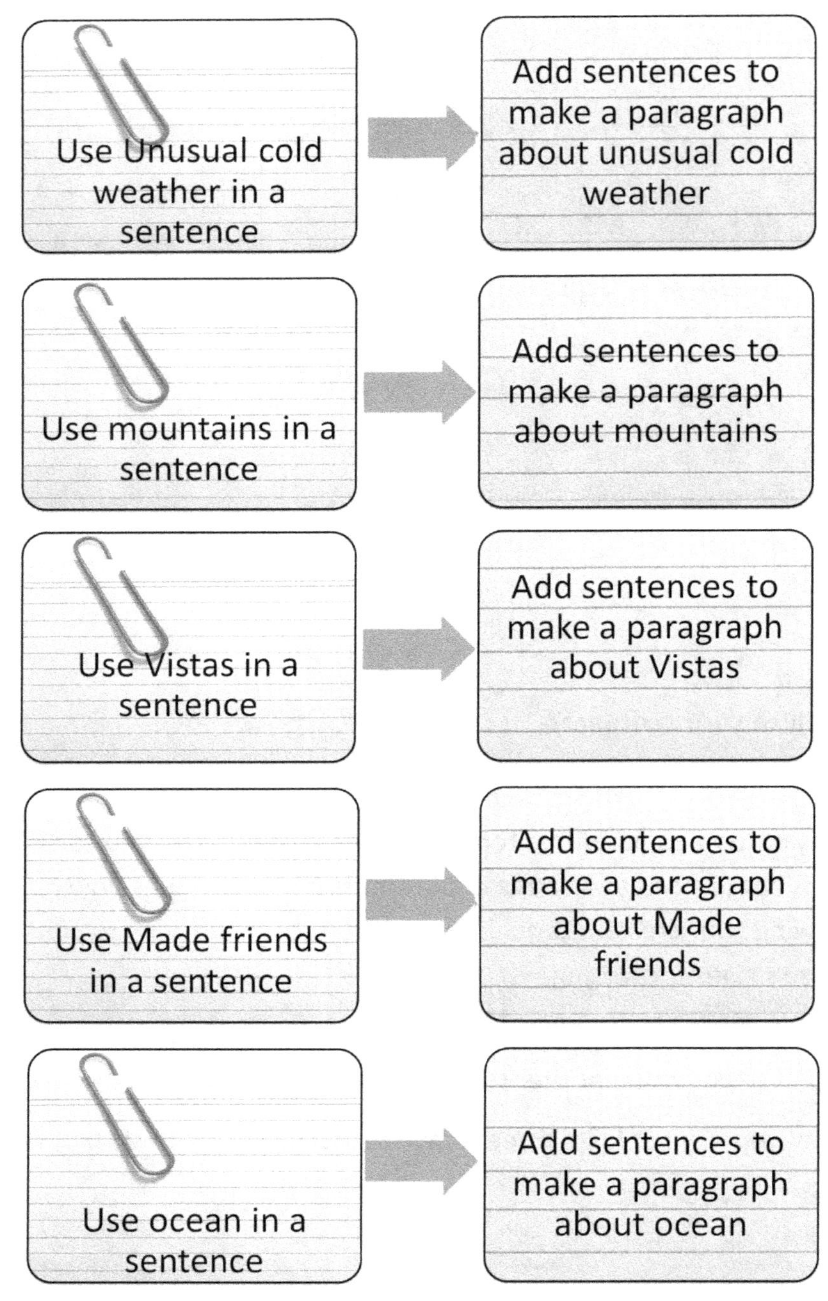
Use Unusual cold weather in a sentence
Add sentences to make a paragraph about unusual cold weather
Use mountains in a sentence
Add sentences to make a paragraph about mountains
Use Vistas in a sentence
Add sentences to make a paragraph about Vistas
Use Made friends in a sentence
Add sentences to make a paragraph about Made friends
Use ocean in a sentence
Add sentences to make a paragraph about ocean

Step 5. Decide on the order for your paragraphs and connect them with transition words.

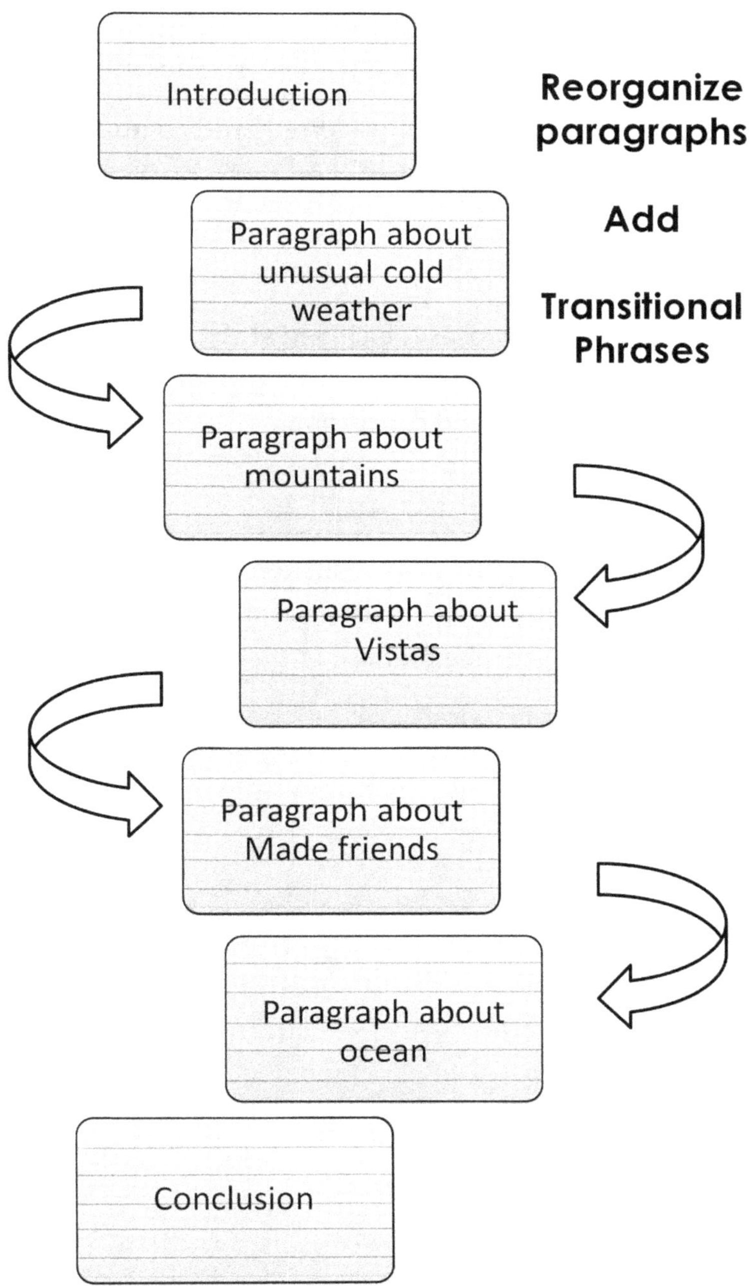

This process allows you to start anywhere in the writing process. It frees up creative thought and encourages the words to flow. The stress of trying to force writing into a set structure can hinder creativity.

A. Look at your paragraphs and decide on the best sequence.

B. Literally tape the paragraphs, in your preferred order, onto another piece of paper, leaving about an inch of space in between.

C. In the space in between the paragraphs, use transition words and phrases* to connect the paragraphs.

*A list of potential transition phrases is included at the end of this section.

Step 6. Write your introduction and conclusion.

(See figure on following page).

Some people find it easier to write an introduction after they've written the body of the paper. The brainstormed ideas in the circle replace the introductory sentence, yet still provide a clear focus for the premise of the writing piece.

Voilà! You have written your first draft!

Add sentences to make a paragraph about unusual cold weather

Add

Add an Introduction

Add sentences to make a paragraph about mountains

Add sentences to make a paragraph about Vistas

Add sentences to make a paragraph about Made friends

Add sentences to make a paragraph about ocean

Add

Add A Conclusion

Step 7. Rewrite your draft.

At this stage, the main ideas for the paper are in place. This is the time to wordsmith, proofread, edit, enhance, clarify, and refine your ideas.

Don't forget to have someone else proofread it for you!

I have been using this clustering strategy for years and I've taught it to my students, my family, and my colleagues. It works well because it allows the writer to focus on the content and honor the flow of creative ideas rather than being constrained by rules that may not capitalize on your learning preferences.

The clustering writing strategy enables you to write a paper better and faster using this easy seven step productivity strategy! Stay tuned for more productivity tips for accelerating your success!

Transition Words for Writing a Paper

To add:

And, again, and then, besides, equally, important, finally, further, furthermore, nor, too, next, lastly, what's more, moreover, in addition, first (second, et cetera)

To compare:

Whereas, but, yet, on the other hand, however, nevertheless, on the other hand, on the contrary, by comparison, where, compared with, up against,

Introduction

Paragraph about Made friends

Paragraph about mountains

Paragraph about Vistas

Paragraph about ocean

Paragraph about unusual cold weather

Conclusion

balanced against, but, although, conversely, meanwhile, after all, in contrast, although this may be true

To prove:

Because, for, since, for the same reason, obviously, evidently, furthermore, moreover, besides, indeed, in fact, in addition, in any case, that is

To show exception:

Yet, still, however, nevertheless, in spite of, despite, of course, once in a while, sometimes

To show time:

Immediately, thereafter, soon, after a few hours, finally, then, later, previously, formerly, first (second, et cetera), next, and then

To repeat:

In brief, as I have said, as I have noted, as has been noted

To emphasize:

Definitely, extremely, obviously, in fact, indeed, in any case, absolutely, positively, naturally, surprisingly, always, forever, perennially, eternally, never, emphatically, unquestionably, without a doubt, certainly, undeniably, without reservation

To show sequence:

First, second, third, and so forth. A, B, C, and so forth. Next, then, following this, at this time, now, at this point, after, afterward, subsequently, finally, consequently, previously, before this, simultaneously, concurrently, thus, therefore, hence, next, and then, soon

To give an example:

For example, for instance, in this case, in another case, on this occasion, in this situation, take the case of, to demonstrate, to illustrate, as an illustration

To summarize or conclude:

In brief, on the whole, summing up, to conclude, in conclusion, as I have shown, as I have said, hence, therefore, accordingly, thus, as a result, consequently, on the whole

Optimize Your Environment for Focus

Your brain cannot process and retain information at full capacity if it is distracted. Do yourself a favor and optimize your environment as much as possible to work with your focus. For example, I have a pair of noise-canceling headphones on my desk in my office. Outside noise distracts me from my task, so I can learn faster and get through my work more quickly when I have them on.

It took me some trial and error to determine what music worked best for my focus. Anything with lyrics was a big no; even Mozart didn't work. Now I have a playlist of songs I listen to that help my brain focus.

Cut visual distractions as much as possible. A lot of clutter or a messy workspace can distract you just as much as a loud conversation. Move things out of view until you find the balance that works best for you.

Of course, you may not have much control over your work environment at the office. Optimize everything you can. Use noise-canceling headphones if you need to focus. Just be sure to explain to your boss or colleagues that they are noise-canceling and not blaring music or YouTube videos.

Working from home allows you to experiment with different focus support options. The same thing won't work for everyone, so don't fall into the trap of comparing yourself with others. Ignore posts on LinkedIn about someone who works at a treadmill desk if that's not going to increase your productivity. Work from bed in your pajamas if that helps your focus. That said, move to a more appropriate space if you'll be interfacing with customers or co-workers on Zoom.

I'll never forget when a networking connection showed up on Zoom in his bed with short shorts on. During our call, I found it quite awkward to be privy to his bare thighs! Needless to say, it was our first and last Zoom meeting.

Pause and Let Your Brain Process What You've Learned

Whenever I'm learning something, I pause at regular intervals and give my brain time to process the information. You don't have to take extended breaks; even two minutes is enough to let you digest information. I take notes or screen grabs for my records. My husband often walks in the garden for five minutes while he processes. Do whatever works best for you.

You'll find that you retain information much better because your brain doesn't become overwhelmed by learning too much too quickly. Instead, when you go back to learning, your brain can build a connection between the information you knew before the break and what you learned after. It builds upon it rather than wiping it clean.

Many people I work with process information best when they're doing other things. I often see people knitting while participating in my training sessions. I like to fold laundry while listening to a webinar. If that is you, I recommend you stop at regular intervals and take notes to refer to later. If you are driving, you could create little voice notes for yourself. The mere act of taking notes helps with learning, even if you don't review them.

Gift Yourself the Time to Review the Course Framework in Advance

Time is the most precious and limited resource we have. So I completely understand why many people don't review course frameworks or summaries in advance. But studying the topics and subtopics in advance can significantly help your brain process and retain information more effectively.

It provides your brain with reference points and allows it to categorize the information while learning. Your brain loves context and can process information better in real time with that context. If there are no topics or subtopics, find an article explaining the basics of what you are about to learn. Just two minutes of preparing your brain can help immensely.

Find Someone to Teach

Many people, especially extroverts, process information best when they relay it to someone else. Try teaching someone how to do the thing you have just learned and see if it helps you learn better. No, you don't have to become that annoying person in the office who tries to teach people things they already know. Teach your toddler, pet, or even houseplant when you get home. Inanimate objects and pets are some of the best students; they don't ask too many questions.

Be open and honest about how you learn the best and the fastest. A neurodivergent colleague elaborated on the problem when she spoke about the embarrassment and fear people struggle with when they don't learn in the way their company requires them to learn. They explained that honesty about how you learn helps the company understand how they can help you. If you work best by teaching other people, you can volunteer to teach your colleague who missed the training session.

Learn How You Learn

The key to unlocking your learning potential is to put effort into learning how you learn. As Michael aptly summarized, "When we were in grade school, there was only one way to learn. But now, the world has caught up with the fact that everyone learns differently." Use that understanding to your advantage and discover what works best for you. Start with trial and error. Watch videos, listen to podcasts, read books, take courses, and note which methods work and which don't.

Recognize when you struggle to learn something and examine what about the process is making it difficult. Try to tweak things and see if you can grasp the information better. Once you have some essential insights into how you learn, you can start researching and find tips that will be effective for you.

How to Approach Your Boss to Discuss Your Needs

This is the most difficult part of getting your needs met at work so that you can perform at your peak. I like to have scripts for what to say so that I'm not stymied when I start the conversation. Here are some ideas for how to approach your boss. Tweak these and make them your own so that you are comfortable opening up the discussion.

- "Hello, [Boss's name], I've been thinking about how we can create an even more inclusive work environment. I have some ideas for accommodations that could benefit not just me, but potentially other team members as well. Could we brainstorm together on how to implement these?"
- "[Boss's name], I'd like to propose a small change in my work setup that I think could improve my focus and output. Would you be willing to let me try [specific accommodation] for a two-week trial period? We could then assess its impact on my performance."
- "Hi, [Boss's name], I recently learned about some workplace strategies that can help neurodivergent employees like myself thrive. I'd love to share this information with you and discuss how we might apply some of these ideas to our team. Do you have some time to explore this topic together?"

When using these scripts, it's important to:

- Be prepared with specific examples of how the accommodations will benefit your work and the team.
- Show willingness to collaborate and find solutions that work for everyone.
- Be open to feedback and alternative suggestions from your boss.
- Follow up the conversation with a written summary of what was discussed and agreed upon.

Remember, the goal is to create a dialogue that emphasizes your commitment to your job and the company's success while also addressing your needs as a neurodivergent employee.

As a professional, your unique perspective and abilities are valuable assets to your organization. By advocating for yourself, implementing these strategies, and continuously refining your approach, you can create a work environment that allows you to thrive and contribute your best work. Embrace your neurodiversity and use it as a strength in your professional journey.

Chapter Nine Reflection Questions

1. How might the concept of finding your voice in self-advocacy be particularly challenging for neurodivergent professionals? What strategies from the chapter could help overcome these challenges?
2. Reflect on the importance of reframing negative thoughts in building confidence for self-advocacy. How might this practice impact both personal and professional growth for neurodivergent individuals?
3. Analyze the role of executive dysfunction in the workplace. How can the solutions presented in the chapter help mitigate its impact on job performance and satisfaction?
4. Discuss the potential benefits and drawbacks of disclosing neurodivergent status in the workplace. How can employees navigate this decision effectively?
5. How can Problem-solution mapping be used as a tool for self-advocacy and problem-solving in the workplace? Provide specific examples based on the chapter's content.
6. Reflect on the clustering writing strategy presented in the chapter. How might this approach benefit neurodivergent individuals who struggle with traditional writing methods?
7. Analyze the importance of optimizing the environment for focus. How can neurodivergent employees effectively communicate their needs for environmental adjustments to their employers?
8. How might the concept of "learning how you learn" impact a neurodivergent professional's career development and job satisfaction?
9. Evaluate the suggested scripts for approaching a boss about accommodation needs. How might these conversations contribute to creating a more inclusive workplace culture?

CONCLUSION

Ditch Conformity and Hire Divergent Thinkers

In the workplace, neurodiversity is an asset, not an obstacle to growth.

Neurodivergence is a spectrum. At one end, there are people who are near-normal (or know how to mask their differences to appear neurotypical). At the far end, there are those who are highly misunderstood.

Do you remember pop artist Andy Warhol? He was a genius who advanced the visual arts. But did you know that he had a neurological disorder? As a child, Warhol suffered from Sydenham's chorea, a disorder commonly known as St. Vitus' dance, characterized by involuntary movements.

Just as Andy Warhol had a genius within, there is genius in each of us.

For some of us, our strengths follow conventional thinking and draw from what we know has worked in the past. But for others, genius lies in thinking in ways that defy convention and sometimes seem outright crazy. I can only imagine that many of our famous inventors, scientists, and innovators heard all too often that their ideas were implausible.
Corporations can benefit from people who refuse to regard company conventions a s cast in stone. The people who dare to think differently often bring the greatest problem-solving, innovation, and efficiency to the workplace.

Divergent Thinkers and the Problem of Conformity

Fears of controversy, parental objection, and lawsuits have moved our schools and colleges away from teaching students to think critically or to question the status quo. For the past two decades, the educational system has sought to standardize thought, achievement, and tests. While this movement is seen as a way to increase the quality of education, it has reduced education to twelve years of learning only what is

The Business Case for Hiring Neurodivergent Talent
Competitive Edge
Unique strengths in problem-solving & pattern recognition.
Innovation Boost
Challenges groupthink & sparks creative solutions.
Diverse Thinking
Identifies value & opportunities others may overlook.
Untapped Talent
Access a highly skilled yet underemployed workforce.
Proven Success
SAP, Microsoft, & IBM report higher innovation & efficiency.
Process Optimization
Neurodivergent minds excel at streamlining systems.
Higher Engagement
Inclusive workplaces improve retention & satisfaction.
Future-Ready Teams
Neurodiverse teams drive adaptability & growth.

required to pass a test. Sadly, many students never learn to think beyond what is needed to achieve the certificate that allows them to go on to the next chapter in their lives.

As can be imagined, neurodivergent students often struggle to rise to this level of conformity. They try to fit into a mold that runs contrary to their natural way of being in the world. As you can imagine, it is glaringly apparent to the other students that they don't fit in. They think differently compared with everybody else and often feel like they were born on the wrong planet.

It's a lonely way to be in the world.

As a result of this push toward conformity, many divergent thinkers find escape in alternative activities like video games, music, or art...or harmful addictions. Sometimes they self-medicate. The tragic loss is that the divergent thinking of these neurodivergent students often holds the solutions the world desperately needs.

For divergent thinkers, our unique way of being in the world is not the product of our upbringing, education, and culture. It develops when neurological variance exists in our thought paths starting from conception or because of life experiences. If society could ditch its expectations of conformity, divergent thinkers' ability to see the world differently would be recognized as invaluable when they are in the right roles solving the right problems.

Despite some neurodivergent individuals being better suited to entrepreneurship than becoming model employees, many have climbed the workplace ladder of excellence despite their questioning, nonconformist attitudes. The world would surely be worse off if this were not the case.

Of course, not everybody (neurotypical or neurodivergent) can reach those heights of excellence or success. However, our contributions at work and to society make a difference.

Acknowledgments

Traci Raymond - This book would not exist without you. Your encouragement to continue writing, coupled with your challenges to improve, elevated this work. Your thorough developmental copy editing took the book to the next level. I'm profoundly grateful for your support and help throughout this process.

Satvika Rampersad - Your insights as a neurodivergent writer and editor were invaluable in ensuring I covered all necessary topics. Your efforts as a beta reader surpassed my highest hopes. Every suggestion you made found its way into this final version. Thank you for your unwavering support and encouragement.

Monica Harding - Your experience as a neurodiversity lead in the corporate sector helped me frame issues appropriately and address them thoroughly for my readers. I expected a quick skim and brief thoughts; instead, you meticulously read every word, offering suggestions and comments throughout. Thank you for challenging me to make this book better.

Samantha Mazzotta - To my dear friend, kung fu sister, and writing partner, your constant support, suggestions, and copy editing over the four years it took to create this work have been invaluable.

Marilyn Marshall - When I worried about not having enough stories, you encouraged me to add more! As my first "any old Joe," I'm grateful you reprised that role for this book.

Mark Levy - You challenged me to think bigger and incorporate my decades of experience into supporting neurodiversity in the workplace. You were the first to recognize that my work in schools made me the perfect person to help corporations create a more neurodiverse culture and learning organization.

Katharine Giovanni, Katie Knall, Joe Curcillo, Reef Karim, and Austin Grammon - Thank you for constantly challenging me, cheering me on, and most importantly, believing in me throughout this writing journey.

Andrew Williams - Before I realized neurodiversity was a topic of interest, you shared one of my articles on LinkedIn. That shared post made me realize the value of neurodiversity in the workplace was finally being recognized, motivating me to write more articles and dive deeper.

Tiina Drissen - You discovered a four-year-old video of me speaking about neurodiversity and recommended me for Janssen's Annual Kick Off Conference. Where Andrew showed me there was interest, you helped me believe this topic was necessary and that I had a role in being part of the change.

To the countless friends, clients, and mentors who have helped me reach this point - while I can't name you all, please know that I am deeply grateful for your support.

Bibliography

Adams, C. A. (2020). *Neurodiversity at work benefits everyone – why companies are hiring autistic people.* The Conversation. https://theconversation.com/neurodiversity-at-work-benefits-everyone-why-companies-are-hiring-autistic-people-146788

ANet Staff. (n.d.-a). *Deficit Mindset.* ANet Resource Center. Retrieved July 4, 2024, from https://www.achievementnetwork.org/resource-center/eduspeak/deficit-mindset

ANet Staff. (n.d.-b). Deficit Mindset. ANet Resource Center. Retrieved July 3, 2024, from https://www.achievementnetwork.org/resource-center/eduspeak/deficit-mindset

AskEARN Editor. (2024). AskEARN. Employer Assistance and Resource Network on Disability Inclusion. https://askearn.org/

Austin, R. D., & Pisano, G. P. (2017a). Neurodiversity as a competitive advantage: Why you should embrace it in your workforce. In *Harvard Business Review* (Vol. 2017, Issue July-August).

Austin, R. D., & Pisano, G. P. (2017b). Neurodiversity as a competitive advantage: Why you should embrace it in your workforce. *Harvard Business Review,* 2017(July-August).

Austin, R. D., & Pisano, G. P. (2017c, May). *Neurodiversity Is a Competitive Advantage.* Harvard Business Review. https://hbr.org/2017/05/neurodiversity-as-a-competitive-advantage

Banner, J. (2016). *Four Ingredients for a People-Centered Workplace - SmallBox.* Small Box. https://www.smallbox.com/blog/four-ingredients-for-a-people-centered-workplace/

Bernick, M. (2022, February 16). *Is Your Company Inclusive of Neurodivergent Employees?* Harvard Business Review. https://hbr.org/2022/02/is-your-company-inclusive-of-neurodivergent-employees

Binns, C. (2020, May 26). *The Hidden Social Advantage | Stanford Graduate School of Business.* Graduate School of Stanford Business. https://www.gsb.stanford.edu/insights/hidden-social-advantage

Blanchard, V. M. A. (2022). *Spectroomz Blog - Content That Helps Autistic Adults Find Jobs.* Spectroomz Blog. https://www.spectroomz.com/blog

Catalyst. (2019). *12 Diversity & Inclusion Terms You Need to Know.* Catalyst Blog. https://www.catalyst.org/2019/05/30/12-diversity-inclusion-terms-you-need-to-know/

CDC Staff. (2024). Data and Statistics on ADHD | *Attention-Deficit / Hyperactivity Disorder (ADHD).* CDC.Gov. https://www.cdc.gov/adhd/data/?CDC_AAref_Val=https://www.cdc.gov/ncbddd/adhd/data.html

Cecile. (2020). *Improve Apprenticeship Retention Rates - Cognassist.* Cognassist Website. https://cognassist.com/insights/improve-apprenticeship-retention-rates/

Cicerchia, M., & Freeman, C. (n.d.). *7 Tips and strategies for working with dyslexia.* Touch-Type Read and Spell. Retrieved July 5, 2024, from https://www.readandspell.com/us/working-with-dyslexia

CIPD, & Ouptimize. (2018). *Neurodiversity at Work.* https://archive.acas.org.uk/index.aspx?articleid=5858

Clark, S. (2020). *Managing Neurodiversity in the Workplace - How to manage neurodiverse employees effectively.* Adjust Services. https://adjustservices.co.uk/specialism/autism/managing-neurodiversity-in-the-workplace/

Cooper, R., Hewlett, K., & Jameson, M. (2018). Neurodiverse Voices: Opening Doors to Employment. In *The Westminster AchieveAbility Commission for Dyslexia and Neurodivergence.* www.equalityhumanrights.com

Datta, N., Krishnamurthy, A., & Mannie, N. (2020, March 9). *3 ways to build lasting apprenticeship programs*. World Bank Blog. https://blogs.worldbank.org/jobs/3-ways-build-lasting-apprenticeship-programs

Delacato, C. H. (1974). *The Ultimate Stranger: The Autistic Child.* APA PsycNet. https://psycnet.apa.org/record/1975-01338-000

DiversityQ Writer. (2019). *How to Use Mind Mapping to Empower Employees with Dyslexia.* DiversityQ Blog. https://diversityq.com/how-to-use-mind-mapping-to-empower-employees-with-dyslexia/

Dominus, S. (n.d.). *An Office Designed for Workers With Autism.* The New York Times. Retrieved July 5, 2024, from https://www.nytimes.com/interactive/2019/02/21/magazine/autism-office-design.html

Downey, S. N., van der Werff, L., Thomas, K. M., & Plaut, V. C. (2015). The role of diversity practices and inclusion in promoting trust and employee engagement. *Journal of Applied Social Psychology, 45, 35–44.*

Doyle, N. (2020). Neurodiversity at work: a biopsychosocial model and the impact on working adults. *British Medical Bulletin,* 135(1), 108–125. https://doi.org/10.1093/BMB/LDAA021

Draaisma, D. (2009). Stereotypes of autism. *Philosophical Transactions of the Royal Society B: Biological Sciences,* 364(1522), 1475–1480. https://doi.org/10.1098/RSTB.2008.0324

Dubiks. (2018). *Urban Dictionary.* Urban Dictionary. https://www.urbandictionary.com/define.php?term=Autist%22%20/

Employer Assistance and Resource Network on Disability Inclusion. (n.d.). *AskEARN | Neurodiversity in the Workplace.* Ask EARN Website. Retrieved February 12, 2024, from https://askearn.org/page/neurodiversity-in-the-workplace

Fitzell, S. A. (n.d.). *How to Create a Company Culture that Embraces Different Thinkers in the Workplace.* SusanFitzell.Com. Retrieved February 8, 2024, from https://susanfitzell.com/how-to-create-a-company-culture-that-embraces-different-thinkers-in-the-workplace/

Fitzell, S. Me. C. (2021). *Improve Learning with Research-based Classroom Lighting Strategies.* SusanFitzell.Com. https://susanfitzell.com/improve-learning-with-research-based-classroom-lighting-strategies/

Forbes Councils Member. (2021). *13 Productive Ways To Support Neurodivergent Employees.* Forbes Coaches Council. https://www.forbes.com/sites/forbescoachescouncil/2021/04/29/13-productive-ways-to-support-neurodivergent-employees/?sh=2d399eb4fa7d

Gain, F. (n.d.). *Workplace neurodiversity: designing for difference - M Moser Associates.* MMoser Associates. Retrieved July 3, 2024, from https://www.mmoser.com/ideas/workplace-neurodiversity/

Giles, K. (2018, May 1). *Why You Mistakenly Hire People Just Like You.* Forbes. https://www.forbes.com/sites/forbescoachescouncil/2018/05/01/why-you-mistakenly-hire-people-just-like-you/?sh=122db1d93827

Glaveski, S. (2019). *Where Companies Go Wrong with Learning and Development.* Harvard Business Review. https://hbr.org/2019/10/where-companies-go-wrong-with-learning-and-development

Golden, D., Sniderman, B., Buckley, N., & Holdowsky, J. (2024, July 12). *The neurodiversity advantage: How neuroinclusion can unleash innovation and create competitive edge.* Deloitte Center for Integrated Research.

Gronseth, S. L., & Hutchins, H. M. (2020). Flexibility in Formal Workplace Learning: Technology Applications for Engagement through the Lens of Universal Design for Learning. *TechTrends,* 64(2), 211–218. https://doi.org/10.1007/S11528-019-00455-6

Gross, J. (2005, February 26). *As Autistic Children Grow, So Does Social Gap.* New York Times. https://www.nytimes.com/2005/02/26/health/as-autistic-children-grow-so-does-social-gap.html

Grosskopf, H. J. (2019). *Increase Productivity and Team Engagement with Mind Mapping - Training Industry.* Training Industry Blog. https://trainingindustry.com/blog/leadership/increase-productivity-and-team-engagement-with-mind-mapping/

Hanson, P. (2024). *Workplace Neurodiversity: The Power Of Difference Case Study.*

Heasman, B., & Gillespie, A. (2019). Neurodivergent intersubjectivity: Distinctive features of how autistic people create shared understanding. *Autism,* 23(4), 910–921. https://doi.org/10.1177/1362361318785172

High Lantern Group. (2024). Neurodiversity in the workplace: Building toward a more inclusive future of work. In *Bank of America.*

Hiller, R. M., Young, R. L., & Weber, N. (2014). Sex differences in autism spectrum disorder based on DSM-5 criteria: evidence from clinician and teacher reporting. *Journal of Abnormal Child Psychology,* 42(8), 1381–1393. https://doi.org/10.1007/S10802-014-9881-X

HM Government. (2020). *What are the benefits of hiring an apprentice?* Apprenticeships. Gov.Uk. Website. https://www.apprenticeships.gov.uk/employers/benefits-of-hiring-apprentice#

Hull, L., Petrides, K. V., Allison, C., Smith, P., Baron-Cohen, S., Lai, M. C., & Mandy, W. (2017). "Putting on My Best Normal": Social Camouflaging in Adults with Autism

Spectrum Conditions. *Journal of Autism and Developmental Disorders,* 47(8), 2519–2534. https://doi.org/10.1007/S10803-017-3166-5/TABLES/2

Ingram, H., Teare, R., Scheuing, E., & Armistead, C. (1997). A systems model of effective teamwork. *The TQM Magazine,* 9(2), 118. https://doi.org/https://doi.org/10.1108/09544789710165563

JAN Staff Editors. (2024). *JAN.* Job Accommodation Network. https://askjan.org/

JazzHR. (n.d.). *Embracing Neurodiversity in the Workplace: A Guide.* Embracing Neurodiversity in the Workplace: A Guide Share This Story LinkedIn Facebook DIVERSITY, EQUITY, & INCLUSION (DEI), WORKFORCE PLANNING. Retrieved April 6, 2024, from https://www.jazzhr.com/blog/neurodiversity-in-the-workplace/

Kaše, R., Saksida, T., & Mihelič, K. K. (2019). Skill development in reverse mentoring: Motivational processes of mentors and learners. *Human Resource Management,* 58(1), 57–69. https://doi.org/10.1002/HRM.21932

KeepingTABS. (2018). *Ultra Testing helps reduce friction between employees.* Medium. https://medium.com/@canvas8/brand-insight-ultra-testing-careers-workplace-1b580d058249

Kessler, R. C., Adler, L., Berkley, R., Biederman, J., Conners, C. K., Demler, O., Faraone, S. V., Greenhill, L. L., Howes, M. J., Secnik, K., Spencer, T., Ustun, T. B., Walters, E. E., & Zaslavsky, A. M. (2006). The prevalence and correlates of adult ADHD in the United States: Results from the National Comorbidity Survey Replication. *American Journal of Psychiatry,* 163(4), 716–723. https://doi.org/10.1176/AJP.2006.163.4.716/ASSET/IMAGES/LARGE/Q326T3.JPEG

Kirby, A. (2021). *Apprenticeship and Neurodiversity – recognising intrapreneurship – FE News.* FeNews. https://www.fenews.co.uk/exclusive/apprenticeship-and-neurodiversity-recognising-intrapreneurship/

Kopp, R. (2011, October 13). *Why do Japanese fall asleep in meetings? - Japan Intercultural Consulting.* Japan Intercultural Consulting. https://japanintercultural.com/free-resources/articles/why-do-japanese-fall-asleep-in-meetings/

Leadem, R. (2017). *How to Help Employees Remember What They Learned in Training | Entrepreneur.* Entrepreneur. https://www.entrepreneur.com/living/how-to-help-employees-remember-what-they-learned-in-training/289499

Liu, Y., Zhao, G., Ma, G., & Bo, Y. (2014). *The Effect of Mind Mapping on Teaching and Learning.*

Lucas, S. (2020, May 19). *Is Displaying Favoritism in the Workplace Illegal?* Live About Dotcom. https://www.liveabout.com/is-displaying-favoritism-in-the-workplace-illegal-4159736

Mahoney, J. (2017, June 5). *How JPMorgan Chase's Autism At Work Program Is Helping To Win Top Tech Talent.* Forbes. https://www.forbes.com/sites/jpmorganchase/2017/06/05/how-jpmorgan-chases-autism-at-work-program-is-helping-to-win-top-tech-talent/?sh=10b179b130bb

Marmorstein, A. (n.d.). *Spectroomz Blog - Content That Helps Autistic Adults Find Jobs.* Spectroomz Blog. Retrieved February 25, 2022, from https://www.spectroomz.com/blog

McGregor, K. P. (n.d.). *What is a Neurodevelopmental Disorder?* DLD and Me. Retrieved February 19, 2024, from https://dldandme.org/what-is-a-neurodevelopmental-disorder/

Morris, M. R., Begel, A., & Wiedermann, B. (2015). Understanding the challenges faced by neurodiverse software engineering employees: Towards a more inclusive and productive technical workforce. ASSETS 2015 - *Proceedings of the 17th International ACM SIGACCESS Conference on Computers and Accessibility,* 173–184. https://doi.org/10.1145/2700648.2809841

Neurodiversity in the Workplace - THINKING DIFFERENTLY AT WORK Toolkit, 62 (2018).

Olkin, R., Hayward, H., Abbene, M. S., & VanHeel, G. (2019). The Experiences of Microaggressions against Women with Visible and Invisible Disabilities. *Journal of Social Issues, 75(3), 757–785. https://doi.org/10.1111/JOSI.12342*

Oswald, T. D. (2020, October 26). *Autism and Trauma: Masking - Tasha Oswald.* Open Doors Therapy. https://opendoorstherapy.com/autism-and-trauma-masking/

Pearson, A., & Rose, K. (2021). A Conceptual Analysis of Autistic Masking: Understanding the Narrative of Stigma and the Illusion of Choice. *Autism in Adulthood : Challenges and Management, 3(1), 52–60. https://doi.org/10.1089/AUT.2020.0043*

Polec, D. (2018). *Ergonomic Design Of Workspaces For Employees With Autism.* The Arc Alliance. https://thearcalliance.org/ergonomic-design-of-workspaces-for-employees-with-autism/

Rodden, J. (2021). *Executive Dysfunction: Sign and Symptoms of EFD.* ADDitude Magazine. https://www.additudemag.com/what-is-executive-function-disorder/

Sanchez-Ruiz, M.-J., Khoury, J. El, Saadé, G., & Salkhanian, M. (2016). Non-Cognitive Variables and Academic Achievement. *Non-Cognitive Skills and Factors in Educational Attainment,* 65–85. https://doi.org/10.1007/978-94-6300-591-3_4

Sharma, D. (2021). *How Dynamic Workplaces Can Help Create Great Employee Experience.* CMSWIRE. https://www.cmswire.com/employee-experience/create-great-employee-experiences-by-building-dynamic-workplaces/

Shepherd, C. (2022). *Five detailed ways to design an office for neurodiversity - Fast Company.* FastCompany. https://www.fastcompany.com/90762205/five-detailed-ways-to-design-an-office-for-neurodiversity

Smith, M. (2024). *Tips for Managing Adult ADHD - HelpGuide.org.* HelpGuide.Org. https://www.helpguide.org/articles/add-adhd/managing-adult-adhd-attention-deficit-disorder.htm

Solomon, M., Miller, M., Taylor, S. L., Hinshaw, S. P., & Carter, C. S. (2012). Autism symptoms and internalizing psychopathology in girls and boys with autism spectrum disorders. *Journal of Autism and Developmental Disorders,* 42(1), 48–59. https://doi.org/10.1007/S10803-011-1215-Z

Spacey, J. (2017). *18 Examples of Ticket Management* -. Simplicable. https://simplicable.com/new/ticket-management

Sparkes, I., Riley, E., Cook, B., & Machuel, P. (n.d.). *Outcomes for disabled people in the UK.* Office for National Statistics. Retrieved July 3, 2024, from https://www.ons.gov.uk/peoplepopulationandcommunity/healthandsocialcare/disability/articles/outcomesfordisabledpeopleintheuk/2021

Staff Writer. (n.d.). *Youth, Disclosure, and the Workplace Why, When, What, and How.* U.S. Department of Labor. Retrieved July 5, 2024, from https://www.dol.gov/agencies/odep/publications/fact-sheets/youth-disclosure-and-the-workplace-why-when-what-and-how

Stillman, J. (2017, April 17). *Yale Researcher to Bosses: Science Proves Job Interviews Are Useless | Inc.com.* Inc. https://www.inc.com/jessica-stillman/yale-researcher-to-bosses-science-proves-job-interviews-are-useless.html

The Institute of Leadership. (2020, July). *Workplace Neurodiversity: The Power Of Difference.* The Institute of Leadership. https://leadership.global/resourceLibrary/workplace-neurodiversity-the-power-of-difference.html

US DOL Staff. (2024). *Section 503 of the Rehabilitation Act of 1973, as Amended.* U.S. Department of Labor. https://www.dol.gov/agencies/ofccp/section-503/law

Van Klink, S. (2021). *Wellbeing and Neurodiversity: Supporting Every Employee With Caring Accommodations.* Grokker. https://www.grokker.com/blog/wellbeing-and-neurodiversity-supporting-every-employee-with-caring-accommodations

VB Staff. (2022). *Report: Companies face a 37% chance of losing IP when employees quit | VentureBeat.* Code42. https://venturebeat.com/data-infrastructure/report-companies-face-a-37-chance-of-losing-ip-when-employees-quit/

Villalon, C. (n.d.). *10 Office Design Trends That Will Keep Employees Happy In 2023 - Alvarez-Diaz & Villalon | Architecture & Interior Design*. Alvarez-Diaz and Villalon Blog. Retrieved July 3, 2024, from https://www.alvarezdiazvillalon.com/blog/7-office-design-trends-for-2017-that-will-make-everybody-happy

Volpone, S. D., Avery, D. R., & Wayne, J. H. (2022). SHAPING ORGANIZATIONAL CLIMATES TO DEVELOP AND LEVERAGE WORKFORCE NEURODIVERSITY. *Neurodiversity in the Workplace: Interests, Issues, and Opportunities,* 16–59. https://doi.org/10.4324/9781003023616-2

Wille, S., & Sajous-Brady, D. (2018). Education the inclusive and accessible workplace. *Communications of the ACM,* 61(2), 24–26. https://doi.org/10.1145/3176410

Williams, C. (2014). *Concentrate! How to Tame a Wandering Mind.* BBC. https://www.bbc.com/future/article/20141015-concentrate-how-to-focus-better

Woo, E. (2019, October 25). *Workplace Neurodiversity | Autism at Work | SAP News Center.* SAP News Center - Corporate. https://news.sap.com/2019/10/workplace-neurodiversity-autism-at-work-program/

Zebra and Ostrich - Symbiotic Relationships. (n.d.). Animalsymbiosis.Weebly.Com. Retrieved September 5, 2022, from https://animalsymbiosis.weebly.com/zebra-and-ostrich.html

Zener, D. (n.d.). Advances in Autism Journey to diagnosis for women with autism Article information. *Advances in Autism,* 5(1), 2–13. https://doi.org/10.1108/AIA-10-2018-0041

Zoe, E. (2019). *What Is Learning Agility, And How Do You Nurture It?* EFront Learning Blog. https://www.efrontlearning.com/blog/2019/03/learning-agility-what-is-how-nurture-it.html

www.ingramcontent.com/pod-product-compliance
Lightning Source LLC
LaVergne TN
LVHW080330110826
845155LV00024B/137

* 9 7 8 1 9 3 2 9 9 5 4 2 8 *